Check Out
Madrid
Granada
Barcelona

D0342146

SPAIN

Contents

Written by Sally Roy
Where to... sections for Madrid, Southern Central Spain and
Andalucía by Josephine Quintero
Additional material for the Where to... sections for Barcelona and
Andalucía by Andrew Benson, Des Hannigan and Clarissa Hyman

Updated by Lindsay Hunt

American editor Tracy Larson

Illustration on pages 22–23 by Sue Climpson of Imageri.com

Edited, designed and produced by AA Publishing
© Automobile Association Developments Limited 2008
Maps © Automobile Association Developments Limited 2008

Published in the United States by AAA Publishing,
1000 AAA Drive, Heathrow, Florida 32746
Published in the United Kingdom by AA Publishing

ISBN-13: 978-159508-245-9

Cover design and binding style by permission of AA Publishing

Color separation by Keenes, Andover
Printed and bound in China by Leo Paper Products

10 9 8 7 6 5 4 3 2 1

A03183

the magazine

A COUNTRY APART

It's hard to pin down what it is that makes Spain feel so different from the rest of Europe – is it the huge empty landscapes, the harsh extremes of climate, the history, the culture, or the passionate people?

Pastoral life remains unchanged in Galicia

The Pyrenees (Pirineos) probably have a lot to answer for. They divide the Iberian peninsula from the rest of Europe, physically isolating Spain and making it difficult in the past for ordinary people to experience anything that was foreign.

Historical factors also play their part. In 711 the Moors swept across the Straits of Gibraltar and northwards through the peninsula, the start of an occupation that was to last in places for more than 700 years. No other European country was inhabited for hundreds of years by a people that was racially, culturally and religiously completely alien. The Moorish occupation was largely peaceful, with tolerance and assimilation on both sides. The Moors gave Christians freedom of religious practice; later, the Christians were to do the same. Despite the ongoing struggles and the forced conversions of the later years of the *Reconquista* (the Christian Reconquest), there was for centuries a genuine cross-cultural exchange.

This was strongest in the south, where the Moorish occupation lasted longest, and is still reflected in the divide between northern and southern Spain. Later historical movements provided the economic north/south split, but the spiritual one is far older. There's a vast gulf between a fiery, fine-boned Andalucían, all passion and *joie de vivre*, and a sombre, hard-working Galician, moulded by grey skies and wet weather. Spaniards rarely see themselves as Spanish, they're from Madrid, or they're Catalan, or Andalucían, or Galician, or Basque…

Perhaps the most straightforward way to view Spain is to see it as a collection of entities, a superb fusion of diverse cultures which evolved behind a mountain range on the fringes of mainstream Europe.

Flamenco epitomises the passionate soul of the south

A sense of regional identity starts early

Romanesque churches in the Pyrenees

A superb fusion of diverse cultures which evolved behind a mountain range on the fringes of mainstream Europe

There's a vast gulf between a fiery, fine-boned Andalucían, all passion and joie de vivre, and a sombre, hard-working Galician

City life – Spanish style

The Autonomías

Under the Spanish Constitution of 1978, seventeen autonomous regions were granted a large degree of self-rule – their own presidents, parliaments and civil administrations. Established partly as a backlash against Franco's repressive centralisation, when even the speaking of regional languages was banned, the *autonomías* have proved a bit of a mixed blessing. While undoubtedly helping to contain what could have become the more rampant and aggressive forms of nationalism in areas like Galicia and Valencia, autonomy has given Catalonia (Catalunya) and the Basque region considerable clout in Madrid, where they held the balance of political power throughout the 1990s at the expense of central government. Politics apart, the plus side has been a growing sense of pride in regional language and culture all over Spain. The flip side of this is a continuation of the lack of national identity that has always been a feature of the Spanish psyche.

¿Se habla español?

It certainly helps if you speak some Spanish when you're travelling around Spain, where few other languages are spoken away from the main tourist centres. Off the beaten track, however, there are some areas where Castilian, which we call Spanish, takes a firm second place to the "minority" language. Autonomy (► panel, page 7) has hugely encouraged the importance of these, and the number of people that speak them.

Look out for:

Catalan This is widely spoken throughout Catalonia, with street and traffic signs, public notices and museum information all in Catalan, often without a Castilian translation. Catalan is a Romance language (one of a group of European languages descended from Latin), with its own vibrant literary tradition, and has similarities with both Castilian and French.

Basque One of the world's most obscure languages, Basque has no apparent linguistic links with any other tongue. You'll see signs and notices everywhere throughout the Basque country in Basque, and it's worth checking up on place names in particular if you're touring. Remembering that Castilian "ch" becomes "tx","k" replaces "c", "y" is "i" and "v" is "b" may help if you're struggling with a menu.

Galician *Gallego* is widely spoken throughout Galicia, with road signs, notices and museum information all in *gallego*, and some small communities speaking nothing else. It sounds like a fusion of Portuguese and Castilian, and has its own body of literature. There are lots of Xs, pronounced "sh", instead of Castilian Gs, Js and Ss; "l" becomes "r", "la" is "a" and "el" is "o".

Valencian This is in general use throughout Valencia for street signs and general information. To outsiders, Valencian has many similarities with Catalan, though the Valencians would disagree.

BC
Phoenician, Carthaginian and Greek trading posts are founded among native Iberian settlements. The **Romans** invade.
5th–6th century AD The Romans are ousted. **Visigoths** invade from Gaul and establish a kingdom.

Boabdil, the last Moorish ruler, expelled from Granada in 149[?]

8th–10th century
Arabic-speaking, Muslim **Moors** invade from the Middle East via North Africa, establishing power bases all over Spain. Córdoba rises to pre-eminence and becomes the capital of the **Western Islamic Empire**. This independent Arab state, known as a caliphate, is ruled by caliphs; there is widespread unity within the caliphate from the 10th to mid-11th centuries, a period considered to be the great age of Moorish Spain. From the 1040s onwards the power of the Cordoban caliphate wanes and it disintegrates into smaller independent states, called *taifas*. Their internal struggles are instrumental in helping the **Reconquista**.

When, Who, What

9th–14th century

The **Reconquista**, the recapture of Moorish territory by Christian states, gradually drives the Moors southwards from Asturias in the north, the only place not to fall to Islam. Christian kingdoms are established as different regions of Spain are regained.

During the Reconquista, city after city fell to the Christians

1492 The Big Date

Granada falls and Spain is finally freed from the Moors. The first monarchs of this newly united Spain are **Ferdinand V of Aragón** and **Isabella I of Castile**, whose marriage in 1479 had united Spain's two largest kingdoms. They are known as **Los Reyes Católicos**, the Catholic

Christopher Columbus, discoverer of the New World

Monarchs, and have immense real and psychological importance in the history of Spain. **Christopher Columbus** discovers America.

16th century

In 1512, Spain becomes a single, politically united country and begins a golden age. This is the time of **Charles V** and Philip II, both Austrian **Habsburgs**. In 1519, the first Habsburg monarch, Charles I, is elected Holy Roman Emperor, taking the title of Charles V and bringing immense power and wealth to Spain from all over Europe. Exploration and annexation of **South America** continues. Philip II makes **Madrid** the capital in 1561. Turks defeated at **Battle of Lepanto** in 1571 – the zenith of Spanish naval power. The **Spanish Armada** is defeated by England in 1588 – the end of Spanish maritime ambitions.

17th century

Habsburg monarchs become progressively weaker.

18th century Bourbons

come to power after the War of Spanish Succession. **Charles III** is the pick of the bunch.

19th century

The **War of Independence** (Peninsular War) (1808–14) is a struggle against the French; the English, also at war with France, help.
The century is marked by opposition to, and revolts against, the monarchy.

20th century

Spain is neutral during **World War I**.
There is **a dictatorship** under Primo de Rivera from 1923. The **king leaves Spain** in 1931.
1936–39 The **Spanish Civil War** is fought between the Republic and the Nationalists; one of the bloodiest and most bitter wars in modern history.
1939–75 The Franco Era.
1975 Death of Franco.
Juan Carlos becomes King of Spain.
1986 Spain joins the **EU**.

King Juan Carlos I

2002 The euro becomes Spain's official currency, replacing the peseta.
2004 Terrorist bombs claim more than 200 lives in Madrid.

¡Fiesta!

Travelling in Spain, there's nothing as serendipitous as arriving in some obscure town or village to find the whole place celebrating. No matter how big or small, every Spanish community devotes at least one day a year to staging the biggest, noisiest, best fiesta it can afford. Fiestas are the perfect antidote to cultural overdose and a great way to get an inkling of what makes Spaniards tick.

Every festival is different, but there are some common strands underlying the celebrations, which can encompass anything from processions of holy images to being chased by running bulls. Most of the biggest have their origins in the key points of the Christian year – the great religious feasts of Lent, Easter and Corpus Christi (a religious feast celebrating the Sacred Host) or individual feast days dedicated to the Virgin or some important saint. Fiestas are mainly focused around a procession or parade, which can be a highly charged religious experience in honour of a particularly revered holy image, or a riotously uproarious display with giant carnival figures, bands and fireworks. Apart from the great pre-Easter processions of Semana Santa (Holy Week), all festivals are imbued with an immense atmosphere of communal rejoicing – helped along by music, dance and mounds of food and drink. These are occasions for people to celebrate their identities and re-affirm their local cultures – so you'll see traditional costume much in evidence, while the music, food, drink and activities are equally specific to the area. Fiestas are celebrations of what it means to be Spanish, to be part of a Spanish community, and to share a common national and local history and culture. These incredible and profligate celebrations are for the Spanish, but everyone's welcome, outsiders being swept along and caught up in the experience.

What is this experience? The answer depends on where you are and what's being celebrated. The whole of Spain is out on the streets for Carnival, when there are parades with giant figures and sumptuous floats, a massive splurge before Lent. The gloom deepens during the Easter Week processions, visually stunning parades of heavy religious tableaux carried by hooded penitents atoning for their sins. This is followed by

Valencian Fallas are huge papier-mâché effigies that are set alight

Opposite: The ceremonial regalia of one of the great religious festivals

the celebrations marking Corpus Christi, a religious feast celebrating the Sacred Host. From now on it's a joyous litany of fun throughout spring and summer, as communities all over the country celebrate in their different ways. Some regions celebrate Spain's culture with week-long festivities and folk music, others concentrate on different themes, such as local produce; you could celebrate the rice crop at a national *paella* competition or the tomato glut in a bizarre and messy tomato-throwing parade.

Wherever you are, look out for fun and games – the memory of an entire town feasting en masse in the main plaza, the scream and thumps of spectacular fireworks and the staccato rhythms of guitar, drums and bagpipes may be among the best memories you'll take home from Spain.

The summertime tomato fiesta

Where and When

Local tourist offices have details of what's on when in their areas. Look out too for posters advertising upcoming fiestas. The biggest ones are:

Carnival Everywhere, with Cádiz best known, February–March.

Fallas de San José Valencia, March.

Semana Santa Everywhere, best at Seville (Sevilla), Málaga, Córdoba, Granada and throughout Castile, March–April.

Feria Seville, April.

Romería del Rocío Huelva, Whit week.

Fiesta de San Fermín Pamplona (Iruñea), July.

Fiesta de Santiago Santiago de Compostela, July.

Mysteri d'Elx Elche (Elx), August.

If you want to attend any of these, you'll need to reserve accommodation well in advance.

Above: A *castell* (human tower), a typically Catalan celebration

Sol y Sombra

Death in the Afternoons

Throughout Spain, the major summer festivals are celebrated by bullfighting, the least understood of all the elements influencing the Spanish psyche. Outsiders see the *corrida* in terms of death, blood and cruelty; *aficionados* see grace, courage and beauty, the fight a potent symbol of man's own life and death.

From the prestigious fights in the big-city rings to the once-yearly event in an improvised bullring in a remote village, the pattern is the same. Six four-year-old bulls, bred on huge estates on the rolling grasslands of Andalucía and Castilla (Castile) are killed during a *corrida*. Until the moment they enter the ring, the 450kg (990-pound) bulls have never seen an unmounted man, spending their lives running free. The young bulls are assessed frequently by their breeders, who look for speed, strength, intelligence and, above all, courage. The greatest accolade a dead bull can be given is to be called "brave", its body cheered as it's pulled from the ring at the end of the fight. The parade, the *picadores*, the *bandilleras*, the music, the glittering costumes, are all subservient to the moment a brave *matador* faces a brave bull. This is the focus of the fight, on which the crowd passes judgement. Working with the *muleta*, a small red cloth, the

The Bulls Will Not Be Killed

In northern Spain, particularly throughout the Basque country, men run with the bulls (►105), pitting their agility against tons of panicky speed. Fights in some places take second place to the running, and the pre-fight posters plainly state "the bulls will not be killed".

matador draws the bull in a series of passes across his body. If man and beast are brave, this is a moment of drama, elegance and breathtaking courage, followed, at best, by a clean kill over the horns and into the heart.

Alien – yes. But the skill and bravery are undeniable, and this stylised dance of death can enthral as easily as appal. Youngsters still queue up to become *matadores*, braving it out at the *novilladas*, fights for novices and lesser bulls. The great *matadores* are national heroes, with fan clubs and web sites. The big fights in Madrid and Seville draw huge television audiences, and will be reviewed on the arts pages of the newspapers. True *aficionados* will spend years studying and analysing the careers of the great fighters and the bloodlines of the great fighting bulls. There is a dawning opposition to the *corrida* however, especially in Catalunya where the Barcelona city council voted in 2004 to ban bullfighting.

A matador can step forward to death or glory

Above: Fighting bulls face man for the first time in the ring

You Need to Know
- The season runs from March to October.
- Buy your ticket at the bullring box office; prices start around €20.
- Fights traditionally start at 5, 6 or 7pm.
- Seats are divided into *sol* (sun) and *sombra* (shade) as the latter are more comfortable in summer, when the heat can be intense. Most of the action occurs in the shade, but *sombra* seats are more expensive.
- *Barreras* (front seats) cost more than the *gradas* at the back.
- Look on www.mundo-taurino.org to learn more.

Art in Spain is part of the fabric of towns and cities. Spain has wonderful galleries and museums, but some of the country's greatest treasures are public buildings, church pictures and furnishings, still performing their original purpose. Some cities' riches date neatly from one epoch, other places have a glorious and heady mix, all forming the perfect, and sensually overwhelming, backdrop to Spanish life.

FROM THE MOORS TO MIRÓ
What's What in Architecture

surviving building types are mosques, *alcázares* (palaces) and *alcazabas* (fortified castles). Moorish architects incorporated water into their designs, either for ritual washing in mosques, or as an architectural

Córdoba's Mezquita is a powerful example of Moorish architecture

element in courtyards and gardens. *Mudéjar* is the name given to work carried out by Moors in the Christian-occupied parts of the country after the *Reconquista*.

Asturian 8th–10th centuries
Asturias, the one part of the peninsula never under Moorish rule, evolved its own style. Churches

Roman 1st century BC– 5th century AD
Look out for monumental public constructions such as aqueducts, theatres, and arches. Roman architectural style was similar all over the Empire, and was typified by solid stonework and classic proportions.

Segovia's Roman aqueduct has survived the centuries

Moorish and mudéjar 8th–15th centuries
Moorish architecture, with its horseshoe arches, intricate plasterwork, and red-and-white brick and stonework is unmistakable. The three main

Symphonies in Stone

Unlike paintings, which require a gallery trip, architecture is a total in-your-face experience, from world-famous buildings and cathedrals to modest gems in tucked-away provincial towns and villages. Mellow golden stone, forbidding granite, light and airy stucco and plaster-work, vibrantly coloured *azulejos* (ceramic tiles) all have their place, contributing to a huge diversity of style and form that evolved from place to place over the centuries. The chances are you'll be content simply to enjoy it all, but a bit of homework helps slot what you see into chrono-logical order. Remembering that rounded means Romanesque, pointed means Gothic, intricate stonework signifies plateresque and illogical curves are a sign of Modernism will add a whole new dimension to sightseeing. Grab a seat in a sunny plaza, order a drink and soak up the glories of Spanish architecture in all its variety.

are modelled on the Latin basilica with soaring lines and Eastern decorative elements.

Mozarabic 8th–14th centuries This is the name for the work carried out by Christians living under Arab rule; it incorpo-rates Moorish and Christian architectural borrowings.

Romanesque 11th–13th centuries The harmonious rounded arches and solid forms that epitomise Romanesque architecture came from Italy to Catalonia, and from France over the Pyrenees and along the pilgrim route to Santiago de Compostela (► 22–24).

Burgos cathedral, a flamboyant example of Spanish Gothic

Gothic and Isabelline 13th–15th centuries Spain's most impressive cathedrals are Gothic, huge structures with no transept, a single nave and pointed stone arches. In time, they became bigger and lavish stone decoration became a feature, a style known as Isabelline.

Renaissance and plateresque 16th century Early Spanish Renaissance architecture is called plateresque, because its ornate stone decoration is reminiscent of silverwork. The style drew on the harmonious proportions of Italian architecture but gave it a distinctly Spanish twist.

Plateresque-style carving at the Monasterio de San Marcos at León

Baroque and Churrigueresque 17th–18th century Architects began looking for ways to soften the austerity of the classical lines of the 16th century, adopting sweeping lines and

Baroque façades in Madrid are stunningly embellished

followed a century or more of derivative architecture, when major town planning changed the face of cities such as Madrid and Barcelona.

Modernism 20th century
Modernism emerged in Catalonia, an ebullient architectural style, part of a whole cultural movement, that used a mixture of modern materials and naturalistic and organic forms, with

hardly a straight line to be seen and surprises at every turn.

The *Modernista* Casa Batlló in Barcelona Below: Madrid's Museo del Prado

forms and adding increasingly lavish decoration. This reached its apogee in the Churrigueresque style with its twisted columns and extravagant stonework.

Bourbon neo-classical late 18th–19th century There

Miró's Woman and Bird

Colour Light and Shade

Great Galleries

The modern façade of Centro de Arte Reina Sofía

It's hard to analyse just what it is that makes Spanish painting so recognisable. Iconography plays a part, for there are few other schools of painting where the subject matter is so infused with passionate religious fervour. The national character makes its own contribution, seen in the piercingly searching portraits of the monarchs and the nobility.

Themes of suffering and death are constantly explored, but equally some artists imbued their work with light and gaiety. It's a heady mix. Spanish painting is not as easily visually accessible as the softer art of France and Italy, but it's worth making the effort, for there are few better ways of understanding the complexity of the Spanish spirit.

Unlike some countries, Spanish painting developed in fits and starts, producing peaks rather than a smooth progression of stylistic growth. Catalonia was dominant in Gothic art, its painters relying heavily on Flanders and the International Gothic school. Foreign artists were also working in Valencia and Castile, and even native painters such as the Berruguete father and son studied abroad and borrowed stylistically from both Italy and the north. It took a foreigner, Domenicos Theotocopoulos (1541–1614), better known as El Greco, to forge one of the first quintessentially Spanish styles. On the super-star level, he was followed by Diego Velázquez (1599–1660), a technical magician with a soul, whose court portraits are some of the finest ever painted.

Contemporaneously, Francisco de Zurbarán (1598–1664) was brilliantly illustrating monastic life, while his fellow-Sevillian Bartolomé Esteban Murillo (1618–82) painted sweet Madonnas and genre pictures, popular all over Europe. The second half of the 18th century through to the 1820s was overshadowed by Francisco Goya (1746–1828), a prolific genius whose work covered a wide range of subject and style. The towering figure of Pablo Picasso (1881–1973) dominated 20th-century art; followed closely, in terms of international importance, by the Surrealist painters Joan Miró and Salvador Dalí, both Catalans.

THE BIG OUTDOORS

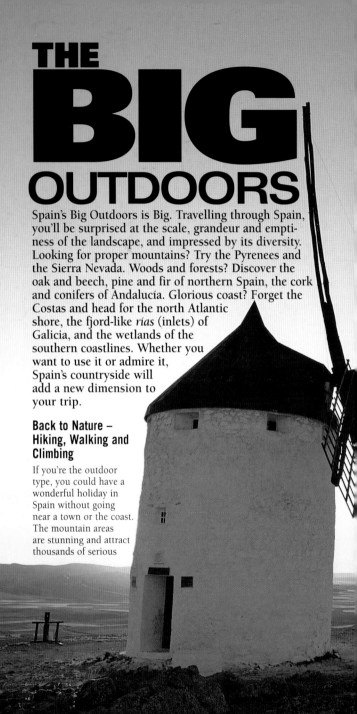

Spain's Big Outdoors is Big. Travelling through Spain, you'll be surprised at the scale, grandeur and emptiness of the landscape, and impressed by its diversity. Looking for proper mountains? Try the Pyrenees and the Sierra Nevada. Woods and forests? Discover the oak and beech, pine and fir of northern Spain, the cork and conifers of Andalucía. Glorious coast? Forget the Costas and head for the north Atlantic shore, the fjord-like *rías* (inlets) of Galicia, and the wetlands of the southern coastlines. Whether you want to use it or admire it, Spain's countryside will add a new dimension to your trip.

Back to Nature – Hiking, Walking and Climbing

If you're the outdoor type, you could have a wonderful holiday in Spain without going near a town or the coast. The mountain areas are stunning and attract thousands of serious hikers and climbers throughout the summer. The Pyrenees in Catalonia and Aragón, the Cordillera Cantábrica, which runs parallel with the northern coast and includes the Picos de Europa, and the Sierra Nevada in the south are the main draws, areas where you can disappear for days, hiking the high trails and sleeping in mountain refuges. All have small towns that act as jump-off points in their foothills, where you can rent equipment, buy excellent maps and guidebooks and plan your route with expert help. Paths and trails are well-marked; the GRs (*Grandes Routes*, the cross-European walking trails), with their red-and-white markers, guide walkers along the extensive and taxing Pyrenean routes. Serious mountaineers use these to access the demanding climbs of the high tops. These are the areas, also, where you're most likely to see Spain's showiest wild animals – chamois, ibex, red and roe deer, wild boar, even wolves and brown bear, though these last two are adept at keeping themselves hidden.

See it in Comfort

If the thought of such high-level activity stresses you out, there's plenty of superb landscape to admire from the comfort of a vehicle. Roads run well into the Pyrenees, the Picos and the Sierra Nevada, so you can explore some of the high country and dramatic gorges with little effort. Another great plus in Spain's empty landscape is that even the most humdrum journey will traverse some splendid country, where you can stop to stretch your legs and sniff the clean air as the fancy takes you. Coastal pottering, beach strolls, picnics beside some of the huge inland reservoirs, and woodland walks all add a further dimension, and even the longest cross-country drive is enhanced by the frequent sightings of great birds of prey.

Early summer brings contrasts of gold and green to the land

**Spain's dramatic rock formations
Left: Windmills in La Mancha**

What Makes Spain Different?

• After Switzerland, Spain is the most mountainous country in Europe.
• The Pyrenees form a natural barrier separating the Iberian peninsula from the rest of Europe – vegetation, flora and wildlife have evolved uniquely.
• There's a wide range of climatic conditions – wet and cool in the north, a mix of bitter winter cold and insufferable summer heat in the centre, typically Mediterranean further east, and veering towards the sub-tropical in the south.
• Spain has larger areas of wild country than other European countries.
• Agriculture is not as intensive as elsewhere, and some traditional methods are still used.

Where to Go, When – Great Places for Twitchers

The Ebro Delta, Catalonia
The lagoon and wetlands with woodlands and rice paddies are at their best during the spring and autumn migration seasons. You can see wildfowl such as coot, teal and grebe, plus resident egret, flamingo, avocet and purple heron. Visitors include the lapwing, oystercatcher and tern.

Picos de Europa, Asturias
This prime site for mountain birds is best from May to October. Head here for the golden eagle, Bonelli's eagle, griffon vulture and rare mountain species such as chough, snow finch and citril.

Doñana National Park, Andalucía
A superb wetland region, this is at its best during migration and winter months. You can see many thousands of over-wintering wildfowl as well as the flamingo, spoonbill, imperial eagle, egret, heron and avocet.

Monfragüe Natural Park, Extremadura
These wooded hills and gorges are best visited in summer to see the range of raptors and migrant visitors. Large raptors including the kite, griffon and black vulture; golden, Spanish imperial and Bonelli's eagle; golden oriole, shrike, hoopoe, bee-eater and roller.

Ordesa y Monte Perdido National Park, Aragón
Access to high-altitude birds in the Pyrenees is easiest in summer months. Ptarmigan, snow finch, chough, eagle owl, vulture, eagle and breeding lammergeier can all be seen here.

Eagles can be spotted in the Pyrenees

The iridescent bee-eater can be seen in southern Spain

Where to Go, When, for Carpets of Wild Flowers

Andalucía

Late winter, spring and early summer are the best months for seeing wild flowers, though the Sierra Nevada is at its peak through to July. Winter-flowering iris, squill and coastal and maritime flora can be found along the Atlantic coast, and daffodils, gentians, tulips, peonies, aquilegia in the mountains. There is excellent *matorral* (maquis) vegetation and large cork and pine forests.

Pyrenees

Superb upland and alpine flora cloaks the Pyrenees throughout the summer months.

Meadows and slopes have huge spreads of spring flowers, including narcissi, pasque-flowers, gentians, lilies, fritillaries; edelweiss and mountain saxifrage can be found at high altitude. There is a wide range of orchid species. Autumn bulbs include cyclamen and crocus.

Asturias and Cantabria

Swathes of oak and beech forest are interspersed with meadowland in this area. There are stunning displays of meadow flowers, spring bulbs, peonies, tulips and purple monkshood as well as myriad different orchid species. Late spring is the best time for the mountains, but coastal flowers start earlier.

The Pick of the Bunch – National Parks

Spain has 13 *parques nacionales* (national parks). Several of these are in the Balearic and Canary islands. The eight mainland ones are:

- **Aigüestortes y Estany Sant Maurici** (Catalonia; tel: 973 69 61 89)
- **Cabañeros** (Castilla-La Mancha; tel: 926 78 32 97)
- **Doñana** (Andalucía; tel: 959 44 86 40)
- **Islas Atlánticas de Galicia** (Galicia; tel 986 85 85 93)
- **Ordesa y Monte Perdido** (Aragón, tel: 974 24 33 61)
- **Picos de Europa** (Asturias, Cantabria and León; tel: 985 24 14 12)
- **Sierra Nevada** (Andalucía; tel: 958 02 63 00)
- **Tablas de Damiel** (Castilla-La Mancha; tel: 926 85 10 97).

For more information contact the Ministerio de Medio Ambiente (Interior Ministry); tel: 915 96 46 00; www.mma.es Spain also has many other kinds of nature reserve, especially *parques naturales* (natural parks), which are locally managed and vary tremendously in size and character.

Red deer prosper in the national parks

THE CAMINO DE SANTIAGO

Look at a Spanish tourist map and you'll see a clearly marked route, stretching across the top of northern Spain from the Pyrenees to the city of Santiago de Compostela near the western Atlantic coast. This footpath, one of the oldest in Europe, is known as the Camino de Santiago, the Way of St James.

Santiago de Compostela • Argua • Vilar de Donas • Villafranca del Bierzo • León • Ponferrada • Sahagun

Stamps on a pilgrim's *credencial* (these pages) trace the route west

St James and Santiago

To medieval Europeans, a pilgrimage was a means of earning extra grace and thus attaining heaven faster; it also meant travel, excitement and fun, an excuse to leave every-day humdrum life and hit the trail. Pilgrimages were made to many holy places, but the great goals were Jerusalem, Rome and Santiago de Compostela, the burial place and shrine of the apostle St James, Santiago in Spanish.

According to legend, he had preached in Spain before returning to martyrdom in Judaea. His disciples brought his body back to northern Spain where it lay hidden until 813, when a hermit was drawn to a particular hillside by starry visions – hence the name Compostela, *campus stellae*, the "field of stars". The King of Asturias, the only part of the peninsula not under Moorish domination, came to pray here and St James, was adopted as the champion of Christian Spain against the Infidel. In 844 he inspired a Christian victory at Clavijo, gaining himself the title of *Matamoros*, the Moorslayer, and a role as patron saint of Spain. By the 11th century pilgrims were travelling from all over Europe to pray at his tomb.

Pilgrims travelled from France, Britain, Germany,

The Camino de Santiago de Compostela

Order, the Camino was policed and waymarked along its length, with hostels, inns and churches offering practical and spiritual sustenance to the travellers. Towns grew up around the stopping points, with their own churches, hospitals and hospices.

Dressed in sandals and a heavy cape, and armed with a stout staff and flask, pilgrims were distinguishable by the scallop shells, an emblem of the saint, they wore in their

Italy and Scandinavia, as well as Spain and Portugal, many of them taking years to complete their journey. By the mid-12th century between 500,000 and 2 million people annually were on the move, a vast number in terms of contemporary population sizes. Roads to Spain threaded their way across the continent, but once across the Pyrenees they joined to follow a well-organised route across the north of Spain, the *Camino de Santiago*. Administered by a special religious military

broad-brimmed hats. There was even a guidebook, written by the French monk Aymery Picaud, which gave routes and useful tips about what the pilgrim might encounter *en route*. On arrival in Santiago, the custom was to enter the cathedral and embrace the golden effigy of the saint placed high above his tomb, while giving alms and thanks in gratitude for the safe completion of the pilgrimage, an act which would guarantee remission of half the pilgrim's time in purgatory.

Since the Middle Ages pilgrims have stopped at churches and monasteries along the Camino

The Camino Today

The custom of walking the Camino died out during the reforming 16th century, to be revived around 1880, though it's really the last 20 years that have seen a phenomenal increase in pilgrim numbers. The governments of the regions along the Camino have invested heavily in upgrading the paths, making new ones to keep pilgrims off the horribly busy main roads, building hostels and restoring some of the historic churches and buildings along the way. Most pilgrims start their journey in the Spanish Pyrenees, from where the distance to Santiago is around 760km (471 miles). You can do the Camino on foot, by bicycle or on horseback, all recognised as means of gaining the *compostela*, the certificate issued by the cathedral authorities in Santiago which confirms the completion of the pilgrimage. The obvious query is how do they know you haven't cheated?

The answer lies in the *credencial*, the pilgrim's passport, a small, multi-page folder that must be stamped by the ecclesiastical and civil authorities at the towns along the Camino. This precious document also entitles the pilgrim to stay for a pittance at the hostels along the way, making the pilgrimage as accessible to everyone today as it was in the Middle Ages.

More than just Flamenco Olé

Flamenco – heart-stopping, passionate, sensuous – is Spain's greatest musical heritage, as vibrant today as it's ever been. But it's not the only folk music to be heard, and guitars and castanets by no means epitomise Spanish musical traditions. Spain embraces different peoples, languages and cultures, and their diversity is nowhere better shown than in their music and dance.

Flamenco

Flamenco was born in southern Spain, evolving from the sounds and rhythms of Eastern cultures fusing with Arab and Jewish elements. Its most famous exponents were often gypsies, a people who perhaps more than others could understand the heart-rending mix of pain and joy which distinguishes life and is expressed in the most sublime flamenco. It is played, sung and danced, often heard at its best when it occurs spontaneously, late at night in some private house or smoke-filled bar. Its ultimate expression is song, particularly the pain-racked *cante*

jondo (deep song), where the singer passionately pours out his soul, inspired and encouraged by the guitars' rhythm and the shouts of the listeners. The lighter side of flamenco is expressed in dance – *tangos*, *fandangos* and *sevillanas* – where the graceful, sinuous body movements contrast marvellously with the furious, staccato footwork. Colour and movement, rhythm and sound, and, above all, passion, are flamenco's hallmarks.

Catalonia

Catalan folk music and song was a major force in helping to keep alive the region's culture and

Stars and Idols

Flamenco	Catalan Music	Galician Music	Basque Music
• El Camarón de la Isla	• Els Setge Jutges	• Milladoiro	• Josepa Tapia
• Paco de Lucía	• Lluís Llach	• Carlos Nuñez	• Kepa Junkera
• Tomatito	• Joan Manuel Serrat	• Cantegueiras Xiradella	• Ruper Ordorika
• Paco Peña	• Raímon	• Palla Mallada	• Benito Lertxundi
• La Chanca		• Matto Congrio	
• Cristina Hoyos		• Xorima	

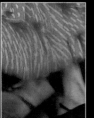

spirit during the Franco years. The *sardana*, the Catalan national dance, came to represent a free Catalonia, and still plays an important role in all festivities. Catalan orchestras have their own style, playing traditional dance music with more than a touch of *salsa* to it – you can hear Spanish America too, in the Cuban-inspired *habanera* songs.

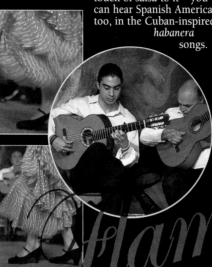

Galicia

Folk music is alive and thriving in Galicia, but don't expect guitars; listen instead for pipes and drums and the steady drone of the bagpipes. Galicians are Celts, and their music has much in common with that of Scotland and Ireland. The worksongs and *jotas* (folksongs) heard here are foot-tapping and robust, while the melancholy yearning held in common by all Celts manifests itself in the traditional love songs.

Euskadi

At the eastern end of Spain's north coast lies the Basque country, with an equally strong indigenous musical tradition. Here, there's a growing fusion of the traditional wild accordion music, *trikitrixa* (the name means devil's bellows), with Celtic and rock elements – fantastic stuff.

Where to hear it

Tourist offices are the best places to get up-to-date information about what's on during your visit to a specific place.

Flamenco

Head for the flamenco clubs or bars, the *tablaos* or *peñas*, where you'll hear it properly performed by professionals – avoid the tourist-trap "flamenco shows".

Catalan Music

The *sardana* is performed at all summer festivals and there are festivals devoted to *habanero* on the Costa Brava and the Costa Blanca.

Galician Music

Track it down at live music clubs and summer fiestas – Santiago hosts an annual folklore festival in July.

Basque Music

For live Basque music, try clubs in Bilbao and throughout the region at festivals – in Asturias there's the Oviedo Folk Festival, where you'll hear the best of Basque and Galician rhythms.

BEST OF...

Mountains, sun, sand and sea at Nerja

Best of the Costas

Coasts **with good family resorts**: **Costa Brava** (130), **Costa Blanca** (► 154–155), **Costa del Sol** (► 174). Or follow the Spanish and try **Costa Verde** (► 97–98), the **Rías Baixas** (► 103) and the **Costa de la Luz** (► 174–175).

Unspoiled Coastlines: explore the off-the-beaten-track stretches of the **Costa Verde** (► 97–98), **Costa da Morte** (► panel, page 104) and **Costa de la Luz** (► 174–175).

Best Cities

For big-city style and buzz: **Madrid** (► 41–66), **Barcelona** (► 111–138), **Valencia** (► 149–151) and **Bilbao** (► 101–102).

For their own unique flavour: **Segovia** (► 75–76), **Salamanca** (► 77–80), **Toledo** (► 144–146), **Santiago de Compostela** (► 94–96), **Seville** (► 164–167), **Córdoba** (► 168–169) and **Granada** (► 170–172).

Let-your-Hair-Down and Dance All Night: it has to be the **Costa Blanca** for Benidorm (► 154–155) and the **Costa del Sol** for Benalmádena (► 174).

Great Beaches: huge sandy expanses along the **Costa Blanca** (► 154–155) and the **Costa de la Luz** (► 174–175); cliffs and coves on the **Costa Brava** (► 130) and the **Costa Verde** (► 97–98).

Activities: play golf on the **Costa del Sol** (► 174) and the **Costa Blanca** (► 154–155); head for the **Costa Blanca** (► 154–155) for **watersports and sailing**; try the **Costa de la Luz** (► 174–175) for some of Europe's best **surfing and wind- and kitesurfing**.

Best Food Markets

Mercado Antón Martín in Madrid (► 65), **la Boquería** in Barcelona (► 122), the **Mercado Central** in Valencia (► 149), the **Mercado Central** in Alicante (► 154–155) and **Mercado de Abastos** in Santiago de Compostela (► 94–96).

Chorizo to suit all tastes – a true taste of Spain

Best Modern Architecture

Fallas figures dwarf the crowds in Valencia

Museo Guggenheim, Bilbao (➤ 101–102), **Fundació Joan Miró**, Barcelona (➤ 123–124) and **La Ciutat de les Arts i les Ciències**, Valencia (➤ 150).

The sinuous silvery curves of Bilbao's Museo Guggenheim

Best Tastes

Rice and seafood combine in paella

Best Fiestas

The Fallas (Valencia, March); **Holy Week** (Seville, Málaga, March/April); **Feria** (Seville, April); **El Rocío Pilgrimage** (El Rocío, Huelva, Andalucía, Whitsun); **Hogueras** (Alicante, June); **San Fermín** (Pamplona, July); **Mystery Play** (Elche, August) and **La Rioja Wine Festival** (Logroño, September).

A jug of refreshing sangría is welcome in summer

Food to try: the bean dishes, roast meats and *cochinillo* (suckling pig) of Castile, seafood and *pulpo* (octopus) in Galicia, asparagus, peppers and game in Navarre, Basque cooking generally; *paella*, *fideuà* (made with pasta) and fruit and vegetables from Valencia and around, fried fish and gazpacho from Andalucía; *jamón* (dry-cured ham), *chorizo* (spicy sausage), Manchego (sheep's milk cheese) and *tortilla* (omelette) almost everywhere.

Drinks to sample: wine – go for the best of what's local; try the cider in Asturias and Cantabria; *sangría*, made with wine, fruit and lemonade, in the coastal areas; sherry in Andalucía; beer and *horchata* (a refreshing summer drink made from tiger nuts) in Valencia.

Finding Your Feet

First Two Hours

Spain has international gateways in all areas of the country, with Madrid, Barcelona, Málaga, Alicante (Alacant), Valencia and Bilbao (Bilbo) being the busiest tourist entry points. Transport into these cities from their airports is by bus, train, metro or taxi. Travellers arriving from the UK by sea will dock at Santander or Bilbao, both on the north coast.

Arriving in Madrid

■ International flights arrive at the **Aeropuerto de Barajas** (tel: 902 40 47 04; www.aena.es) 13km (8 miles) north-east of the city. Most international flights arrive at the new Terminal 4, which has doubled the airport's capacity. Facilities include a Tourist Information Office (tel: 913 05 86 56, Mon–Fri 8–8, Sat–Sun 8–2), a 24-hour currency exchange, a RENFE office for booking train tickets, car hire offices, post office and hotel reservations desk.

■ **Taxis**, leaving from outside all the terminals, are the easiest way to get into the city centre. The journey costs up to €25, depending on traffic.

■ The next best bet is the **metro link** (daily 6am–2am; cost under €2). Take Line 8 and change on to Line 4 at Mar de Cristal.

■ **Shuttle buses** run every 10–15 minutes from 4:45am–2am from outside each terminal into Plaza de Colón, where you can connect with the metro system at Serrano. The journey takes between 30 and 50 minutes, depending on traffic and costs under €3.

Tourist Offices

✉ Plaza Mayor 27
☎ 915 88 16 36
🕐 Daily 9:30–8:30

✉ Calle del Duque de Medinaceli 2
☎ 914 29 49 51
🕐 Mon–Fri 9–7, Sat 9–3

✉ Mercado de Puerta de Toledo
☎ 913 64 18 76
🕐 Mon–Fri 9–7, Sat 9–3

✉ Estación de Chamartín
☎ 913 15 99 76
🕐 Mon–Fri 8–8, Sat 9–3

The general telephone number for Madird tourist offices is 902 10 00 07; for information in English dial 010. Useful websites include:
www.esmadrid.com
www.munimadrid.es
www.madrid.org/turismo
www.madrid.es

Arriving in Barcelona

■ Barcelona is served by the **Aeroport El Prat de Llobregat** (tel: 932 98 38 38; www.aena.es), 13km (8 miles) southwest of the city. There are three terminals, and international flights arrive at each. All have Tourist Information Offices (open daily 9–9), car rental offices and exchange facilities.

■ The **taxi trip** into the centre takes around 30 minutes and costs around €25; taxis leave from outside all terminals.

■ **Trains** run every 30 minutes to the city centre from 6:15am–10:15pm and cost under €3. The journey time is approximately 30 minutes and will take you to Estació-Sants.

■ The **airport bus** departs every 12 minutes from outside each terminal, 6am–midnight, and costs under €4. The journey time is 30–40 minutes to the centre, where the bus stops at Plaça d'Espanya, Gran Via, Plaça de la Universitat, Plaça de Catalunya and Passeig de Gràcia.

- If you're **arriving by train** from another Spanish destination, Barcelona's main station is Estació-Sants, where you can pick up metro Line 3 or take a taxi from outside the station. There are also stations at Estació de França, Plaça de Catalunya, Arc de Triomf, Plaça d'Espanya and Passeig de Gràcia. All connect with the metro system.

Tourist Offices
- ⊠ Plaça de Catalunya
- ☎ 807 11 72 22
- ⊕ Daily 9–9

- ⊠ Ajuntament, Plaça de Sant Jaume
- ☎ 906 30 12 82
- ⊕ Mon–Fri 9–8, Sat 10–8, Sun 10–2

- ⊠ Estació-Sants
- ⊕ Apr–Sep daily 8–8; Oct–Mar Mon–Fri 8–8, Sat–Sun 8–2
- ⊠ Palau Robert, Passeig de Gràcia, 107
- ☎ 932 38 40 00
- ⊕ Mon–Sat 10–7, Sun 10–2

Useful websites include:
www.barcelonaturisme.com
www.bcn.es
www.gencat.net/probert

Arriving in Málaga
- **Aeropuerto de Málaga** (tel: 952 04 84 84) is 10km (6 miles) southwest of the centre. It has exchange facilities and car rental offices. The offices of some budget car rental companies are a short distance from the terminal building; they normally run a free pick-up service from the airport.
- The easiest way to reach the city centre is by **train**, which runs every 30 minutes from 7am–11:45pm, costs under €2, and takes about 10 minutes. Reach the station by going up to the *Salidas* (Departure) hall and follow the *Ferrocarril* signs across the pedestrian overpass. Use the platform furthest away from you for Málaga trains and stay on the train to Centro-Alameda.
- **Taxis** cost around €15 and leave from outside the terminal with a journey time into the centre of around 20–30 minutes.
- The **airport bus** runs from outside the terminal every 30 minutes from 7am–midnight, with a journey time of 20 minutes, and costs €1.
- **Trains** arrive from other Spanish cities at the RENFE station, a short distance from the centre of town.

Tourist Offices
- ⊠ Pasaje de Chinitas, 4
- ☎ 952 21 34 45
- ⊕ Mon–Fri 9–8, Sat–Sun 10–2

- ⊠ Plaza Marina 11
- ☎ 952 12 20 20
- ⊕ Apr–Oct Mon–Fri 9–7, Sat–Sun10–7; Nov–Mar until 6

www.malagaturismo.com

Arriving in Alicante (Alacant)
- **Alicante Aeropuerto El Altet** (tel: 966 91 90 00) is 12km (7.5 miles) southwest of the centre, with exchange facilities and car hire offices: note that some of the budget hire companies have their offices in mobile trailers in the car park outside the terminal building.
- You can pick up a **taxi** outside the terminal; the journey time to the centre is around 20 minutes and costs around €15.
- **Airport buses** leave every 40 minutes from 7am–11pm, take around 30 minutes to reach the centre and cost under €2.
- The main **train station** is the Estación de Madrid, Avenida Salamanca; if you're **connecting** to one of the Costa Blanca resorts, coastal services leave on the FGV line from Playa de Postiguet.

Tourist Office
✉ Avenida Rambla de Méndez
Núñez, 23
☎ 965 20 00 00

🕔 Mon–Fri 9–8, Sat 10–2, 3–8
www.alicanteturismo.com

Arriving in Valencia

- The **Aeropuerto de Manises** (tel: 961 59 85 00) is 8km (5 miles) west of Valencia; there are exchange facilities and car hire offices.
- **Airport buses** run every 20 minutes from outside the terminal (from about 6:30am–midnight) to the city centre; the journey takes around 45 minutes and costs under €3.
- **Taxis**, which cost around €15–20, leave from outside the terminal, with a journey time of about 30 minutes.
- **Trains arrive** from other Spanish destinations at the Estación del Nord, close to the city centre.

Tourist Office
✉ Plaza de la Reina 19
☎ 963 15 39 31
🕔 Mon–Sat 9–7, Sun 10–2

www.turisvalencia.es

Arriving in Bilbao (Bilbo)

- The **Aeropuerto de Bilbao** (tel: 944 86 93 00) is 12km (7.5 miles) north of the city centre; it has a currency exchange, a tourist information kiosk and car rental offices.
- Bilbao centre is around a 30-minute **taxi** ride away which costs around €20; taxis leave from outside the terminal.
- **Airport buses** leave from outside the terminal every 30 minutes between 6:15am and midnight for the 40-minute trip to town and cost under €2.
- The **main train station** is the Estación de Abando where you'll arrive from other regions of Spain. If you're **moving on along the coast**, use either the Estación Atxuri, or, for FEVE services to Santander, the Estación de Santander.
- **Ferries from the UK** (Portsmouth) dock at Santurtzi on the river mouth to the north of the centre. Buses and trains run from the docks to the city centre; if you're **driving** you can join the A8 *autopista* (motorway) from the docks.

Tourist Offices
✉ Plaza Ensanche II
☎ 944 79 57 60
🕔 Mon–Fri 9–2, 4–7:30

✉ Museo Guggenheim
🕔 Jul–Aug Mon–Sat 10–7, Sun 10–3; Sep–Jun Tue–Fri 11–6, Sat 11–7, Sun 11–2

Arriving in Santander

Ferries from the UK (Plymouth) arrive at the Estación Maritima de Ferries at the Puerto Grande. You'll have to follow the signs for Oviedo or Bilbao and negotiate the city to join the main coastal highway, the N634.

Tourist Office
✉ Jardines de Pereda s/n
☎ 942 20 30 00
🕔 Jun–Sep daily 9–9; Oct–May

Mon–Fri 9:30–1:30, 4–7,
Sat–Sun 9:30–1:30

www.santanderciudadviva.com

Getting Around

Spain is a big country, and if you're planning an extensive trip, it's worth considering using internal flights. The slower option, the national rail network, supplemented by some private lines, covers the whole country, as does the bus system. In terms of speed and cost, there is often little to choose between trains and buses, remoter places being served only by buses.

Domestic Air Travel

■ Spain's national carrier, Iberia (tel: 902 40 05 00; www.iberia.com) offers **internal flights** throughout the country, as does Air Europa (tel: 902 40 15 01; www.air-europa.com), which has a useful **shuttle service** between Madrid and Barcelona. Each region of Spain has at least one airport.

Trains

■ RENFE (www.renfe.es) is the Spanish rail company, operating three main types of **train services**. *Cercanías* are local commuter trains in and around the main cities; *regionales* connect cities, and *largo recorrido* express trains cover the long-distance routes. Spain has a multiplicity of high-speed trains, including the Intercity, Estrella and Talgo, all with many variations. At the top of the range is the AVE, which runs from Madrid to Seville and Malaga in one direction, and will soon extend as far as Barcelona in the other. The Euromed runs from Barcelona to Alicante (Alacant). All these services have greatly shortened travelling times through Spain. FEVE is a private rail line which runs along the north coast from Donostia (San Sebastián) to Ferrol; it connects at various places along its route with RENFE trains. FGC and FGV operate services in Catalonia and Valencia respectively.

■ **Advance reservations** are essential on the *largo recorrido* trains; this can be done at the window marked *venta anticipada* at main stations or at any travel agent displaying the RENFE sign. Many large towns have their own RENFE office or you can reserve via the **website** (www.renfe.es). Be aware that different **timetables** are issued for different train categories, so there may be more services to a destination than you think at first glance.

■ **Prices** vary considerably depending on the category of train; fares on the faster *largo recorridos* cost more than double those on the *regionales*. **Discounts** are available on return fares and also for children, senior citizens and travellers with disabilities. RENFE accepts InterRail and Eurail **passes**, and has its own pass, the Tarjeta Explorerail for passengers aged under 26. **FlexiPass**, available only to visitors resident outside Europe, gives 3–10 days unlimited first- or second-class travel within a 2-month period (current prices start at US$155 for 3 days second-class travel, plus US$30 for each subsequent day). Children (4–11) travel for half-fare. Before you invest in a rail pass, check how much train travel you intend to do. Note that supplements may be payable on the faster services.

Buses

■ Spanish **buses** are reliable, air-conditioned and comfortable. There are dozens of companies, most of which operate from the various provincial capitals. Ask at the tourist offices for more information. **Sunday and holiday services** are few and far between.

Taxis

- Taxi services in both rural and urban areas are inexpensive and reliable. Either go to taxi ranks or call in advance; outside Madrid and Barcelona it is not usual to hail a taxi on the street. Supplements are payable for extra passengers and luggage and late-night trips. Tipping is discretionary, but a few euros will suffice.

Driving

- **Drivers** in Spain must hold an **EU driving licence**; US and Canadian licences are also accepted. For peace of mind, North American visitors might want to invest in an **International Driving Licence**. UK visitors whose licences do not comply with the EU format should carry photo ID with them or obtain an International Driving Licence. These are obtainable through the AA and RAC in the UK and similar driving organisations in other countries. Carry your licence with you at all times when driving. Drivers must be 18 or over.
- **Third-party insurance** is compulsory in Spain. If you're bringing your own car, you will need a **green card** from your insurers; a **bail bond** is recommended. Take your **vehicle registration document** with you.
- **Spanish major roads** are generally good, though remote roads in rural areas can have bad surfaces and, in mountainous regions, precipitous drops. Tolls (*peajes*) are levied on some motorways (*autopistas*).
- City traffic can be hectic; it's a good idea to negotiate the approaches to a strange city during siesta time, when the streets are quiet.
- **Check regulations before you travel** – www.theAA.com has comprehensive European driving information.

Driving Know-how

- Drive on the **right-hand side** of the road.
- **Seat belts** are compulsory in the front of the car and rear seat belts, if fitted, must be worn; **children under 12** are not meant to sit in the front unless the seat has a special belt.
- The blood **alcohol** limit is 0.05 per cent (0.03 per cent for new drivers).
- **Yield** to vehicles coming from the right.
- **Speed limits** are 50kph (31mph) on urban roads, 90kph (56mph) outside built-up areas, 120kph (75mph) on motorways; speed traps are common.
- On-the-spot **fines** are levied for all traffic offences. Obtain a receipt.
- **Vehicle crime** is widespread: never leave anything visible in the car, remove the radio and be prepared to pay extra at city-centre hotels for parking to avoid leaving your car on the streets.
- Make sure you know what the **breakdown procedures** offered by your own insurer or car rental company are before you start your trip. The Spanish Motoring Club (*Real Automovil Club d'España*) has reciprocal agreements with the AA, US AAA, Australian AAA, CAA and NZAA.

Renting a Car

- Cars can be rented by **drivers over 21** who have held a licence for at least a year on presentation of a **full driving licence**.
- The **cheapest deals** are to be had by booking in advance with rental firms, or as part of a **fly-drive package**. It's worth shopping around on the **internet** to compare rates and find local companies.
- You will usually have to pay a **deposit**; this is normally charged on your credit card and refunded when you return the car.
- All the **major rental companies** have offices at airports as well as in city centres.

Urban Transport

You can walk around the main sights in most of the Spanish cities; historic centres are small, many are pedestrianised, and walking gives a great feel for any new place. Madrid, Barcelona, Valencia and Bilbao (Bilbo) have metro systems, all towns have efficient bus services, and taxis everywhere are plentiful and relatively inexpensive.

Madrid

- The **metro** runs daily from 6am–2am, serves most of the places you'll want to get to, and is clean and efficient. The **flat-fare tickets** are also valid for use on buses; a 10-trip ticket (*bono de diez viajes*) will save you money. There are 12 colour-coded lines, the direction of travel shown by the name of the terminus station. You can pick up a free **map of the system** (*plano del metro*) at any station.
- Madrid's **bus system** is comprehensive, but more complicated to understand than the metro. Use it when there's no nearby metro station to your destination. Buses run from 6am–midnight, with services on more than 20 routes throughout the night. **Flat fare and 10-trip tickets** are interchangeable with metro tickets. Pick up a **plan** at the information offices in the Plaza de la Cibeles and the Plaza Puerta del Sol. Tickets must be validated by punching them in the machine on board the bus.
- **Taxis** are white with a red stripe and show a green light on top when they are available. **Supplements** are charged for luggage, train and bus station and airport trips, and journeys outside the city limits. You can hail a taxi in the street, from a taxi rank or call 914 05 55 00 or 914 47 55 00.
- Madrid Vísion runs **tourist buses** around the main sights with tickets that allow you to get off and on (Calle San Bernardo 23, tel: 917 65 10 16; www.madridvision.es).

Barcelona

- Barcelona's excellent **metro system** runs Sun–Thu 5am–midnight (Fri–Sat 5am–2am) on six lines, which are shown on the **public transport map** available at tourist information offices. You can buy single or multiple (*targeta T1/T10*) **tickets** which must be validated before you board. Tickets are interchangeable with bus tickets. You can also buy **travel passes** lasting up to five days.
- **Bus routes** are colour-coded and marked at bus stops as well as on the transport map; **ticketing** is the same as for the metro system. The daytime system, which runs from 5am–10:30pm, is supplemented on the main routes by a night bus service from 10pm–4am.
- Barcelona also has a **commuter train line**, the FGC, with stations at Plaça de Catalunya and Plaça d'Espanya. To get up Montjuïc, there's the option of the **funicular railway** and **cable-car** (▶ Inside Info, page 124).
- **Taxis** are black and yellow and show a green roof light when they are available for hire. Hail them in the street, find a taxi stand or ring 933 30 08 04, 933 03 30 33 or 933 30 03 00.
- The **bus turistic** (tourist bus) links all the main sights and allows you to get on and off as often as you like. The service starts in the Plaça de Catalunya; red buses head north, and blue south; the ticket price includes the funicular and cable car, and discounts to some attractions.

Admission Charges

The cost of admission for museums and places of interest mentioned in the text is indicated by the following price categories:
Inexpensive under €3   **Moderate** €3–€10   **Expensive** over €10

Accommodation

Spain has an excellent cross-section of competitively priced accommodation, ranging from small family-run *hostales* (modest hotels) to *paradores* (the state-owned chain of luxurious hotels). Away from the more popular tourist destinations, you can usually find a room at short notice, particularly at a *hostal* or *pensión*. During the summer, however, it is always wise to reserve ahead, even if you are heading for somewhere off the beaten track.

Types of Accommodation

- If you can afford it, *paradores* are wonderful places to stay. Many are converted castles, palaces and monasteries, which have successfully retained the historical character of the building, while incorporating all the amenities you would expect from a luxury hotel. There are about 90 paradores throughout Spain. Advance reservations are recommended. Some agencies offer good rates: in the UK, try Keytel International (tel: 020 7616 0300; enquiries@keytel.co.uk; www.keytel.co.uk) or in the US, California-based Petrabax Tours (tel: 1/800 634-1188; www.petrabax.com). Alternatively, book online at www.parador.es, or contact Central de Reservas, Calle Requena 3, 28013, Madrid (tel: 902 54 79 79; www.parador.es).

- Spanish **hotels** are regionally classified with one to five stars (*estrellas*) depending on the amenities. A **5-star hotel** is truly luxurious, with prices and facilities to match. A **4-star hotel** is only slightly less deluxe and still offers first-class accommodation. A **3-star hotel** is considerably lower in price but the rooms are perfectly adequate and will include TV and air-conditioning, while a **1-** or **2-star hotel** is more basic and relatively inexpensive. On-line hotel booking facilities are available on the following websites: http://interhotel.com/spain/es, www.madeinspain.net and the global (but including Spain) www.all-hotels.com and www.travelweb.com.

- *Hostales,* small, family-run establishments, often provide better accommodation and value than inexpensive hotels. *Hostales* are also categorised from 1 to 3 stars. A *hostal* with 3 stars is the equivalent of a 2-star hotel.

- A *pensión* is more like a boarding house. Rooms are clean but spartan, and you often have to share a bathroom. Often a *pensión* will require you to take either full-board (three meals) or half-board (breakfast, plus lunch or dinner). Check when booking what is included in the price.

- *Camas/habitaciones* are the closest equivalent to a bed-and-breakfast, usually advertised in the windows of private houses and above bars and *ventas* (rural restaurants), perhaps with the phrase *camas y comidas* (bed and meals). Don't expect an en-suite bathroom.

- A *fonda* is a small inn offering basic no-frills accommodation.

- All Spanish **campsites** are routinely inspected and approved by the Spanish tourist authority and classified under four categories according to their amenities. The *Guía de Campings* provides a comprehensive list of campsites in Spain. Camping is forbidden on beaches and at tourist resorts. Always check with the local tourist office before you start hammering in the pegs or you may be subject to a fine.

Finding a Room

- If you haven't reserved ahead, visit the **local tourist office** as it will have a list of accommodation with prices. In towns or villages where there is no tourist office, head for the main plaza or centre of town where you're likely to find the greatest concentration of hotels and *hostales*.

- You will be asked to show your passport when you **check in**; this will be used to complete a registration form. Ask to see the room first, especially in cheaper accommodation.
- **Check-out** is normally at noon in hotels, although at some *hostales* and *pensiones* it is 11am. Always find out in advance, to avoid paying an extra day. Likewise, if you plan to leave early in the morning, advise the front desk and if necessary, pay in advance, otherwise you may find there is no one around to settle the bill.
- Hotels will normally store your luggage until the end of the day. *Hostales* are not always as accommodating, however, due to lack of lobby space.

Seasonal Rates

Minimum and **maximum rates** are established according to the season, as well as the facilities provided. In popular summer resorts, July and August are the high season (*temporada alta*) when room rates can increase by 25 per cent. In winter resorts, like the Sierra Nevada (Granada), high season is logically over the winter period. During national holidays and local fiestas (such as the April *feria* in Seville), accommodation can cost as much as three times more. Outside the main season, many hotels offer low, half- or full-board rates, and some will have reduced prices at weekends.

Addresses

The abbreviation s/n signifies a house or building that doesn't have a street number (*sin número*). Urb. (short for *urbanización*) is used as part of the address for new developments.

Food and Drink

While eating habits and hours are more or less uniform throughout Spain, there is no national cuisine, as such, aside from a few dishes such as *paella* (rice, saffron, chicken and/or seafood), *tortilla española* (potato omelette) and *gazpacho* (chilled tomato, pepper and garlic soup), which are popular nationwide. Indeed, each Spanish region guards its culinary traditions as jealously as its regional dialects and languages.

The misty and mountainous region of Galicia, for example, is appropriately home for the robust *caldo gallego* soup (with beef, beans and spinach) and the finest veal in Spain, whereas Asturias is known for its legendary bean dish *fabada*, and *queso cabrales*, a deliciously strong blue cheese. Basque cooking concentrates on fish dishes, such as stuffed king crab *shangurro* and squid in a rich ink sauce. Due east, Catalonia is known for its inventive and exciting cuisine, such as lobster with chicken in a hazelnut sauce and meat and poultry dishes prepared with local fruits.

In the interior areas of Spain, such as Madrid, Castilla and La Mancha you find the best baby roast meats, *chorizo* (spicy sausage) and what is central Spain's best-loved dish, *cocido*, an enticing chick-pea and sausage stew.

In Valencia eating rice is a way of life. This is the home of *paella,* with dozens of variations, including meat, fish, snails or vegetables while, further south, food is prepared with the same abandon and simplicity with which people live their lives. Fried fish is native to Andalucía, as well as *gazpacho*.

Meal Timetable

- **Breakfast** (*desayuno*) is usually coffee with toast (*tostada*), which locals prefer topped with olive oil instead of butter. Other toppings include pork lard (*manteca*), coloured a lurid orange by the addition of paprika, and crushed tomato with olive oil (*tomate y aceite*), often served with a garlic clove on the side. *Churros* (strips of deep-fried dough) and hot chocolate are another popular choice. Most Spaniards drink coffee in the morning, either strong and black (*café solo*), with hot milk (*café con leche*), or black with a dash of milk (*café cortado*). If you find the coffee too strong, you may prefer the more diluted *americano*.

- **Lunch** (*almuerzo*), usually served between 2pm and 4pm, is the most important meal of the day. There are usually three or four courses, starting with soup and/or salad, followed by a seafood or meat dish with vegetables. Often the choice of desserts is limited to caramel custard (*flan*), ice-cream or fresh fruit.

- **Tapas** (snacks) are an integral part of the national culinary tradition, found in even the smallest bar in the tiniest village. Most *tapas* will usually be available in larger *media ración* and *ración* size.

- **Dinner** (*cena*) is eaten any time from 9:30pm onwards and is generally a lighter meal than lunch. Few restaurants offer their cut-price menu in the evening. Instead, you can choose *à la carte*.

Budget Eating

Many restaurants and bars offer an economical lunchtime *menú del día* which will include a starter, main dish and choice of dessert or coffee. The baguette-style sandwiches made by the national chains, *Bocata* and *Pans & Company*, are equally filling and cheap. *Tapas* are also a good budget option, especially if you head for the bars frequented by locals.

Tipping

The Spanish tip an average of five per cent but there is rarely any arithmetic involved. It's more a matter of just leaving spare change. IVA (value added tax) is normally included in the price of meals, usually stated on the menu.

What to Drink

- **Beer** (*cerveza*) is extremely popular and many Spaniards prefer it to wine. A *cervecería* is a bar that specialises in beer and usually has several brands on tap, plus a wide range of bottled and imported beers.

- **Wine** (*tinto and blanco*) Rioja is world-famous, but there are 40 other wine denominations in Spain. You may want to try a house wine (*vino de la casa*) or, for a refreshing alternative, a *tinto de verano* of red wine with lemonade (*gaseosa*).

- **Sherry** is produced in the Jerez region of Andalucía. *Fino* and *manzanilla* are dry, straw-coloured sherries; *amontillado* is medium dry, and *oloroso* is sweet and dark.

- **Spirits** are much cheaper in Spain than in many other countries and the measures are generous. Spanish spirits cost far less than international brands and there is little difference in quality. However, Spanish whisky is better avoided!

- The usual choice of **non-alcoholic** drinks is available, including ubiquitous brands such as Pepsi, Coca-Cola and Seven-Up. Other non-alcoholic drinks include fruit juice (*zumo*) and *Bitter Kas*, the latter similar in flavour to Campari. For something different, try ice-cold *horchata*, a nutty milk-like beverage made from tiger nuts (*chufas*), available at most cafés.

Shopping

Since Spain joined the European Union, the country's shopping scene has been transformed with the opening of numerous shopping centres and hypermarkets. Despite this, there is a fierce loyalty among the Spanish to support the small family-run *tiendas* (shops), which consequently still seem to flourish, particularly in the *pueblos* (small towns).

Opening Hours

Shopping hours in Spain can vary depending on the region, city or town and the type of shop. There are no statutory closing days or hours for retail outlets, except in Catalonia where shops must close by 9pm. Small shops throughout the country still tend to close from 1 or 2pm to 4 or 5pm for the afternoon siesta, although some shops in the larger cities, such as Madrid and Barcelona, as well as supermarkets, souvenir shops and department stores stay open all day.

What to Buy

- Among the best buys in Spain are the **handicrafts**. These are wonderfully diverse and include ceramics, embroidery, fans, glassware, ironwork, damascene (decorative metalwork), jewellery, lace, paintings, porcelain, rugs and carved woodwork. Most of the handicrafts reflect a regional variation, with many products found close to where they are made.
- **Leather goods** are not as cheap as they once were but the quality is dependably high. You can also save on fashionable Spanish exports such as Camper shoes when you buy in Spain.
- **Spanish fashion** reflects the Spanish character and is audacious, colour-ful and stylish. Zara, the darling of fashionistas, is the world's third largest clothing retailer and has nationwide boutiques, while the more mature Mango has an excellent range of smart and stylish fashion for women. Two of the more popular menswear chains are Massimo Dutti and the slicker, more expensive, Adolof Domínguez.

Department Stores

El Corte Inglés is a nationwide Spanish institution and Europe's second-largest department store chain. The stores are huge and stock the best and most famous Spanish and international products. Most outlets also have an excellent but expensive supermarket, with an emphasis on imported and exotic foods.

Markets

There are several kinds of market in Spain. Virtually every village and town will have a daily fresh produce market, selling everything that is in season in the countryside. Weekly street markets, particularly in the tourist resorts, can be a good place to pick up inexpensive pottery and household goods. The city flea markets such as Madrid's Rastro (► 61–62) sell everything from jewellery and ornaments to second-hand clothes.

Payment

The Spanish generally pay cash when shopping, although credit and debit cards are widely used. Personal cheques, even local ones, are rarely accepted. Avoid carrying your money around too conspicuously and watch your handbag in crowded shopping streets, especially Madrid, Barcelona and Seville, all of which are notorious for bag snatching.

Entertainment

There is no shortage of entertainment in Spain, and you don't necessarily have to dig too deep into your pocket to enjoy it. For example, try to time a visit to coincide with one of the more than 3,000 festivals or fiestas held throughout the country. This is one of the best ways to appreciate at first hand the *alegría* (joy) that is an integral part of the Spanish character, and could well cost you no more than the price of a drink.

Music

Spain has a wealth of traditional folk music and dance, particularly flamenco and classical guitar made famous by, among others, Andrés Segovia and Carlos Montoya.

Young Spaniards enjoy a lively and varied music scene, with the Catalans recognised as the country's most serious music lovers. Jazz has a large following thoughout the country and there are annual jazz festivals in many cities, including Barcelona and Santander.

Madrid, Barcelona and Valencia all stage classical music seasons in winter; Granada's summer International Festival of Music and Dance takes place against the magical backdrop of the Alhambra Palace, and the Autumn festival in Madrid includes concerts, opera, drama and ballet. Top international bands, orchestras and soloists perform year-round in Spain.

Advance Tickets

Advance ticket sales for concerts, theatres and other events can often be bought from national savings banks. In Madrid, Caja de Cataluña and Caja Madrid have the most advanced telesales operations, while La Caixa's booking agency ServiCaixa operates throughout Spain. Contact 902 33 22 11, www.servicaixa.com for exact locations. Most branches of El Corte Inglés and FNAC also have a ticket phone line for reserving seats at local concerts/performances.

Nightlife

Spain is famous for its vibrant nightlife, especially in the major cities and resort areas. Most clubs don't start to warm up until after midnight. Some actually open at daybreak, while others are in business non-stop from Friday night until Monday afternoon. A few have early evening sessions for teenagers. Live music is common in music bars. Most have a small dance floor and offer free entrance, but charge more for drinks.

Sports and Outdoor Activities

Spain is the second most mountainous country in Europe and has more than 30 **ski resorts**, including the spectacular Sierra Nevada in Granada.

Golfers are similarly well catered for with more than 200 courses. The majority are along the western Costa del Sol from Málaga to Cádiz, an area dubbed the Costa del Golf (www.golf-andalucia.com is useful).

Watersports enthusiasts have plenty of scope for **wind- and kitesurfing**, **water-skiing**, **jet-skiing**, **surfing** and **sailing**. For information about marinas and competitions, contact the Real Federacíon Española de Vela (Spanish Sailing Federation, tel: 915 19 50 08; www.rfev.es).

The greatest number of top tennis players in Europe can be found in Spain and there are now thousands of courts at tennis and country clubs, hotels, *urbanisations* and municipal and private sports centres. You can expect to pay around €8 an hour for a court.

Madrid

Getting Your Bearings

Spaniards themselves – as long as they come from neither place – would agree it's debatable whether Madrid or Barcelona is bigger, better or livelier. Whatever you think, since 1561, when Philip II decreed it, Madrid has been the capital of Spain, giving it an automatic edge over its Catalonian rival.

Madrid is noisy, vibrant and chaotic, a city where great wealth exists side by side with grinding poverty. Since Franco's death in 1975 *Madrileños* have embraced the values and ideals of the late 20th century with enthusiasm. The result is an exuberant and fast-moving city, with still enough of the old-style way of life to provide a sharp, if elusive, contrast.

For sightseeing, the city handily divides into three historic areas, lying around the hub of the Puerta del Sol. Viejo Madrid (Old Madrid) is centred around the Plaza Mayor, the Barrio de Oriente lies to the east of the Palacio Real (hence its name), while the heart of 18th-century Bourbon Madrid is the sweeping avenues around the Prado museum. Exploring all this gives a wonderful sense of contrast, enhanced by the green open spaces of the city's parks – Madrid has more than any other European capital. However, the city has much more than museums and monuments going for it. It's divided into *barrios*, best described as neighbourhoods, each completely individual, with its own characteristics and charm. *Madrileños* associate the different *barrios* with different activities and atmosphere, and are fiercely loyal to their own *barrio*, though opinions frequently differ about where one ends and the next starts. *Barrios* are both distinct and elusive, and even a short visit to Madrid can result in an attachment to a particular one. Each has its own shops stuffed with the best of its own particular Spanish style, there are literary and artistic associations everywhere, and the entire city seems sports mad. Above all, it's the nightlife that amazes first-time visitors – Madrid really does party all night, with things hotting up well after midnight and traffic jams at 4am.

Previous page: Frescoes enhance the façade of the Casa de la Panadería in the Plaza Mayor. The building is now home to the city's main tourist office

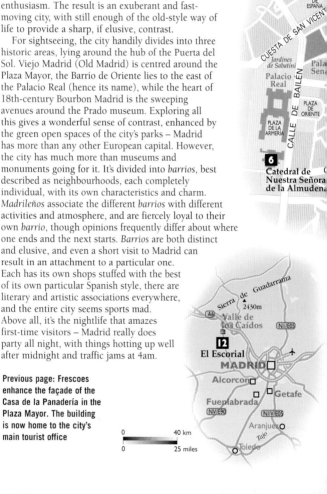

★ Don't Miss

At Your Leisure

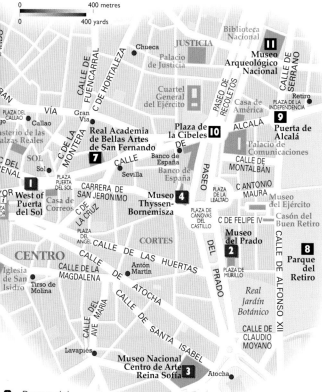

Three days is not long to explore a capital city, but it is just enough to do Madrid's main sites justice and soak up some of the distinctive atmosphere of its different *barrios*, before heading out to explore its major outlying attraction, the monastery of El Escorial.

Madrid in Three Days

Day One

Morning
Take the metro to the **1 Puerta del Sol** (➤ 46–48) and walk west to the **Plaza Mayor** (➤ 46–47), where you can visit the tourist office to pick up maps and information. Head west on the Calle Mayor, pausing to admire the **Plaza de la Villa** (➤ 47). Turn right up Calle de Bailén to see the **6 Catedral de Nuestra Señora de la Almudena** (➤ 56) and the splendid **Palacio Real** (➤ 47–48). Have lunch at the Café de Oriente on the **Plaza de Oriente** (➤ 48), one of Madrid's loveliest open spaces.

Afternoon
Head east from the Plaza de Oriente to the **Monasterio de las Descalzas Reales** (right, ➤ 48) before a stroll down the monumental Gran Vía, Madrid's commercial heart, lined with fine early 20th-century buildings and thronged with shoppers. When you've had enough, take the metro to Retiro for an early evening stroll in the **8 Parque del Retiro** (➤ 57) and look at the **9 Puerta de Alcalá** (➤ 57). The park frequently has entertainment on offer, particularly at the weekend.

Day Two

Morning
Head for the superb collections at the **2 Museo del Prado** (➤ 49–52), one of the world's great art galleries. If Old Masters aren't your thing, take the metro to Atocha and concentrate on the modern masterpieces at the **3 Museo Nacional Centro de Arte Reina Sofía** (➤ 53). Then take the metro or a taxi to Serrano, to have a late lunch in the *barrio* de Salamanca, Madrid's designer shopping district, with plenty of chances for window shopping and people watching.

Afternoon

Round off a day's culture by spending time in the **4 Museo Thyssen-Bornemisza** (above, ➤ 54–55), then stroll up the Paseo del Prado towards the **10 Plaza de la Cibeles** (➤ 57–58), pausing for a drink en route at a *terraza* (outdoor bar) in summer.

Day Three

Morning

Take an early train from Estación de Atocha for the 50km (31-mile) journey to San Lorenzo de El Escorial, from where a local bus runs regularly up the hill to the monastery of **12 El Escorial** (right, ➤ 59–60). Built by Philip II, it is the largest Spanish building of the Renaissance. Spend the morning there before heading back to San Lorenzo for lunch.

Afternoon

Catch the direct bus from El Escorial to **Valle de los Caídos** (➤ panel, page 60), Franco's monument to the dead of the Civil War. Head back via San Lorenzo de El Escorial to Madrid in time to arrive for the evening *paseo*, and stroll with the locals.

Evening

Spend time exploring some of the bars and *tascas* (taverns) in either the Santa Ana and Huerta *barrio* between Puerta del Sol and Museo del Prado, or the Rastro (➤ 61–62).

West of Puerta del Sol

Plaza Puerta del Sol (Gateway of the Sun) marks the epicentre of Spain, a constantly bustling space dear to the heart of every *Madrileño*, from where historic thoroughfares lead to some of the capital's most brilliant architectural ensembles and artistic delights. Rich in history, the area to the west of Sol contains some of Madrid's most important monuments, dating from the 16th–18th centuries, while recent renovations have added a sparkle of sophistication to the entire neighbourhood.

Plaza Puerta del Sol, until 1570 the site of one of Madrid's entrance gates, is dominated by the neo-classical Casa de Correos (1768) and its clock-tower (built later). During the Franco years it housed the headquarters of the feared security police; today, it's the seat of the Madrid regional government. The clock officially ushers in New Year, when *Madrileños* try to eat a grape on each stroke to ensure 12 lucky months. Sol's two other landmarks are the equestrian bronze of Charles III and the statue of the city's emblem, a bear and *madroño* (arbutus) tree.

Top: Madrid's city symbol
Below: Philip III surveys the grandeur of his Plaza Mayor

The old processional route of Calle Mayor runs west from Sol. Off here you'll find the **Plaza Mayor**, its harmonious brick façades punctuated with elegant stonework, the ground-floor arcades designed for shelter. Planned by Philip II, it was

The imposing façade of the Palacio Real

built in the early 1600s by Philip III as a focus for the new capital, and was used for state occasions throughout the 17th and 18th centuries. The oldest building is the Casa de la Panadería (Bakers' Guild) on the north side; recognise it by its frescoed façade. It is now the main tourist office.

Further west and just off the Calle Mayor, you'll find **Plaza de la Villa**, the city's oldest square. The plaza's oldest structure is the Torre de los Lujanes, built in the 15th century, with a fine, though much-restored, *mudéjar* tower. This is balanced by the 1537 Casa de Cisneros, now the mayor's office, richly ornamented in the plateresque style, which simulated the intricate designs of *plateros*, or silversmiths. On the west side of the plaza stands the Casa de la Villa, finished in 1693 to house the city council, a function it still fulfils. The statue in the centre is the 16th-century naval hero, the Marquis of Santa Cruz.

North of the end of the Calle Mayor looms the huge bulk of the grandiose **Palacio Real** (Royal Palace), the high spot of this part of Madrid. No longer the actual home of the royal family, the palace is still used for state entertaining, its opulence the perfect backdrop for official functions. It stands on the site of the 9th-century Moorish Alcázar which became the royal residence when the court moved to Madrid in 1561, remaining so until a fire destroyed it in 1734. Philip V started the rebuilding process, completed in 1764 under Charles III.

The trek across the Plaza de la Armería to the entrance gives you time to take in the colonnaded south front and the gardens of the Campo del Moro. The opulent main staircase, all golden stucco and heroic frescoes, leads to the Salón de los Alabarderos (Halbardiers' Room), with its wonderfully vertiginous ceiling by Tiepolo, and the tapestried Salón de las Columnas (Columned Hall). The next highlight is the Salón del Trono (Throne Room), which still preserves its original 18th-century Bourbon décor. High above the red velvet-swagged walls and gilded furniture, Tiepolo's mighty 1764 ceiling illustrates *The Grandeur of the Spanish Monarchy*, an over-the-top *tour de force* of staggering perspective and swirling draperies. The next three rooms were Charles III's private apartments; look out for the two pairs of fine Goya royal portraits. The delights of the Sala de Porcelana (Porcelain Room) follow, where over a thousand green, white and gold pieces of 18th-century porcelain from the Buen Retiro factory are displayed. Then follows the Comedor del Gala (State Dining Room), still used for banquets, the Capilla Real (Royal Chapel), and outside the main building, the fascinating Armería Real (Royal Armoury) and 18th-century Farmacia (Pharmacy).

Fronting the palace, you'll find the **Plaza de Oriente**, one of Madrid's most pleasant open spaces. East from here lies the **Monasterio de las Descalzas Reales** (Monastery of the Barefoot Royal Ladies), one of the city's great hidden treasures. It was founded in 1564 by Juana de Austria, Philip II's sister, as a convent for aristocratic ladies seeking, or being forced into, the religious life. Pious and wealthy, the nuns and their families endowed and decorated chapels – 33 of them, each more opulent than the last. The two levels of the cloister, each lined with chapels, are connected by a magnificent staircase. The monastery is still home to sisters of the barefoot Franciscan order.

TAKING A BREAK

Finish your tour of the Palacio Real at the elegant **Café de Oriente** (Plaza de Oriente 2). The café's lavish décor and superb views of the palace have established its exclusive reputation.

Plaza Puerta del Sol
➕ 194 C3 ✉ Puerta del Sol 🚇 Sol

Plaza Mayor
➕ 194 C3 ✉ Plaza Mayor 🚇 Sol

Plaza de la Villa
➕ 194 B3 ✉ Plaza de la Villa 🚇 Sol/La Latina/Opera

Palacio Real
➕ 194 A3 ✉ Calle de Bailén ☎ 914 54 88 00 🕐 Apr–Sep Mon–Sat 9–6, Sun 9–3; Oct–Mar Mon–Sat 9:30–5, Sun 9–2

💰 Expensive; free on Wed for EU citizens
🚇 Opera

Plaza de Oriente
➕ 194 B3 ✉ Plaza de Oriente 🚇 Opera

Monasterio de las Descalzas Reales
➕ 194 C3 ✉ Plaza Descalzas Reales 3 ☎ 914 54 88 00 🕐 Tue–Thu and Sat 10:30–12:45, 4–5:45, Fri 10:30–12:45, Sun 11–1:45; guided tours only, some in English
💰 Moderate; free on Wed for EU citizens
🚇 Callao/Sol

MADRID: INSIDE INFO

Top tips Plan your visiting times carefully to hit everything you want to see during opening hours.
• If time is short, **concentrate on the Palacio Real**; you can take in most of the other sites en route.
• **Keep a close eye on your money and personal belongings** at all times – tourists are a prime target around Puerta del Sol.
• Some guides **rush** through the tour of the Descalzas Reales; do your best to **slow** them down, so you can appreciate the treasures on display.

One to miss Skip the **guided tour** at the Palacio Real. It's better to wander at your own speed along the fixed route, though bear in mind that labelling throughout the palace is poor.

2 Museo del Prado

The Museo del Prado, Madrid's most-visited attraction, is one of the world's great museums and a showcase for the finest collection of Spanish paintings, as well as outstanding works by every major European artist. You may find your visit overwhelming, mind-blowing or frustratingly crowded, but you won't forget it. Pace yourself, be selective, and remember you can always come back.

More than most national museums, the Prado represents the personal taste of the monarchs through the centuries and is thus immensely strong in some areas, less so in others, with a noticeable emphasis on religious and courtly paintings. It's particularly focused on Spanish painting, and very rich in

Italian High Renaissance and Flemish art – reflecting the aesthetics of the royal family, whose paintings form the nucleus of the collection. The splendid neo-classical building, designed by Juan de Villanueva in 1785, was finally opened in 1819, when Ferdinand VII moved the royal painting collection here. Amid this vast treasure-house, the Spanish works shine brightest, culminating in *Las Meninas* (*The Maids in Waiting*) by Velázquez, often described as "the finest painting in the world". Goya's work occupies many rooms, as do Italian pictures by Fra Angelico, Botticelli, Titian and Tintoretto. The surreal work of the Flemish painters Hieronymous Bosch and Peter Brueghel the Elder, are other highlights, and there are fine 17th-century French pictures by Poussin and Lorraine. Notable sculptures and dazzling jewellery are on display, while the separate Casón del Buen Retiro houses 19th-century works.

Lofty gallery space shows off the Prado's treasures to their best advantage

Las Meninas

Las Meninas, (below), one of the world's most famous, and certainly greatest pictures, was painted in 1656 by Diego Velázquez, Philip IV's court painter. No other picture so perfectly traps a single moment in time, capturing a transient scene with such precision that you feel you're part of it, standing in Velázquez's own studio in Philip IV's palace. He's possibly painting a portrait of Their Highnesses, who are standing directly in front of you – their reflections can be seen in the mirror on the back wall. Beside the artist stands the royal couple's little daughter, the Infanta Margarita, heir to the throne, surrounded by her maids, the much-loved court dwarfs and a manservant. A favourite dog lies quietly settled. Just outside the room a courtier surveys the scene – or is he about to disturb it? It is this sense of fleeting time that makes *Las Meninas* such a great picture. Reams have been written about the handling of perspective, light, colour and space, the superlative, loose brush work – well worth close inspection, but what you'll remember is the moment. The great Impressionist artist Manet probably summed it up best when he saw the painting and commented "After this I don't know why the rest of us paint".

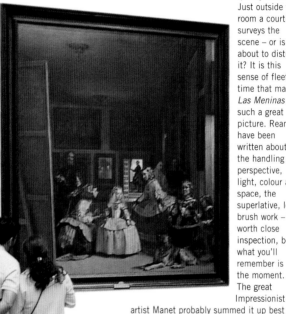

Tackling the Prado

Owing to space problems only about 1,500 of the museum's vast number of works are on display, but even so you can't hope to do justice to everything. In addition, the museum is in the midst of ongoing renovation, which will greatly expand its exhibition space and generally bring it into line with the other great European galleries. So things are very much in a state of flux and you'll need to pick and choose to get the best out of your visit. There's no obvious or set route

The Prado Plan

Renovation has been ongoing at the Prado since the 1980s and there's still much more to come. The refurbishment of the main building is largely complete, but far more dramatic plans are afoot for the Casón del Buen Retiro and other nearby buildings. The Casón is being extended underground, while the neighbouring church of San Jerónimo el Real is scheduled to provide additional exhibition space and also to gain a stunning, glass-fronted office building to one side. The Prado is also going to take over the old Museo del Ejército, the largest surviving part of Philip IV's Palacio del Buen Retiro, on the other side of the Casón. This will eventually house paintings, jewellery and *objets d'art* in keeping with the splendid 17th-century building.

round the museum, but each room is clearly marked with a Roman numeral above the door – though the eye-level signs on the door frames are perhaps easier to spot.

Pictures are frequently moved around, or lent to other museums, but the big stars are normally on view; though some pictures, particularly those by Velázquez and Goya, attract big crowds and you may have to wait to see them. Information is poor throughout the museum – this haughty indifference to visitors may be part of the allure, but it makes sense to buy a guide and spend time working out your priorities before you tackle the actual galleries. As a general guide, the first floor is home to European Renaissance paintings and the pick of the Spanish stars – head here for the Velázquez and Goya rooms. There are more works by Goya on the second floor, while the ground floor is devoted to earlier masterpieces.

TAKING A BREAK

El Dolores (Plaza de Jesús 4) is a short stroll away from the museum and, with its atmospheric interior, ceramic-tiled bar and complimentary olives with your tipple, makes a pleasing alternative to the Prado's basement café.

Francisco de Goya

The Prado's collection of works by Francisco de Goya (1746–1828) is the largest in the world – around 140 paintings and more than 500 drawings and engravings. They cover every aspect of Bourbon Spain's greatest artist's output, from the light-hearted, sunny tapestry cartoons to the apocalyptic pessimism of the *pinturas negras*, the dark pictures. Born in Fuendetodos, Zaragoza, Goya studied in Italy, returning to Spain to work at the Royal Tapestry Workshops before becoming court painter to Charles IV in 1789. Deaf from 1792, his style became increasingly intense and troubled as he became isolated from the world around him. He moved to France in 1824, where he died four years later.

Star Paintings

The Tapestry Paintings – *Spring, Summer, Autumn, Winter; The Clothed Maja; The Naked Maja; The Family of Charles IV; Self-portrait; The Third of May 1808; Saturn Devouring One of his Sons*

Pick of the Prado

Nobleman with his Hand on his Chest – El Greco
(Domenicos Theotocopoulos)
Las Meninas – Diego Velázquez *The Immaculate*
Conception – Bartolomé Esteban Murillo *The Clothed Maja*
– Francisco de Goya *The Naked Maja* – Francisco de
Goya *The Third of May 1808* – Francisco de Goya
The Annunciation – Fra Angelico *Madonna with a*
Fish – Raphael *Ecce Homo* – Titian
Christ Washing the Disciples' Feet – Tintoretto
The Garden of Delights – Hieronymous Bosch
The Triumph of Death – Peter Brueghel the
Elder *The Three Graces* – Peter Paul
Rubens *Artemesia* – Rembrandt
Self-portrait – Albrecht Dürer

Right: This fine bronze pays tribute
to Velázquez, one of Spain's most
revered artists

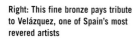

✚ 195 E2 ✉ Paseo del Prado ☎ 913 30
28 00; www.museoprado.es 🕐 Tue–Sun 9–8
💰 Moderate, free on Sun; reduced entrance
fee with the Paseo del Arte ➤ Top Tips below
🚇 Banco de España/Atocha

MUSEO DEL PRADO: INSIDE INFO

Top tips Arrive as **early** as you can to escape the worst of the crowds caused by guided tours, and **be prepared to wait** to get near the star draws.
• If you can, avoid **Saturday afternoons and Sundays** when the museum is extremely busy.
• Pictures are frequently moved around or lent to other museums, so pick up an **up-to-date floorplan** on your way in.
• The **illustrated guidebook** is both informative and well-produced.
• If you're visiting all three museums on the Paseo del Prado, the elegant boulevard which is home to Museo del Prado, the Museo Nacional Centro de Arte Reina Sofía (➤ 53) and the Museo Thyssen-Bornemisza (➤ 54), it's worth buying the **Paseo del Arte ticket**, on sale at all three, which gives a worthwhile discount on entry price.

One to miss Unless you're hooked on **19th-century painting**, don't bother with the pictures in the Casón del Buen Retiro, a separate building to the east.

Getting in There are **two main entrances**. The **Puerta del Goya** on Calle de Felipe IV has an **upper and lower** entrance; take the lower if you want to tackle the museum chronologically, the upper leads straight to the main Spanish collections. The **queues are often shorter** at the **Puerta de Murillo** on Plaza de Murillo at the other end of the building and opposite the Real Jardín Botánico.

3 Museo Nacional Centro de Arte Reina Sofía

One of Madrid's most exciting galleries and exhibition spaces, the Museo Nacional Centro de Arte Reina Sofía is a series of light and airy galleries, the perfect backdrop for the numerous large-scale works that form the backbone of the collection. Here hang works by the greatest Spanish exponents of the different movements of 20th-century art, while pride of place goes to Picasso's great *Guernica*, a timeless allegory on the barbarity of war.

Picasso's *Guernica* is displayed in a modern gallery

Once a hospital, the museum complex was created in the 1980s to provide a stunning setting for art works by luminaries such as **Solana**, **Dalí** and **Miró**. The development of 20th-century art is traced from the Spanish perspective, with enough key works from other countries to put it in international mainstream context. The second and fourth floors house the **permanent collection**; the first- and third-floor galleries are devoted to **changing exhibitions** of contemporary art and design.

Most visitors come here to see Picasso's huge *Guernica* (second floor), one of the 20th century's greatest paintings. Painted in 1937 during the Civil War, *Guernica* finally came back to Spain, on Picasso's wishes, following the restoration of democracy in 1981. Commissioned for the Spanish Republic's pavilion at the 1937 Paris Exhibition, it was inspired by the bombardment of the defenceless town of Guernica by Nationalist and German forces. Packed with symbolism that has provided art historians with decades of debate – Picasso was reluctant to discuss the painting – it is a stunning indictment of the futility of war.

TAKING A BREAK

You'll find a **café**, **bar** and **restaurant** in the basement.

➕ 195 E1　✉ Calle de Santa Isabel 52　☎ 917 74 10 00　🕐 Mon and Wed–Sat 10–9; Sun 10–2:30
💲 Moderate, free Sat pm and Sun; reduced entrance fee with the Paseo del Arte ▶ Top tips, page 52
🚇 Atocha

4 Museo Thyssen-Bornemisza

If the Prado is among the world's great royal art collections, the Museo Thyssen-Bornemisza has to be one of the world's greatest private treasure troves, a stunning array of art amassed over 80 years by the German-Hungarian father-and-son industrial magnates, Heinrich and Hans Heinrich Thyssen-Bornemisza. This highly personal collection, covering nearly every major artist and movement, is brilliantly exhibited in a beautifully remodelled 18th-century building opposite the Prado.

Seeking a new home for his paintings in the early 1990s, Baron Thyssen was undoubtedly influenced by his Spanish wife, Tita. The site, opposite the Prado, also played a part, and in 1993, fighting off competition from Prince Charles, the Getty Foundation and others, the Spanish state successfully secured the collection at a knock-down price of US$350 million.

The Thyssen's treasures are worth a close inspection

The core of the **14th–18th century collection** was purchased during the 1920s and 1930s by the present Baron's father; pictures, sculpture, and objets d'art. On his death in 1947 the collection was split between his heirs. The present Baron bought back some works and began buying on his own account. He started with **old masters**, but from the 1960s concentrated on **German Expressionism, Cubism, Futurism and 19th-century American art**. The reunited, stellar collection of **European old masters** includes four superb Renaissance portraits by Raphael and Hans Holbein. There are Dürers and Cranachs, their linear northern style the perfect contrast to the acidic Mannerism of the El Grecos and the voluptuous colourwork of Titian, Tintoretto and Canaletto.

Moving down from the second floor the museum changes gear, with rooms devoted to cool **Dutch** interiors, **neo-classical** painting and **European Romanticism**. The Impressionists are well represented; don't miss Monet's light-drenched *Thaw at Vétheuil* and Degas's *Race Horses in a Landscape*. Here too you'll find the finest collection of 19th-century **American painting** outside the US, displayed in rooms 29 and 30. Romantic landscapes by Thomas Cole typify the American dream of the virgin land, while Frederick Remington's taut action pictures pay homage to the native people. There's a charming portrait by Gilbert Stuart, set off by sea and river scenes by Winslow Homer, themselves the perfect foil for the brittle sophistication of John Singer Sargent's society portraits.

On the ground floor you'll find **20th-century art** up to the 1970s, with the accent on Cubism – look out for Picasso and Braque. There are pictures too by such luminaries as Jackson

Pollock, Francis Bacon and Roy Lichtenstein, one of the few places in Spain where you can see their challenging work.

In this gallery 20th-century art is displayed to its best advantage

TAKING A BREAK

Try **Viridiana** (► 64), a great little restaurant with some of the most innovative cuisine in town.

🕂 195 E3 🖂 Paseo del Prado 8 ☎ 913 69 01 51; www.museothyssen.org
🕐 Sep–Jun Tue–Sun 10–7 💷 Moderate; reduced entrance fee with the Paseo del Arte ► Top Tips, page 52 🚇 Banco de España

---

MUSEO THYSSEN-BORNEMISZA: INSIDE INFO

Top tips Buy the **well-illustrated guidebook** to help you get the most out of your visit; there's also a **free floor plan**.
• Over 200 new works will soon be on show in this museum after 16 new galleries are opened.

At Your Leisure

5 Museo de América

The Museo de América (America Museum) is one of the best places in Spain to help put the Spanish Conquest in context. This stunning collection of pre-Columbian art and artefacts owes its origins to the treasures first brought home by the *conquistadores*; wonderful objects from the Mayan, Aztec and Inca civilisations. The museum is arranged thematically and spreads over two floors; follow the suggested route to get the best out of your visit. There are displays on history and geography, society, religion and communication, as well as a fascinating section on ideas and myths about America. Don't miss the Quimbayas Treasure, a collection of gold objects from Colombia, or the Trocortesiano Maya Codex, which records the arrival of the Spaniards in the New World. More ghoulishly inclined visitors should seek out the shrunken heads and the Parácos mummy.

🚼 194 off A5 ✉ Avenida de los Reyes Católicos 6 ☎ 915 49 26 41 🕒 Tue–Sat 9:30–3, Sun 10–3 💷 Moderate, free Sun 🚇 Moncloa/Plaza de España

6 Catedral de Nuestra Señora de la Almudena

Madrid's cathedral, dedicated to Our Lady of the Almudena, was consecrated by Pope John Paul II in 1993, more than a century after the original plans were drawn up. Its neo-classical façade was designed to match the neighbouring Palacio Real (➤ 47), its interior, all cool pastel colours, was based on 13th-century Gothic architecture. On the exterior south wall stands the image of the Almudena Virgin, said to have been brought to Spain by St James. Hidden from the Moors, the figure was rediscovered by Alfonso VI when he reconquered Madrid at the end of the 11th century.

🚼 194 A3 ✉ Calle de Bailén ☎ 915 42 22 00 🕒 Daily 9–8:30. Crypt 10–8 💷 Free 🚇 Opera

7 Real Academia de Bellas Artes de San Fernando

Philip V was responsible for instituting the Real Academia de Bellas Artes de San Fernando (Royal Academy of Fine Arts), which has occupied the same building since 1773. For those not sated with the treasures of the Prado (➤ 49–52) and Thyssen (➤ 54–55), this is a treat – one of Spain's most important galleries, crammed with painting and sculpture. The stars here are Spanish, with Velazquez, Murillo, Goya and Picasso well represented, but there is also

The Palacio de Cristal in the pretty Parque del Retiro

exhibitions, and folk dancers often perform on Sunday.

➕ 195 F2 ✉ Calle de Alcalá, Calle de Alfonso XII, Avenida de Menéndez y Pelayo, Paseo de la Reina Cristina 💷 Free 🚇 Retiro/Atocha

French and Italian art.

Goya's self-portraits deserve close scrutiny, as does *Spring* by the Italian Arcimboldo – the sitter's features are entirely composed of fruit and vegetables.

➕ 195 D3 ✉ Calle de Alcalá 13 ☎ 915 24 08 64 ⏰ Tue–Fri 9–7, Sat–Mon 9–2:30 💷 Moderate, free on Wed 🚇 Sevilla

8 Parque del Retiro

The Parque del Retiro (Retreat Park) was laid out in the 1630s as part of an immense French-style pleasure gardens, complete with palace and lake, designed as a royal playground. The palace's ballroom, the Casón del Buen Retiro still survives, and houses the Prado's 19th-century collection (➤ panel, page 51); most of the rest was destroyed during the Napoleonic Wars. Since 1868, when the Retiro became municipal property, it has been Madrid's favourite park, bright with flowers, scattered with statues and fountains, and *the* place for the Sunday *paseo*. Many people head straight for the lake, dominated by an ornate statue of Alfonso XII, but there's plenty more, including the Palacio de Cristal, a wonderful 19th-century glass palace, an 18th-century parterre, the world's only statue of Lucifer, *El Angel Caído*, and drifts of roses. There's always a good programme of concerts and

9 Puerta de Alcalá

Surrounded by roaring traffic, the Puerta de Alcalá (Alcalá Gate) is a symbol of Madrid, a fine example of neo-classical architecture, and one of the first things to catch the eye on the way in to the city. Standing on the site of the old city walls, the gateway was completed in 1778 for Charles III as the main entrance to Madrid. It's on a monumental scale, with five grandiose arches topped by lion heads, cherubim and coats of arms.

➕ 195 F4 ✉ Plaza de la Independencia 🚇 Retiro

10 Plaza de la Cibeles

Glistening buildings on an epic scale surround the Plaza de la Cibeles; prosaically, the one most resembling a wedding cake is home to the main post office, while the others are the Army HQ, the Banco de España and the Casa de América (Palacio de Linares), a showcase for Latin American visual arts. For many *Madrileños*, the plaza's ebullient architecture is a real symbol of the city, with the central fountain taking star billing. This depicts the goddess Cibeles in her chariot and was completed in 1792 for Charles III. Cibeles's lions

Lions draw Cibeles's chariot in a superb fountain in the Plaza de la Cibeles

are called Hipponomes and Atlanta, and her fountain is a popular bathing spot for victorious Real Madrid fans.

🔢 195 E4 ✉ Plaza de la Cibeles ⓜ Banco de España

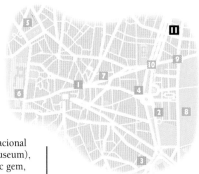

ⓜ Museo Arqueológico Nacional

The Museo Arqueológico Nacional (National Archaeological Museum), an archaeological and artistic gem, occupies part of the massive neo-classical building housing Spain's National Library. The collection sets out to trace the evolution of human culture from pre-history to the 15th century, concentrating mainly on pieces from excavations in Spain, and ranging from Roman and Greek to Islamic finds. This is the place to see rare Celto-Iberian busts, like the enigmatic Dama de Elche from the region of Valencia, and a fabulous

Visigothic treasure, the Guarrazar Crowns, found near Toledo. Don't miss the reconstruction of the Altamira prehistoric cave paintings (➤ 99–100); they are in the garden to the left of the main entrance.

🔢 195 F5 ✉ Calle de Serrano 13 ☎ 915 77 79 12 🕐 Tue–Sat 9:30–8, Sun 9:30–2:30 💶 Moderate, free Sat and Sun pm ⓜ Colón

For Kids

• There's plenty to keep children occupied in the **Parque del Retiro** (➤ 57), with the advantage that it's right in the middle of town. You can rent a boat, sample the playgrounds, or enjoy a **puppet show in the summer**.

• For the best range of kids' activities head for the **Casa de Campo**, to the west of the Palacio Real (🔢 194 off A4, metro: Batán). This big park is home to the **Zoo-Aquarium** (tel: 915 12 37 70, open summer daily from 10:30–8, winter from 11–5:30, admission expensive). There is also a boating lake and the **Parque de Atracciones** (tel: 914 63 29 00, www.parquedeatracciones.es, open Apr–Sep daily noon–dusk, Oct–Mar Sat–Sun noon–dusk, check website for precise schedule). It is moderate without rides, expensive with unlimited access to rides. Older children will love *La Lanzadera*, a vertical drop, and the white-water raft ride, *Los Rápidos*. There's an open-air auditorium and plenty of parades to watch. Across the Parque is the **Teleférico**, a cable-car ride which gives great views of the city (Paseo del Pintor Rosales, tel: 915 41 74 50, www.teleferico.com/madrid, open summer daily noon–dusk, winter Sat–Sun noon–dusk, admission inexpensive, metro: Argüelles).

• Also good for children is the **Museo de Ciencias Naturales** (🔢 195 off F5, Calle José Gutiérrez Abascal, tel: 914 11 13 28, open Tue–Fri 10–6, Sat 10–8, Sun 10–2:30, admission inexpensive, metro: Nuevos Ministerios), where there are hands-on exhibits and audiovisual displays.

• At **Imax Madrid** (🔢 195 off F1, Calle Meneses s/n, Parque Enrique Tierno Galván, tel: 914 67 48 00, www.imaxmadrid.com, several shows a day from noon, admission moderate, metro: Méndez Alvaro) there's a choice of three giant screens showing mainly wildlife and adventure documentaries.

Further Afield

⓬ El Escorial

The big must-do excursion from Madrid is the 50km (31-mile) trip to the Sierra de Guadarrama and the massive religious complex known as El Escorial. One of the most impressive monuments in Spain, and the largest Renaissance building in the country, this huge and severe building gives a true insight into the extraordinary wealth and power of the 16th-century Spanish monarchy.

In 1557 the Spanish forces of Philip II defeated the French at St Quentin. In thanksgiving Philip, a deeply religious man, conceived the idea of building a monastery dedicated to San Lorenzo (St

The stern lines of El Escorial encapsulate the power of the Spanish monarchy

Lawrence), which would also serve as a royal palace and burial place. From here, he planned to live the life of a monk, ruling the world "with two inches of paper". Between 1563 and 1584 some 1,500 builders worked on the vast structure designed by Juan Bautista de Toledo and Juan de Herrera.

Externally, **El Escorial** is rectangular, but its ground plan is patterned on a grid, said to recall the gridiron on which St Lawrence was martyred; you can see the saint's statue, complete with gridiron, over the west gate. Nearly 210m (229 yards) long, the monastery has more than 1,200 doors, 2,600 windows and 16 courtyards. The severe structural lines of the building are accentuated by the granite used in

its construction, and the clear air has kept the stone and tiles pristine.

The **Patio de los Reyes** (Courtyard of the Kings) fronts the huge **basilica**, with its 40 side altars and Philip's collection of holy relics. The church is on a monumental scale, with a 30m (98-feet) high altarpiece whose onyx, marble and jasper columns are punctuated by bronze sculptures. Below lies the **Panteón de los Reyes** (Royal Pantheon), where the majority of Spanish kings from the time of Charles V onwards are buried. Most of the religious treasures are kept in the rooms around the basilica, including paintings by El Greco, Titian, Tintoretto and Veronese.

The **Salones Reales** (Royal Apartments) were extended by the Bourbon monarchs; their sumptuous interiors and tapestries are a marked contrast to the simplicity of Philip II's private apartments. These restrained rooms have direct access to the church, and here, dying of gangrene caused by gout, Philip could participate in the Mass from his sickbed.

The second-floor **Biblioteca** (Library) links the secular and religious areas of the monastery. Here you'll see shelves of rare wood, marble tables and a mind-boggling ornate ceiling. After all this, there's still the picture museum to tackle; its highlights, among numerous works by Rubens, Titian and Tintoretto, are

Getting There

• **Avoid visiting** on Wednesday, when entrance is free, to escape the worst of the crowds.

• The **best time** to hit the Royal Apartments is just before lunch.

• You can combine El Escorial and Valle de los Caídos by taking a **guided tour** from Madrid – try Juliatour (Gran Vía 68, tel: 915 59 96 05); Pullmantour (Plaza de Oriente 8, tel: 915 41 18 05) or Trapsatur (Calle San Bernardo 5/7, tel: 915 41 63 21).

• If you've got your **own transport**, it's worth driving the 7km (4.3 miles) along the Ávila road to the **lookout point** at Silla de Felipe II. This rocky outcrop is supposedly the point from which Philip watched the construction of his monastery and there are splendid views of the buildings and surrounding countryside.

Roger van der Weyden's thought-provoking *Calvary* and the gaunt angularity of El Greco's marvellous *Martyrdom of St Maurice*.

✚ 199 D2 ✉ Calle Juan de Bourbón y Battemberg s/n, San Lorenzo de El Escorial ☎ 918 90 59 02 🕐 Apr–Sep Tue–Sun 10–6; Oct–Mar 10–5 💰 Expensive; free on Wed to EU citizens 🚉 From Atocha 🚌 Autocares Herranz (tel: 918 96 90 28); buses leave from Moncloa bus station

Valle de los Caídos

A beautiful valley, deep in the Guadarrama mountains, is the setting for Franco's chilling monument **Valle de los Caídos** (Valley of the Fallen). Ostensibly a memorial to the Civil War dead of both sides, the basilica complex was built by survivors of the Republican army between 1940–58, an austere and grandiose building aimed clearly at the glorification of Franco and his regime. The dictator is buried behind the high altar; the only other named tomb is that of his Falangist model, José Antonio Primo de Rivera. An immense cross stands on the mountain above the basilica surrounded by giant figures – take the funicular up to enjoy the superb views.

✚ 199 D2 ✉ Carretera de Guadarrama, Valle de Cuelgamuros 🕐 Apr–Sep Tue–Sun 9:30–6:30; Oct–Mar 10–5:30 🚌 From El Escorial Tue–Sun at 3:15 💰 Moderate; free on Wed to EU citizens; combined ticket with El Escorial.

THROUGH THE RASTRO

Walk

DISTANCE 3.2km (2 miles) **TIME** 3 hours, allowing time for El Rastro (time this walk for Sunday if possible, when the flea market takes place) and the Real Jardín Botánico
START POINT Plaza Puerta del Sol ⓢ Sol ✛ 194 C3
END POINT Real Jardín Botánico ⓜ Atocha ✛ 195 F2

This walk takes you from the elegance of the Plaza Mayor through the exuberant working class districts of El Rastro and Lavapiés, which are now becoming increasingly fashionable. The vibrant weekend street life, with the famous Rastro Sunday market, makes a good contrast with the fine 18th-century architecture and the expanses of green you'll also encounter on this walk.

1–2

Stand in the **Plaza Puerta del Sol** (➤ 46) with your back to the **Casa de Correos**, built in 1768 and the city's post office until 1847. You're standing at the epicentre of Spain, since all distances are measured from the stone slab below the clock tower, known as Kilómetro Cero (Kilometer Zero). Turn left down **Calle Mayor**, and take the fourth turning on the left into the **Plaza Mayor** (➤ 46–47).

2–3

Leave the Plaza Mayor in the southwest corner and head down the **Calle de Toledo**, a typically *Madrileño* street with wonderfully idiosyncratic shops. As you reach the Plaza de Segovia Nueva, the huge building on the opposite left-hand corner is the **Iglesia de San Isidro**. The church was built as the Jesuits' Spanish powerhouse in 1622–33 and was part of the Colegio Imperial. Charles V fell out with the Jesuits in 1767, annexing their property, and the church was rededicated to San Isidro, Madrid's patron saint. It served as the city's cathedral from 1886–1993.

3–4

Follow the signposted **El Rastro** route south from San Isidro down Calle de los Estudios to the Plaza de Cascorro and across this into **Calle de la Ribera de Curtidores**, the heart of the Rastro district and site of the famous flea market. Rastro means "stain", a reference to

the blood from two slaughterhouses which once stood here. Curtidores is quietish on a weekday, but becomes a sprawling, vibrant market on Sundays. You'll find everything imaginable on sale, a great atmosphere, and some of the city's liveliest bars. Watch your bag, and leave cameras and jewellery back at the hotel.

4–5

Turn left down Calle de San Cayetano and continue until you reach the parallel street, **Calle de Embajadores**, with the 1761 church of **San Cayetano**, one of the area's patrons, ahead of you across the road.

5–6

Head down Embajadores and take the sixth turning left, **Calle de Tribulete**, to walk past **La Corrala**. This traditional 19th-century tenement block, with its balconies opening on to a central courtyard, provides some of the area's most characteristic housing. In summer the

turning left, Calle del Doctor Fourquet. Turn right at the bottom to reach the **Museo Nacional Centro de Arte Reina Sofía** (▶ 53).

7–8

From the Reina Sofía, use the Atocha station underpass system to reach Calle del Doctor Velasco on the north side of the Paseo de la Infanta Isabel. Head north to the **Real Jardín Botánico**, founded in the 18th century and restored in the 1980s to house over 30,000 plant species from around the world. It's a peaceful spot, with shady paths, benches and hothouses crammed with tropical plants and vines.

patio is used for *zarzuela*, Spain's own version of Gilbert and Sullivan, which incorporates elements of opera with bawdy music-hall songs and jokes.

6–7

From La Corrala, continue along Tribulete until you reach **Plaza de Lavapiés,** a square which was the medieval centre of the Jewish quarter. Turn diagonally right into Calle de Argumosa, taking the third

Taking a Break

You'll find plenty of places in the streets around El Rastro market to pause. **El Tempranillo** (🛏 194 B2, Calle de Cava Baja 38, open noon–4, 8–1) serves good *tapas* and wines by the glass.

When

Sunday is the day for El Rastro market. If you can't make the Sunday, don't worry – this is an atmospheric neighbourhood any day of the week. Start at around 10am to hit the Rastro as things get going.

Places to Visit

San Isidro

🛏 194 C2 ⊠ Calle de Toledo 37–39
🕐 Mon–Sat 7:30–12:30, 6–8:30, Sun 8:30–2:30, 5:30–8:30 🚇 La Latina 🎫 Free

El Rastro

🛏 194 C2 ⊠ Calle de la Ribera de Curtidores
🕐 Sun 10–3 🚇 La Latina 🎫 Free

Real Jardín Botánico

🛏 195 F2 ⊠ Plaza de Murillo, 2 🕐 Daily 10–dusk (depending on season) 🚇 Atocha
🎫 Inexpensive

Where to... Stay

Prices
Expect to pay per person per night
€ up to €50   €€ €50–€90   €€€ €91–€120   €€€€ over €120

Bauzá Hotel €€€

This is one of Madrid's most stylish hotels, a haven of minimalist luxury. Walls throughout are in tones of grey and pale blue with the occasional splash of red. Rooms have modern facilities, including internet access. There's an excellent restaurant which serves adventurous Mediterranean food.

⊞ 195 off F5 ⊠ Calle de Goya 79
☎ 914 35 75 45; www.hotelbauza.com
Ⓜ O'Donnell/Goya

Hostal Lido €

A great-value *hostal*, the Lido is on one of Madrid's most happening streets. There are ten rooms with a choice of shared or en suite bath-room. Heating fans and fridges are included in the price. Singles are a real bargain at around €25 a night.

⊞ 195 D3 ⊠ Calle de Echegaray 5, 2º Izqda ☎ 913 69 46 43;
www.hostallido.com Ⓜ Sevilla/Antón Martín

Hostal Persal €€

A facelift has brightened up this old-fashioned hotel in a grand old building perfectly situated between buzzy Plaza Santa Ana and Plaza Mayor. The spacious rooms have TV, air-conditioning, bathrooms and small balconies over a pretty leafy square.

⊞ 195 D3 ⊠ Plaza del Angel 12
☎ 913 69 46 43;
www.hostalpersal.com Ⓜ Sol

La Macarena Hostal €€

This elegant cream-and-white building sits on one of the city's most charming old streets across from several famous 18th-century *tascas* (bars), just west of the Plaza Mayor. All 23 rooms have satellite TV and cheery yellow paintwork. Try to request a room with a balcony, particularly recommended is number 303 for its extra size. There's a lively café downstairs where you can join the locals for breakfast.

⊞ 194 B3 ⊠ Calle Cava de San Miguel 8 ☎ 913 65 92 21; fax: 913 64 27 57 Ⓜ Sol/Opera

Hotel Mora €€

This 1930s hotel is conveniently placed near the Prado and Botanical Gardens. The bright, airy lobby has an original skylight and marble-look columns, and there's an adjoining café, which is popular with locals as well as residents. The tastefully decorated, modern rooms are spacious and practical, with plenty of useful gadgets. Some have views over the museum and gardens. Double-glazing helps to block out traffic noise.

⊞ 195 E2 ⊠ Paseo del Prado 32
☎ 914 20 15 69; www.hotelmora.com
Ⓜ Atocha

Westin Palace €€€€

This classic *grande dame* of Spanish hotels, dating from 1912, is part of Starwood Hotels. The hotel décor is fittingly palatial, with prices to match. The entrance lobby and surrounds are wonderfully sumptuous – particularly eye-catching is the stained-glass domed ceiling in the entrance salon where you can sit and sip a sherry even if you can't afford to stay. The hotel covers an entire city block with more than 400 rooms, plus a panelled library, restaurants, bars and a modern fitness centre.

⊞ 195 E3 ⊠ Plaza de las Cortés 7 ☎ 913 60 80 00;
www.palacemadrid.com
Ⓜ Sevilla/Banco de España

Where to...
Eat and Drink

Prices

Expect to pay per person for a meal, including wine and service

€ up to €12   €€ €12–€30   €€€ over €30

Casa Ciriaco €€

This traditional Castilian taverna near the Royal Palace offers a range of unpretentious fare such as *gallina en pepitoria* (chicken in egg and saffron), *cocido madrileño* (a hearty stew, made with chorizo sausage) and *perdriz con judiones* (partridge with broad beans). There is a good wine list too.

➕ 194 B3 ⌑ Calle Mayor 84 ⌦ 915 48 06 20 ⏱ Thu–Tue 1–4:30, 8–12:30; closed Aug Ⓜ Opera

El Olivo €€–€€€

It took a Frenchman, Jean Pierre Vandelle, to open a restaurant honouring two of Spain's most revered culinary resources – olive oil and sherry. You can choose from more than 60 regional olive oils to dribble on chunks of bread. These are best accompanied by an ice-cold *fino*, from a selection of more than 90 different sherries stocked at the bar. Specialities on the menu include a variety of fish dishes with sauces based on olive oil, including four preparations of salt cod served with a chilli sauce.

➕ 195 off F5 ⌑ General Gallegos 1 ⌦ 913 59 15 35 ⏱ Tue–Sat 1–4, 9–midnight; closed August 15–31 and Easter week Ⓜ Cuzco

El Estragón €–€€

Expect generous helpings at this vegetarian restaurant. Dishes include risotto verde, and some have an Eastern tang. The restaurant stands on one of Madrid's most attractive and ancient squares, and is now a fashionable meeting place for the younger set. There's an inexpensive *menú del día* during the week, and two sittings for dinner. The imaginative desserts are well worth trying.

➕ 194 B2 ⌑ Plaza de la Paja 10 ⌦ 913 65 89 82 ⏱ Daily 1:30–5, 8–midnight Ⓜ La Latina

Restaurante Botín €€–€€€

Botín is one of the city's original old taverns, complete with smoke-blackened brick walls, wood-fired oven and low ceilings. The speciality is suckling pig and roast meats of every description. You can expect to pay a minimum of €30 a head for a memorable gastronomic experience.

➕ 194 B3 ⌑ Cuchilleros 17 ⌦ 913 66 42 17 ⏱ Daily 1–4, 8–12 Ⓜ Sol/Tirso de Molina

San Mamés €€

San Mamés is a typical *tasca* – noisy, crowded and cramped with just nine tables spread over two small rooms. Hearty Castilian fare is the mainstay, marvellously prepared with an emphasis on barbecued meats and fish, as well as haricot bean stew, garlic soup and tripe *a la madrileña*.

➕ 194 off C5 ⌑ Bravo Murillo 88 ⌦ 915 34 50 65 ⏱ Mon–Fri 1:30–4, 8:30–11, Sat 1:30–4 Ⓜ Cuatro Caminos

Viridiana €€–€€€

There's nothing run-of-the-mill about this restaurant. Aside from having an exceptional wine cellar with wines from all over the world, owner Abraham García is movie mad and the walls are covered with big screen stills. The innovative food is based on traditional Castilian dishes. Try the steak with black truffles for a real taste-bud treat.

➕ 195 F3 ⌑ Calle Juan de Mena 14 ⌦ 915 23 44 78 ⏱ Mon–Sat 1:30–4, 8:30–midnight Ⓜ Retiro

Where to... Shop

One of the delights of shopping in Madrid is exploring the idiosyncratic small shops. Many have remained in the same family for several generations and are a nostalgic reminder of the days before bland high street chains. The sheer diversity of shops is fascinating, and the personal service an added bonus.

At the centre is Plaza Mayor where, amongst the inevitable souvenir bazaars, are located such gems as **Casa Yustas** (tel: 913 66 50 84, metro: Sol), an extraordinary emporium founded in 1894, selling everything from sombreros to army caps. A short walk away, **Casa Hernanz** (Calle de Toledo 18, tel: 913 66 54 50, metro: Sol) is famous for its espadrilles, while **Gonzapur** (Calle de Esparteros 18, tel: 915 22 27 96, metro: Sol) is one of the best places for Spanish shawls, fans, hair combs and *mantillas*. **Capas Seseña** (Calle de la Cruz 23, tel: 915 31 68 40, metro: Sevilla) is equally famous for its wool capes, reputedly worn by Picasso, Miró and Chelsea Clinton, among others, while **Loewe** (Gran Vía 8, tel: 915 22 68 14, metro: Gran Vía) dates from 1846 and is easily Spain's most elegant leather store.

In the more upmarket class, Calle Ortega y Gasset is home to **Giorgio Armani** (No 16, tel: 915 76 10 36, metro: Núñez de Balboa) and the more affordable **Kenzo** (No 15, tel: 914 35 65 93, metro: Núñez de Balboa). **Zara** (Calle de la Princesa 45, tel: 915 41 09 02, metro: Ventura Rodríguez), the darling of fashionistas has made Spanish creator, Ortega, the second richest man in the European rag trade with stores in 34 countries. Top designers are copied, to give "fast fashion" that is stylish and at a price that won't burn a hole in your pocket! A few doors away, **Mango** (Calle de la Princesa 69, tel: 915 44 46 96, metro: Ventura Rodríguez) is marginally more up-market and expensive, and virtually next door, **Massimo Dutti** (Calle de la Princesa 79, tel: 915 43 74 22, metro: Ventura Rodríguez) sells trendy, good value menswear. Calle Serrano also has many smart fashion outlets.

DEPARTMENT STORES

The city's biggest one-stop shop is **El Corte Inglés**, providing all the goods you expect in a department store, plus hair and beauty treatments, a supermarket, and a restaurant. There are several branches throughout the city, the most central being at Calle de Preciados 1–4 (tel: 913 79 80 00, metro: Sol).

MARKETS

For sheer shopaholic rapture, the Sunday market at El Rastro (▶ 61–62) is obligatory. Open from dawn to approximately 2pm, the country's most famous flea market sells everything from glorified junk to genuine antiques. It is also a pickpocket's paradise so be extra vigilant. The fruit and vegetable markets are worth visiting for their atmosphere and colour. In the centre, follow the shopping baskets to **Mercado San Miguel** (Plaza de San Miguel, metro: Sol) or, even better **Mercado Antón Martín** (Calle de Santa Isabel 5, metro: Antón Martín) with its old-style tiled frontage and mouth-watering produce displays.

CAKES AND PASTRIES

Casa Mira (Carera de San Jerónimo 30, metro: Sevilla) dates from 1842 and still prepares *turrón* (nougat) and other delicious sweets, while **La Mallorquina** (Plaza Puerta del Sol 8, metro: Sol) has a café upstairs, where you can enjoy a slice of local life along with the delicious cakes and pastries made on the premises.

Where to...
Be Entertained

Pick up *In Madrid*, a monthly free magazine, to see what's going on, or buy the glossy *Broadsheet*, which has a useful classified section. There is also the weekly Spanish language *Guía del Ocio* magazine with entertainment, cinema and restaurant listings.

NIGHTLIFE

Madrid must be one of the few cities in the world where you can get caught in a traffic jam at 4am on a Sunday morning. Dusk-to-dawn partying is the norm in Europe's nocturnal capital.

The mainstay in Madrid's music scene are the **discobars** which have small dance floors. There is seldom a cover charge, unless there is live music, although drinks will cost more than usual bar prices.

Discobars are located throughout the city, with the most eclectic, trendy mix concentrated in the areas around Sol and Santa Ana.

Among the best is, **El Viajero** (Plaza de la Cebada, metro: La Latina), a fashionable late-night hang-out with a good music mix and pool tables.

Jazz enthusiasts go to **Café Central** (Plaza Ángel 10, tel: 913 69 41 43, metro: Antón Martín) with nightly concerts at 10, and **Café Jazz Populart** (Calle Huertas 22, tel: 914 29 84 07, metro: Antón Martín); open from 6pm, music from 11pm.

Disco diehards have seven floors to choose from at **Kapital** (Calle de Atocha 125, tel: 914 20 29 06, metro: Atocha). The **Palacio de Gaviria** (Calle del Arenal 9, tel: 915 26 60 69, metro: Opera) provides a fabulous baroque setting and varied music in a choice of rooms.

CLASSICAL MUSIC AND THEATRE

For unrivalled elegance, try Madrid's **Teatro Real** (tel: 915 16 06 00, metro: Opera), a revamped former theatre on Plaza de Oriente and the city's principal opera house. The city is also the home of *zarzuela*, comparable to a more spirited version of the Viennese operetta and best enjoyed at the **Teatro de la Zarzuela** (Calle Jovellanos 4, tel: 915 24 54 00, metro: Banco de España).

Classical music buffs can check out the programme at the **Teatro Monumental** (Calle de Atocha 65, tel: 914 29 21 81, metro: Antón Martín), which is also open to the public on Thursday mornings at rehearsal time. Serious theatre (as well as music and dance) can be seen at several venues in Madrid, with the greatest variety available during the **Festival de Otoño** (Autumn festival, Oct–Nov).

FLAMENCO

Flamenco has recently undergone an enthusiastic revival in Madrid and there are several authentic *tablaos* (shows) in town. Among the best is the one at **Café de Chinitas** (Calle de Torija 7, tel: 915 47 15 02, metro: Santo Domingo), where some of Spain's top dancers perform in 17th-century surroundings.

For an Andalucian atmosphere, head for **Al Andalus** (Calle del Capitán Haya 19, tel: 915 56 14 39, metro: Cuzco) where the post-floor show sees the mainly Spanish audience dancing *sevillanas* until dawn. If you want a chance to practise first, try **Almonte** (Calle de Juan Bravo 35, tel: 915 63 54 04, metro: Núñez de Balboa). There's no live show, but plenty of flouncing frills and foot-stomping on the dance floor.

Castilla and León

Getting Your Bearings

If your vision of Spain has been shaped by the sun 'n' sand Costa image, you'll find no greater antithesis than Castilla (Castile) and León. Here there's nothing but mile after mile of rolling, empty countryside beneath immense skies, outcrops of isolated mountains and thread-like rivers, the plains and valleys dotted with a few remote towns. From this lonely landscape rise the great cities of Spain's central plateau – Burgos, Segovia, Salamanca and León, rich monuments to a great past.

In European terms, distances here are big, and often seem greater because of the emptiness of the land. But the long drives between the cities give a real sense of what oases they are – entering a beautiful, historic place after hours on the road gives a real buzz. If you're not up for a lot of driving, aim to concentrate on the square formed by the main cities of Burgos, Segovia, Salamanca and León. This way you'll see the best in terms of cathedrals and monuments and also get a taste of Spain's upland interior.

Away from these major centres, picturesque villages like Covarrubias lie in quiet countryside, and once-major cities, such as sleepy walled Ávila, make a civilised contrast to the scenic

delights of the Sierra de Guadarrama, Madrid's outdoor playground. Travelling around is easy:

Previous page: Autumn vineyards clothe Castile's rolling hillside

Left: Majestic medieval walls completely enclose the city of Ávila

★ Don't Miss

At Your Leisure

Further Afield

roads are, on the whole, excellent and uncrowded, and the entire area is relatively undiscovered by foreign tourists. Your main problem may be trying to decide what to miss, or not having as much time as you'd like in each place.

With time to spare, you could explore the regions to the east and north of the area. The rolling countryside of La Rioja, famed for its vineyards, contrasts with the diverse delights of the neighbouring province of Aragón, whose highlights include the majestic scenery of the high Pyrenees and its capital, Zaragoza.

**Walkers in the hills of the
Sierra de Guadarrama**

There are some longish drives between the four great cities of the Castile and León region, which will give you a good idea of the size and scale of the *meseta*, the great Spanish upland central plateau. Seeing Burgos, Segovia, Salamanca and León in five days will help you appreciate their diversity and the wonderful contrast between these bustling centres and the empty outlying countryside.

Castilla and León in Five Days

Day One

Morning
Spend the morning exploring the historic centre of ❶ Burgos (➤ 72–74), visiting the **cathedral** (detail of the façade right) before having lunch at one of the restaurants along Calle de la Paloma, perhaps La Taberna de Quico (➤ 73).

Afternoon
Head across the river to visit the **Real Monasterio de las Huelgas** (➤ 73), returning to the centre in time for some shopping before joining the strolling evening crowds along the **Paseo de Espolón**. Have a pre-dinner drink at one of the bars on **Plaza Rey San Fernando** near the cathedral before sampling a local restaurant, such as El Mesón del Cid (➤ 86).

Day Two

Morning
Take the N1 south towards Segovia, detouring perhaps on to the N234 to visit ❺ Covarrubias (➤ 83) and **Santo Domingo de Silos** (➤ 83), where you could have lunch.

Afternoon
Continue south on the N1, then turn southwest on the N110 to ❷ Segovia (➤ 75–76). Get your bearings by strolling around the city and viewing the **aqueduct** before visiting the **cathedral** and the **Alcázar** (➤ 75).

Evening
A drink at one of the outdoor cafés on the **Plaza Mayor (➤** 76) makes a
good start to the evening; follow it up with dinner and a late-night stroll.

Day Three

Morning
Leave Segovia via **Iglesia de la Vera Cruz (➤** 75–76), then head southwest
to **7 Ávila (➤** 83), where you could have lunch before walking a section of
the walls.

Afternoon
Take the
N501 north-
west to
8 Salamanca
(➤ 77–80)
arriving in
time to walk
to the **Plaza
Mayor** (right)
as the shops
open and the
city starts to
gear up for
the evening.

Day Four

Morning
Spend the morning tackling Salamanca's big sights, the **cathedral**
(➤ 78–79) and the **university**, before relaxing over lunch in the Plaza Mayor.

Afternoon
You'll have time to take in some of the city's churches and monasteries
before heading north on the N630 to arrive in **4 León (➤** 81–82) in time for
a typically late Spanish dinner.

Day Five

Morning
Get up early to see the morning light on the **cathedral** before exploring the
interior. Then it's time to visit **San Isidoro (➤** 82) and the **Panteón (➤** 82)
before lunch at Boccalino (➤ 87) on the plaza outside.

Afternoon
Head down into modern León to do some window-shopping before ambling
through the riverside gardens to treat yourself to a drink at the bar in the
parador at **San Marcos (➤** 82 and 86).

Evening
Spend the evening back in the historic centre, dining and experiencing the
atmosphere in the bars around **Plaza San Martín (➤** 82).

❶ Burgos

Rising from the plains of Castile, historic Burgos and its great cathedral are inextricably linked with the glory days of the *Reconquista* and the pilgrim path to Santiago. Thriving modern Burgos pulsates with civic pride, its historic buildings and riverside setting forming the perfect backdrop to the pleasures of a prosperous provincial capital.

Burgos was the capital of Castile from 1037–1492; from here, Ferdinand III recaptured Murcia, Córdoba and Seville from the Moors, and it was he who commenced the building of the cathedral. Get your bearings by wandering around the pedestrianised centre to the arcaded **Plaza Mayor**, keeping an eye out for the sweeping glass-galleried frontages of so many of the buildings, typical of this part of Castile.

The City Centre

Two historic bridges cross the River Arlanzón. For the El Cid connection, head for the **Puente de San Pablo**, a stone-figure-lined bridge dominated by a dramatic equestrian statue of El Cid (➤ panel, page 74) at its far end. From here, the tree-lined Paseo de Espolón, scene of Burgos' evening promenade, leads down beside the river to the **Puente de Santa María** bridge and the great white **Arco de Santa María**. This gateway was once part of the town walls and was castellated and decorated with statues in the 16th century – you'll be able to spot El Cid here as well.

The Arco leads to the lovely plazas surrounding the **cathedral** – a nice place to pause at a café table. From here, you'll get your first close-up of the astounding forest of spires, pinnacles, stone carving and statuary adorning this **masterpiece of Gothic art**. Founded in 1221 by Ferdinand III, the cathedral is Spain's third largest, and, architecturally, covers the evolution of the Gothic style from the 13th–15th centuries. Inside, northern elements are fused with Hispano-Moorish features in a mind-boggling profusion of doorways, chapels, vaulting and sculpture. Burgos impresses with its complexity, not as a unified whole. So concentrate on the individual highlights, the simple **tombstone of El Cid** beneath the transept crossing, the superb **star-vaulting** – a Moorish borrowing – and, above all, the chapels, large enough to be

Right: The gloriously ornate main altar of the Real Monasterio de las Huelgas

Below: The soaring façade of Burgos cathedral

churches in their own right. Best of these is the octagonal **Capilla del Condestable** behind the high altar, founded in 1482 and largely the work of Simon of Cologne, a second-generation Hispano-German architect. Nearby, you can admire the splendid **Escalera Dorada** (Golden Staircase), a double stairway in the north transept. The **Capilla del Santo Cristo**, just off the southeastern corner of the nave, though far plainer, contains a much-venerated image of the crucified Christ, a 14th-century figure endowed with human hair and covered with buffalo hide to resemble human skin.

Real Monasterio de las Huelgas

The Real Monasterio de las Huelgas, set in a tranquil backwater across the river, was founded in 1187 as the resting place for Alfonso VIII and his English wife Eleanor of Aquitaine, daughter of Henry II. This lovely **monastery** was one of the most powerful in Spain and the burial place of many Castilian monarchs. It is renowned for its **mudéjar craftmanship**, which you'll see on the ceiling of the main Gothic cloister – look out for the typical star patterns and peacock designs (a bird revered by the Moors). Its museum contains fine medieval textiles and jewellery, the church is splendid and there's a cult statue of St James with an articulated right arm for dubbing knights.

TAKING A BREAK

Near the cathedral you'll find stylish **La Taberna de Quico** (Calle La Paloma, tel: 947 27 19 73), where you can enjoy sophisticated *tapas*, *bocadillos*, and salads.

El Cid

Fact or fiction, goodie or baddie – who was the legendary hero El Cid? He certainly existed and was born near Burgos in the mid-11th century. Motivated chiefly by cash, he was a mercenary soldier, happy to fight for whomever would pay, and fought during his career for both Christians and Muslims, though he earned his sobriquet from the Moors; *sidi* means "lord" in Arabic. He was first employed in Castile, but his most famous victory was the capture of Valencia in 1094. He died in 1099, his widow holding Valencia for another three years before fleeing to Castile with her husband's body. They were buried near Burgos and in 1921 their ashes were finally interred in Burgos cathedral.

✚ 199 D3

Tourist Information Office
✉ Plaza Alonso Martínez 7
☎ 947 20 31 25; www.aytoburgos.es
🕐 Mon–Fri 9–2, 5–7, Sat–Sun 10–2, 5–8

Cathedral
✉ Plaza Santa María

☎ 947 20 47 12 🕐 Mon–Sat 9:30–1, 4–7, Sun 9:30–11:45, 4–7 💷 Moderate

Real Monasterio de las Huelgas
✉ Compases ☎ 947 20 16 30 🕐 Tue–Sat 10–1, 3:45–5:30, Sun 10–2 💷 Moderate, guided tours mainly in Spanish, free Wed

BURGOS: INSIDE INFO

Top tips Use the **English-language audioguide** to get the most out of your visit to the cathedral.
• If you're **visiting Las Huelgas**, ask at the ticket desk if your guide on the tour **speaks English**; if not, it may be worth waiting for the next one.
• Climb up behind the cathedral for wide **city views** from the **Mirador del Castillo**.

Hidden gems Pause to admire the **planting along the river** where wildflowers, trees, shrubs and grass provide one of the most tranquil city-centre elements you'll ever see.

2 Segovia

Beautiful Segovia, crammed with mellow stone monuments, churches, mansions and squares, spreads along a rocky ridge against the stunning backdrop of the Sierra de Guadarrama. Retaken from the Moors in the 11th century, it was here that Isabel the Catholic was proclaimed Queen of Castile in 1474; the finest buildings date from these centuries. Intimate yet sophisticated, grand but cosy, Segovia is rightly one of the top choices for anyone exploring Castile and León.

The great Roman **acueducto** (aqueduct) constructed in the 1st century AD brought water from over 15km (9 miles) away. Towering above the Plaza de Azoguejo in Segovia's lower town, the 166 granite arches of this remarkable structure, 800m (875 yards) long and 30m (98.5 feet) high, have stood firm with no cement or mortar, though traffic and pollution are taking their toll.

Centuries later, in 1525, work started by the order of Charles V on the **cathedral**, the last important Gothic building constructed in Spain, built over more than 200 years. Outside, pinnacles, domes and flying buttresses soar skywards; inside, the space is filled with the heavy central green marble *coro* (choir). The rooms surrounding the cloisters contain the cathedral **museum**, while to one side, the free-standing tower looms over the whole fantasy.

Still more fantastic is Segovia's **Alcázar**, complete with pointed turrets and sloping roofs, which stands at the opposite end of the ridge from the aqueduct. Originally built in the 14th–15th centuries and once a royal residence, today's whimsical castle – used as a model for the original Disneyland castle – is largely an 1862 reconstruction, following a fire. It's well worth exploring the interior, all gilding and *mudéjar*-style friezes, as much for the fine views as for the pictures and furniture. You'll get even better vistas from the **top of the tower** – 141 steps up and no lift.

Below the walls and outside the city stands one of Spain's most remarkable ecclesiastical buildings, the 12-sided **Iglesia de la Vera Cruz** (The True Cross), built for the Knights Templar in the 13th century. Modelled on the Church of the Holy Sepulchre in Jerusalem, its form is unique in Europe.

The fairy-tale silhouette of Segovia's Alcázar

The powerful arches of Segovia's Roman aqueduct tower above the plaza below

Inside, there's a two-storied central temple, where Templars once kept vigil. Awe-inspiring in its antiquity, redolent with mysticism, Vera Cruz deserves to be better known.

TAKING A BREAK

Head for **La Concepción** (Plaza Mayor 15, tel: 921 46 09 30) to taste the very best of Castilian regional cooking and imaginative *tapas* while you watch the world go by.

✚ 199 D2

Tourist Information Office
✉ Plaza Mayor ☎ 921 46 60 70; www.segoviaturismo.es ◷ Summer daily 9–8; winter Mon–Fri 9–2, 5–8, Sat–Sun 10–2, 5–8

Cathedral
✉ Calle Marqués de Arco ☎ 921 46 22 05 ◷ May–Sep daily 9:30–6:30; Oct–Apr 9:30–5:30 🎟 Museum: inexpensive

Alcázar
✉ Plaza de la Reina Victoria Eugenia ☎ 921 46 07 59 ◷ Apr–Sep daily 10–7; Oct–Mar 10–6 🎟 Moderate; free Tue to EU citizens

Iglesia de la Vera Cruz
✉ Carretera de Zamarramala ☎ 921 43 14 75 ◷ Apr–Oct Tue–Sun 10:30–1:30, 3:30–7; Dec–Mar Tue–Sun 10:30–1:30, 3:30–6; closed Nov 🎟 Inexpensive

---

SEGOVIA: INSIDE INFO

Top tips You can rent an **English language audio-guide** at the **Alcázar**; there's also an informative English leaflet.
• Make a point of **walking out** along the roads surrounding the city for **ever-changing views** of the cathedral and Alcázar. **Best overall views** are about 2km (1 mile) out to the north on the Cuéllar road.
• Spend time just **wandering around**; you'll come across hidden corners and splendid buildings at every turn.
• Make sure you have an outside table at one of the **cafés in the Plaza Mayor** – soak up the atmosphere and do some great people-watching.

In more depth If you're keen on **Romanesque churches** head for **San Martín, La Trinidad, San Millán and San Justo**; be warned though, that only La Trinidad and San Millán are open outside service times. La Trinidad has superb capitals on the pillars of its double-arched apse; San Millán has the characteristically Segovian open portico and a *mozarabe* tower (► 15).

One to miss Unless **weapons and artillery** really fascinate you, **skip** the Royal Artillery Museum at the Alcázar.

3 Salamanca

Salamanca's wonderful mix of graceful churches, mansions and plazas, its ancient university and tradition of scholarship all combine to make it one of Spain's most seductive cities. It is a city on a human scale, made even more alluring by the glowing honey-coloured stone of its buildings. There's plenty to see, but one of the chief pleasures is wandering the streets and absorbing the atmosphere of a city that is more than the sum of its parts.

The best place to start exploring Salamanca is the **Plaza Mayor**, built in the 18th century by Philip V, and one of the world's great squares. The symmetry of the three-storey, arcaded buildings around this harmonious space is punctuated on the north side by the grander mass of the Ayuntamiento (Town Hall). Above the arcade arches you'll notice a series of portrait medallions of Spanish monarchs and famous men – look out for El Cid and Christopher Columbus. Constantly criss-crossed by locals and tourists alike, the Plaza is the real hub of Salamanca.

Cross the road on the south side to head down the Rúa Mayor, which leads towards many of the city's finest monuments. Halfway down, on a corner on the right, is the beautiful **Casa de las Conchas** (The House of the Shells), a mellow 15th-century building whose exterior walls are decorated with

The façade of the Ayuntamiento enhances the line of the architecture around the Plaza Mayor

more than 400 stone cockle shells, a reminder of the pilgrimage to Santiago de Compostela (➤ 22–24). Opposite here looms the church of the **Clerecía**, a 17th-century baroque building, built for the Jesuits, with an impressive cloister.

The University of Salamanca

Salamanca's **university** was founded in the 13th-century and quickly made its mark as one of Europe's intellectual powerhouses, renowned for its freedom of thought and its huge academic prowess. It thrived for more than five centuries, its influence only waning under the attack of 18th-century extreme clericalism and the depredations of the Napoleonic troops. Today, it's outshone by the universities of Madrid and Barcelona, but retains its social prestige.

The tiny **Patio de las Escuelas**, flanked by a lovely courtyard, stands opposite the university's main entrance, a good place to admire this elaborate plateresque **façade** (1534). It is covered with superb decoration, a riot of foliage, heraldic decorations and medallions – the central one shows Isabel and Ferdinand, the Reyes Católicos (Catholic Kings). See if you can spot the tiny carved frog – good luck comes if you find it unaided. (Cheats should concentrate halfway up on the right pilaster.)

The entrance leads into a courtyard, surrounded by the old lecture halls, still in use today, from where you can explore the rest of the complex. Pick of the bunch is the **Aula Fray Luís de León**, which still retains its 16th-century furnishings. It was to here that Fray Luís returned in 1578 after five years in the hands of the Inquisition, starting his lecture with the words "Dicebamus hesterna die…" (as we were saying yesterday). On the upper floor you'll find the 18th-century **library**, lined with some 40,000 incunabula (early books) and 16th–18th century books.

The Cathedrals and Beyond

There's more plateresque work on the entrances to the **Catedral Nueva** (New Cathedral), just behind the university. Started in 1513, the New Cathedral acted as both a statement of Salamanca's prestige and a buttress to the Romanesque **Catedral Vieja**

Honey-coloured stone and superb plateresque carving are the hallmarks of the Catedral Nueva

(Old Cathedral), which was in danger of imminent collapse. It's the wonderful contrast between the two buildings, one ornate and flamboyant, the other simple and serene, that makes the complex so special. The New Cathedral was largely complete by the 1560s, with later baroque additions. A door in the south aisle leads into the stunning Old Cathedral, all light and lofty golden stone. Glowing behind the main altar hangs the huge 15th-century *retablo* (altarpiece) by Nicolás Florentino, with 53 panels showing scenes from the Life of Christ and the Virgin. The adjoining cloister is surrounded by chapels, many of which were used as overflow university lecture rooms. Star of the show is the **Capilla de Anaya**, with its two exquisite alabaster tombs and a quirky little organ, said to be the oldest in Europe.

Behind the cathedral there's a contrast in the form of the **Museo Art Nouveau y Art Deco** (Museum of Art Nouveau and Art Deco). It contains lovely glass and porcelain, lamps and furniture but it's the building itself, the Casa Lis, which takes top prize. Filled with light and colour, it was built largely of coloured glass for an enthusiast in the early 1900s.

More Churches

East from here, the **Convento de San Esteban** (St Stephen) boasts a splendid plateresque façade, a beautiful portico and fine 16th-century Gothic-Renaissance cloisters. Inside, the east end is dominated by a baroque *retablo* by José Churriguera, a riot of decorative columns, statuary and ornate decoration.

There are more cloisters at the **Convento de las Dueñas**, perhaps the most striking in Salamanca. Climb the creaky stairs to the upper level for a fabulous view of the cathedral, framed by the irregularly shaped cloisters themselves.

To the north, the **Convento de Santa Clara** is crammed with treasures, many of which hid under whitewash for years until rediscovery in the 1980s. The most riveting find was the

Facing page: Statuary and coats of arms emphasise the historic importance of Salamanca's university

orginal 14th-century ceiling of the church, decorated with the castles and lions of Castile and León, which had been covered by a baroque false ceiling.

TAKING A BREAK

Choose from one of the restaurants surrounding the Plaza Mayor, all of which serve *tapas*. **Don Mauro** (Plaza Mayor 19, tel: 923 28 14 87) is one of the best.

🔢 198 C2

Tourist Information Office
✉ Plaza Mayor 32 ☎ 923 21 83 42;
www.salamanca.es ⏰ Summer Mon–Fri
9–2, 4:30–8, Sat 10–8, Sun 10–2; winter
closes at 6pm

Casa de las Conchas
✉ Calle Compañia ☎ 923 26 93 17
⏰ Apr–Sep Mon–Fri 9–9, Sat 9–2, 5–8, Sun
5–8; Oct–Mar Mon–Fri 9–9, Sat 9–2, 4–7, Sun
10–2, 4–7 💰 Free

La Clerecía
✉ Calle Compañia ☎ 923 26 46 60
⏰ Apr–Sep Tue–Fri 10:30–1, 5–7, Sat
10–1:30, 5–7:30, Sun 10–1:30; Oct–
Mar Tue–Fri 10:30–1, 4–6, Sat 10–1:30,
4–6:30 💰 Inexpensive

Universidad
✉ Patio de Escuelas ☎ 923 29 44 00
⏰ Mon–Fri 9:30–1:30, 4–7, Sat 9:30–1:30,
4–6:30, Sun 10–1:30 💰 Moderate

Catedral Nueva
✉ Plaza de Anaya ☎ 923 21 74 76
⏰ Daily 9–8 💰 Free

Catedral Vieja
✉ Plaza de Anaya ☎ 923 21 74 76
⏰ Daily 9–8 💰 Moderate

Museo Art Nouveau y Art Deco
✉ Calle Gibraltar ☎ 923 12 14 25
⏰ Tue–Fri 11–2, 5–9, Sat–Sun 11–9
💰 Moderate

Convento de las Dueñas
✉ Plaza Concilio de Trento ☎ 923 21 54 42
⏰ Apr–Sep Mon–Sat 10:30–12:45, 4:30–6:45,
Sun 11–12:45, 4:30–6:45; Oct–Mar Mon–Fri
11:30–12:45, 4:30–5:30, Sun 11:30–12:45,
4:30–5:30 💰 Inexpensive

Convento de San Esteban
✉ Plaza Concilio de Trento
☎ 923 21 50 00 ⏰ Apr–Sep daily 9–1, 4–6;
Oct–Mar 9–1, 4–5 💰 Inexpensive; free Mon
am

Convento de Santa Clara
✉ Calle Santa Clara ☎ 923 26 96 23
⏰ Mon–Fri 9:30–2:30, 4–7, Sat–Sun 9–3
💰 Inexpensive

SALAMANCA: INSIDE INFO

Top tips If you're pushed for time concentrate on the **Plaza Mayor**, the **cathedrals** and the **university**. Be sure to leave an hour or so simply to wander.
• The best time for a drink in the **Plaza Mayor** is after dark, when the square is beautifully **floodlit**.
• The Convento de las Dueñas still sells delicious **cakes and biscuits** made by the enclosed nuns. Ring the bell beside the hatch in the entrance hall, put in your order and money and the goods will **appear on the turntable**.

One to miss The religious art collection at the **Museo de Salamanca** (Bellas Artes) is pedestrian, though the exterior of the 15th-century mansion is superb.

Hidden gems It is worth the stroll down to the **Puente Romano** behind the cathedral; this 400m (440-yard) long, graceful bridge has superb views back to the old city on the hill above.

4 León

First a Roman settlement, then the capital of the northern Christian kingdom during the *Reconquista*, León's power reached its peak from the 11th–13th centuries. Its finest monuments date from this time, grouped, with one exception, in the compact huddle of the old quarter. Around this nucleus, a lively modern city spreads down to the River Bernesga, with everything you would expect from a stylish provincial capital with a big university presence.

Left: Glowing stained-glass is the glory of León cathedral

Inset: Vibrant stone figures crowd the cathedral's façade

León's great buildings are graphic examples of how French Romanesque architecture crept over the Pyrenees and through northern Spain in the wake of the pilgrims following the Camino de Santiago (➤ 22–24). León was a stopping point along the route, where pilgrims worshipped in the cathedral, founded in 1255, and rested before one of the hardest sections.

The soaring **cathedral**, with its flying buttresses and great rose windows, might easily have been transported straight from France – go inside for the assault of glowing colour from **Spain's finest stained glass** and you'll be even more struck by the similarities to French Gothic cathedrals. But here, the colours are less muted, vibrant reds and yellows replacing the soft pinks and blues found in France. Outside, two towers rise above the **central doorway** with its lively scenes of the Last Judgement.

A 10-minute walk northwest through the old city from the cathedral lies the complex of **San Isidoro**, dating from the mid-11th to 12th centuries. The church, with its Moorish arches, was built after the **Panteón** next door, constructed by Ferdinand I as a mausoleum. The vaulted roof is covered with **12th-century paintings** portraying Christ Pantocrator and the Evangelists, surrounded by biblical scenes and decoration. The rural scenes representing the months of the year are as appealing as the day they were painted.

West again and well outside medieval León, stands the **Hostal de San Marcos**, founded in 1168 as a pilgrim hostel. The original building was replaced in the 16th century when it became the headquarters of the Knights of Santiago – look out for St James tackling the Moors above the main entrance. Behind the extravagant **plateresque façade** there is a beautiful cloister; part of the *parador* now occupying San Marcos. The monastery's church is still open to visitors, although much of the complex is currently undergoing renovation.

TAKING A BREAK

If you're near the cathedral, head for the popular **Restaurante Catedral Bar** (Calle Mariano D Berrneta 17, tel: 987 21 59 18) where you'll find excellent *tapas* at the bar and full meals served in the restaurant behind.

🚩 198 C4

Tourist Information Office
✉ Plaza de la Regla 3 ☎ 987 23 70 82; www.aytoleon.com 🕐 Jul–Aug Mon–Fri 9–7, Sat–Sun 10–8; Sep–Jun Mon–Fri 9–2, 5–7, Sat–Sun 10–2, 5–8

Cathedral
✉ Plaza de la Regla ☎ 987 87 57 70; www.catedraldeleon.org 🕐 Jul–Sep Mon–Sat 8:30–1:30, 4–8, Sun 8:30–2:30, 5–8; Oct–Jun Mon–Sat 8:30–1:30, 4–7, Sun 8:30–2:30, 5–7

Museo Diocesano
✉ Plaza de la Regla ☎ 987 87 57 70 🕐 Jun–Sep Mon–Fri 9:30–2, 4–7:30, Sat 9:30–2, 4–7; Oct–May Mon–Fri 9:30–1:30, 4–7, Sat 9:30–1:30 🎟 Moderate

Panteón y Museo de San Isidoro
✉ Plaza de San Isidoro ☎ 987 87 61 61 🕐 Jul–Aug Mon–Sat 9–8, Sun 9–2; Sep–Jun Mon–Sat 10–1:30, 4–6:30, Sun 10–1:30 🎟 Moderate; free Thu pm

Iglesia de San Marcos
✉ Plaza San Marcos ☎ 987 24 50 61 🕐 May–Sep Tue–Sat 10–2, 5–8:30, Sun 10–2; Oct–Apr Tue–Sat 10–2, 4:30–8, Sun 10 –2, 🎟 Inexpensive

---

LEÓN: INSIDE INFO

Top tips Don't miss Antonio Gaudí's (➤ 127) neo-Gothic **Casa de Botines**, opposite the 16th-century Palacio de los Guzmanes on the edge of the old town.
• The best way to visit **Hostal de San Marcos** and see its lovely cloister is to **stay there** – but anyone can have a drink in the bar.
• Head for the streets around the **Plaza San Martín** for León's liveliest and most atmospheric bars and restaurants.
• If you are driving, park by the river, which is convenient for all the major sights.

One to miss Unless you are interested by ecclesiastical museums, **skip the cathedral museum**, though it's worth popping in to look at the cloister.

At Your Leisure

5 Covarrubias and Surrounding Area

Covarrubias, southeast of Burgos, is a pretty, small town, complete with an historic church and picturesque half-timbered buildings, whose flower-draped walls shelter cool arcades. From here you could head south again to take in the Benedictine abbey of **Santo Domingo de Silos**. Its great double-storeyed Romanesque cloister was built in the 11th century and is one of the loveliest in Spain. The sculptural reliefs are outstanding, as are the capitals of its columns, but what you'll chiefly remember is the atmosphere of peace and the lazy splash of water in the central fountain. The abbey's monks are famed worldwide for Gregorian chant. Sung Mass is on Sundays at noon.

✚ 199 E3

Monasterio de Santo Domingo de Silos
✚ 199 E3 ✉ Valle de Tabladillo
☎ 947 39 00 68 ☺ Tue–Sat
10–1, 4:30–6, Sun–Mon 4:30–6
☺ Moderate

6 Sierra de Guadarrama

The range of mountains known as the Sierra de Guadarrama stretches to the northwest of Madrid, a natural barrier between Madrid and Castile, and a favourite recreational area for *Madrileños*. These beautiful hills enclose two regional parks (Peñalara and La Pedriza), which have kept large areas relatively unspoiled. You could take the little train which runs from **Cercedilla** to **Puerto de Navacerrada**, the heart of the ski area, or visit **Manzanares el Real**. Across the range, the highlights are the two Bourbon summer palaces of **La Granja**, with its spectacular fountains, and **Riofrío**, surrounded by a deer park.

✚ 199 D2

7 Ávila

Ávila is famous on two counts – its wonderfully preserved city walls and its home-grown saint, the mystic St Teresa. Alfonso VI's Muslim prisoners built the walls in the 1090s following the re-capture of the city from the Moors. These massive structures, still complete with their 88 watch towers, encircle the old city, and walking at least one section should be high on your list. Ávila's architectural hotch-potch of a cathedral backs on to them; started in the 11th century, the apse is actually an integral part of the walls. There are several convents and muse-ums associated with St Teresa – she is the joint patron saint of Spain along with Santiago (St James).

✚ 199 D2

Tourist Information Office
✉ Plaza de Pedro Dávila 4
☎ 920 21 13 87; www.avila.net or
www.avilaturismo.com ☺ Jul–Sep
Mon–Thu 9–8, Fri–Sat 9–9; Oct–Jun
daily 9–2, 5–8

Murallas (City Walls)
✉ Puerta del Alcázar, Puerta
del Rastro ☺ Tue–Sat
10–2, 4:30–7:30, Sun
10:30–2
☺ Moderate

Cathedral
✉ Plaza de la Catedral
☎ 920 21 16 41 ☺ Mon–Sat
10–8, Sun 12–6 ☺ Moderate

Further Afield

8 La Rioja

Vineyards in the rolling landscape along the valley of the River Ebro produce Spain's best-known quality wine, Rioja. Wine-lovers could easily spend a couple of days following the wine trails in the area, sampling along the way. **Haro** is the obvious place to start; here you'll find the state-of-the-art **Estación Enológica y Museo del Vino** (Oenology Centre and Wine Museum), which explains the entire production process, with information on soil and climate, grape varieties and vintages. Haro is a down-to-earth working town with some lovely old buildings and plenty of opportunities for wine-tasting. **Logroño**, further down the valley, is a prosperous city with a fine cathedral and a clutch of wineries.

➕ 199 E3

Tourist Information Office, Haro
➕ 199 E4 ✉ Plaza Monseñor Florentino Rodríguez ☎ 941 30 33 66; www.beronia.org ⏱ Jul–Sep Tue–Sat 10–2, 4:30–7:30, Sun 10–2; Oct–Jun Tue–Sat 10–2, Sun 4–7

Estación Enológica y Museo del Vino, Haro
➕ 199 E4 ✉ Calle Breton de los Herreros ☎ 941 31 18 00 ⏱ Closed for renovation

Tourist Information Office, Logroño
➕ 199 E4 ✉ Paseo del Espolón ☎ 941 29 12 60; www.logrono.es ⏱ Daily 10–2, 4–7

9 Zaragoza

Zaragoza, the capital of Aragón, stands on the banks of the River Ebro. Its civic centrepiece, the Plaza del Pilar is one of the most impressive complexes in northern Spain. Two great religious buildings dominate this huge expanse, with its graceful buildings, statuary and fountain, the Basílica de Nuestra Señora del Pilar (Our Lady of the Pillar) and La Seo, the old cathedral. The Pilar was built in the 1760s to house the sacred pillar on which the Virgin was said to have descended from heaven in an apparition; the Seo is much older with exquisite *mudéjar* details. There's more Moorish work at the Aljafería, the 11th-century palace of the region's Moorish rulers, which now houses the Aragonese parliament.

Tourist Information Office
➕ 200 A3 ✉ Plaza del Pilar ☎ 976 39 35 37; www.turismozaragoza.com ⏱ Mon–Sat 10–8, Sun 10–2

Basílica de Nuestra Señora del Pilar
✉ Plaza del Pilar ☎ 976 39 74 97 ⏱ Summer daily 5:30–9:30; winter 5:30–8:30 🎟 Free

Palacio de la Aljafería
✉ Calle Diputados s/n ☎ 976 28 96 83 ⏱ Apr–Oct Mon–Wed and Sat 10–2, 4:30–8, Sun 10–2; Nov–Mar Mon–Wed and Sat 10–2, 4–6:30, Sun 10–2 🎟 Moderate, free Sun

Left: Rioja wine country, in the fertile valley of the River Ebro

Where to... Stay

Prices

Expect to pay per person per night

€ up to €50   €€ €50–€90   €€€ €91–€120   €€€€ over €120

El Mesón Del Cid €€€

In the very heart of the old city, this comfortable, well-appointed hotel has a wonderful position facing the cathedral and overlooking the Plaza Santa María. The rooms are light and airy – try to get one in the main building, though those in the nearby annexe share the view and are up to a similar standard. The private parking is a real bonus; the staff are friendly and efficient and the attached restaurant is a good choice if you don't want to venture out.

✚ 199 D3 ⊠ Plaza Santa María 8
☎ 947 20 87 15; fax: 947 26 94 60;
www.mesondelcid.es

Norte y Londres €€

Pretty balconies and the glass-fronted galleries so typical of Burgos adorn the facade of this fine hotel on Plaza Alonso Martínez, not far from the cathedral in the centre of town. The 50 spacious, wood-floored rooms are simply furnished in classic style, and the whole property has recently been upgraded.

✚ 199 D3 ⊠ Plaza Alonso Martínez 10 ☎ 947 26 41 25;
www.norteylondreshotel.com

Acueducto €€

If you're looking for a modern and well-run place to stay, head for this slightly out-of-town hotel in the shadow of the aqueduct – you can have breakfast with a view. The spacious public rooms and a bar, and rooms are all a good size, there are you can walk to the town centre (uphill) in around 10 minutes.

✚ 199 D2 ⊠ Avenida Padre Claret 10 ☎ 902 25 05 50;
www.hotelacueducto.com

Infanta Isabel €€

This lovely hotel has to be top choice in Segovia for its wonderful position overlooking the Plaza Mayor and cathedral. Add to this the elegant, 19th-century interior and comfortable rooms, the professional service and you've got the ideal base for discovering Segovia.

✚ 199 D2 ⊠ Plaza Mayor
☎ 921 46 13 00;
www.hotelinfantaisabel.com

Las Sirenas €

This is a modest place with an elegant stone façade on a lovely old plaza. Some of the rooms have balcony views of the handsome church opposite. Inside antiques and ornaments lend a pleasantly old-fashioned air. Rooms are well-maintained, with decent beds and neat bathrooms. Breakfast only is served, but that is not a problem with this central location.

✚ 199 D2 ⊠ Calle Juan Bravo 30
☎ 921 46 26 63;
www.hotelsirenas.com

Petit Palace Las Torres €€€€

Appearances are deceptive. The Petit Palace Las Torres may be housed inside an historic building on the Plaza Mayor, but once you step inside you are greeted by a tastefully modern boutique hotel. The rooms are stylish and hi-tech including computers complete with ADSL connections, and flat-screen TVs.

✚ 198 C2 ⊠ Calle Concejo 4
☎ 923 21 21 00;
www.petitpalacelastorres.com

Where to...
Eat and Drink

Prices

Expect to pay per person for a meal, including wine and service

€ up to €12 €€ €12–€30 €€€ over €30

Rua Hotel €€

An elegant hotel near Plaza Mayor which offers excellent reductions for longer stays and at certain times of the year. The refurbished rooms are decorated with shiny light wood and breezy blue-and-yellow colours. The parking is a plus in this city. Breakfast is served in a charming stone-faced bar.

➕ 198 C2 ✉ Calle Sanchez Barbero 11 ☎ 923 22 72 72;
www.hotelrua.com

LEÓN

Hostal Guzmán el Bueno €

The comfort of this small *hostal*, situated in a quiet street in the historic old town, far exceeds its price. Many of the 25 modern, well-equipped rooms, all with bathrooms, are grouped around an interior courtyard, so ask for one of these if you're looking for peace and quiet.

➕ 198 C4 ✉ Calle López Castrillón 6 ☎ 987 23 64 12;
www.infohostal.com

Hotel La Posada Regia €€

The welcome is warm and the level of comfort high in this small hotel. It is ideally situated just off the pedestrian-only main street in the old town. The hotel has comfortable brick-clad rooms and its own restaurant specialising in local dishes.

➕ 198 C4 ✉ Calle Regidores 9–11 ☎ 987 21 31 73; www.regialeon.com

Parador Hostal San Marcos €€€

One of Spain's great hotels, this luxurious *parador* dates from the 16th century, but the facilities are entirely contemporary. Most of the rooms are in a more modern annexe, but the public rooms of this former pilgrims' hostel have tapestries, carpets and pictures that create a living museum, while the superb cloisters surround a monastic calm. Service and comfort are of the highest standard.

➕ 198 C4 ✉ Plaza San Marcos 7 ☎ 987 23 73 00;
www.parador.es

BURGOS

Casa Ojeda €€

This cosy, popular place offers classic Burgos fare in a setting of Moorish tiles and low ceilinged rooms full of interesting nooks and crannies. The upper restaurant is in two sections. Typical dishes include Basque-style hake, roast lamb or chicken in garlic. A house speciality is *alubias con chorizo y morcilla* (white beans and spicy sausage).

➕ 199 D3 ✉ Calle Vitoria 5 ☎ 947 20 90 52 🕐 Mon–Sat 1:30–4,
9–11:30; Sun 1:30–4

El Mesón del Cid €€

This long-established restaurant, in a building facing the cathedral, specialises in traditional Castilian cooking. Dishes include *olla podrida* (a stew of chickpeas, brisket, ham and marrow bones), pork *morcilla*, black pudding and various *bacalao* (salt-cod) dishes. Try the *queso fresco*, an unfermented cottage cheese made from ewe's milk, traditionally served with honey or *membrillo* (quince paste) for pudding. The wine list is excellent.

➕ 199 D3 ✉ Plaza Santa Maria 8 ☎ 947 20 87 15 🕐 Mon–Sat 1–4,
9–11:30, Sun 12:30–3:30

Mesón de Candido €€

Eating is a serious matter in this historic 15th-century building beneath the Roman aqueduct. The traditions of the best Castilian country cooking are upheld in this long-established restaurant. The local *judiones de la Granja*, oversize broad white beans, often served with pigs' ears and trotters, are a speciality. As are roast suckling pig and baby lamb. The suckling pig is so tender that the waiters traditionally carve it at your table using the edge of a plate. Try the *tarta de ponche segoviano*, an alcohol-soaked cake, to complete the feast. The restaurant is extremely popular, so make reservations in advance.

✚ 199 D2 ⊠ Plaza Azoguejo 5
☎ 921 42 59 11 ⓦ Daily 1–4,
9–midnight

Tasca La Posada €–€€

Don't be put off here by the approach down a narrow alley off the Plaza Mayor, nor the apparently rough nature of the bar, but go through to the restaurant to enjoy the very best of traditional Castilian cuisine. Try the *sopa Castillana* (a tasty soup with egg, bread and lots of garlic), bean dishes enriched with pigs' trotters, and Segovia's famous *cochinillo asado* (roast suckling pig). The front bar serves some great *tapas*, as well as more substantial *raciones* or a full *menu*.

✚ 199 D2 ⊠ Judería Vieja 19
☎ 921 46 21 71 ⓦ Daily 1–4,
9–11:30

Meson Las Conchas €–€€

Eat very inexpensively at this *tapas* bar and restaurant surrounded by enticing shops on one of the city's most attractive pedestrian-only streets. Fronted by a spit-and-sawdust bar dishing up wedges of tortilla and cheese, upstairs is the surprise of a restaurant with black bow-tied waiters and elegant furnishings. The menu is vast including salads, vegetarian, seafood and more meat dishes.

✚ 198 C2 ⊠ Rúa Mayor 16,
☎ 923 21 21 67
ⓦ Daily 9–9

Restaurante El Mesón €€€

A flight of steps leads down into the pleasant vaulted dining rooms of this temple of Salamancan gastronomy, founded more than 50 years ago. The decor is restrained, with well-spaced tables, and the service attentive. *Cochinillo asado* (roast suckling pig) is the speciality, but other meat dishes, mainly roasts, reflect the attention paid to the highest quality ingredients.

✚ 198 C2 ⊠ Plaza del Poeta
Iglesias 10 ☎ 923 21 72 22
ⓦ Mon–Sat 1–4, 9–midnight, Sun 2–5

Boccalino €–€€

Perfectly placed for a relaxing meal after a trip to the complex of San Isidoro, this attractive restaurant, airy and spacious inside, also has tables for outside dining in the beautiful square. *Tapas* and salads, local specialities are on offer, or ring the changes with pizza, pasta and *tortillas*. There's a wide choice of better-than-usual puddings and ice- cream, all served with professionalism and friendliness.

✚ 198 C4 ⊠ Plaza de San Isidoro 9
☎ 987 22 30 60 ⓦ Daily 1–4, 9–midnight

Restaurante El Palomo €€

Pass through the pretty bar area to the welcoming, though slightly cramped, dining room, meticulously run by the highly professional owner. There are a few well-priced set menus of typical Leonese dishes, with the chance to eat fresh trout and some traditional vegetable specialities. The wine list is serious, with some outstanding Riojas.

✚ 198 C4 ⊠ Calle Escalerilla 8
☎ 987 25 42 25 ⓦ Daily 1–4,
9–11:30

Where to...
Shop

SEGOVIA

Segovia has a small selection of **local handicrafts** – textiles, ceramics and leatherwork – which you'll find in the shops opposite the cathedral. Here, you'll also find great pastry shops offering *ponche segoviano* (a liqueur-dipped custard-filled cake topped with marzipan), and the big local favourite, *yemas* (sugared egg yolks); **Limón y Menta** (Calle Isabel la Católica, tel: 921 46 21 41) is the best choice for these.

SALAMANCA

Salamanca has more sweet delights: the specialities are *turrón* (hard nougat made from honey and almonds), *paciencias* (almond cakes) or *chochos* (almond and chocolate cakes). Salamanca is also home to one of the great gastronomic shrines, **Hermanos Hoyos** (Rúa Mayor 16, tel: 923 21 43 24), where splendid hams hang from the ceiling. Food aside, Salamanca's shops are better-than-average; **Artesanía Duende** (Calle San Pablo 33, tel: 923 21 36 22) has superb crafts, including exquisite music boxes and traditionally embroidered regional dresses.

BUYING RIOJA

Look out for the Gran Reserva wines, aged for at least two years in oak casks and a further three in the bottle. Next in quality come the Reservas, select wines that have spent three years maturing, one of which has been in oak. Crianzas are two years old and have been aged in wood, while the light, fruity Joven matures in just one year. Both 1995 and 1996 were exceptional years for Rioja wine.

Where to...
Be Entertained

Evening entertainment is primarily aimed at locals – the provincial centres having a reasonable programme of **classical music, plays and opera**, while late-night bars and discos cater for younger Spaniards. If you want to hit a club, bear in mind that weekends are the time when you'll be able to dance until dawn, then round it all off with hot chocolate and *churros*. Things tend to get going exceptionally late by foreign standards, so if you're heading for a concert don't expect it to start much before 10:30 or 11pm.

Most tourists are happy to while away the evening enjoying the *paseo* (the early-evening promenade) with the locals and having a drink and a good dinner – after dark, the main buildings are often floodlit, making a drink in the balmy evening air gazing at some stupendous façade quite enough to satisfy most people. In some smaller towns and villages, this will probably be all that is on offer.

If you're looking for culture, however, the best place for information will be the **tourist offices**, who will have full lists of what is happening. All cities have their major **fiesta weeks** when things really come alive in a riot of noise, festivity and celebration – these are the weeks when the main **bullfights** will be staged (▶ panel, page 13). Apart from Semana Santa (Easter Week), which is big in León, most festivals take place during the summer; again, the tourist office will advise you what is happening and when.

The Atlantic Northern Regions

Getting Your Bearings

The Atlantic and the mountains define Spain's northern coastal regions; the tides rising and falling, the weather systems beating in from the west, the very different rhythm of life from the sun-drenched south, all adding up to utter magic.

The scenery is stunning, an ever-changing pattern of water and coastline, green fields and woodland, hills and mountains. This is countryside for exploring – walking on a near-empty beach, dawdling in some laid-back Costa Verde village, following the indented shores of the Rías Baixas. It includes Galicia, with its distinctive character and scenery – hills, white-sand beaches and deep fjord-like

Previous page:
An Asturian fishing village

Above: The beautiful Costa Verde

inlets. East lies the enchanting Costa Verde, with its verdant turf, smooth sandy beaches and aquamarine sea. This lovely coast is backed by the green hills of Asturias and Cantabria and the superb mountains of the Picos de Europa.

East again lies the Basque heartland, thriving and individual, with its friendly people and instantly recognisable sense of identity. The Basque country spills inland from the coast into neighbouring Navarra (Navarre), well worth exploring if you've got time. Its diverse landscape is dotted with historic cities and towns such as Pamplona and tiny Puente la Reina.

Apart from all this, the region has some lovely towns and great cultural treasures. Santiago de Compostela is one of Spain's most perfect medieval cities, Santillana del Mar one of its prettiest villages, Bilbao an increasingly dynamic centre, while the

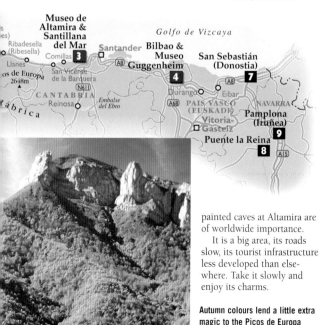

painted caves at Altamira are of worldwide importance.

It is a big area, its roads slow, its tourist infrastructure less developed than elsewhere. Take it slowly and enjoy its charms.

Autumn colours lend a little extra magic to the Picos de Europa

You have to be selective in Spain's green north, and pick and choose what minor sights will best balance the main draws. This region has some of the country's most beautiful scenery, well worth exploring, and it pays to concentrate on this, with Santiago and Bilbao providing the cultural and urban balance. An alternative to moving constantly would be to spend one night in Santiago then base yourself for several days on the Costa Verde, taking day trips out to Altamira, Santillana del Mar, the Picos de Europa and Bilbao.

The Atlantic Northern Regions in Five Days

Day One

Morning
Spend the morning visiting ❶ Santiago's **cathedral** (right, ➤ 94), the **Museo y Tesoro de la Catedral** (➤ 94) and the buildings around the **Praza do Obradoiro** (➤ 95).

Afternoon
Once the museums open up again, head for the **Museo das Peregrinacións** (➤ 95), perhaps following this up with an hour in the **Museo do Pobo Gallego** (➤ 95).

Evening
Don't miss the *paseo* before dining in the old town. After dinner, head for the Praza do Obradoiro to see the **floodlighting** and perhaps to listen to some buskers playing Galician music.

Day Two

Morning
Leave Santiago after breakfast and take the E1 *autopista* towards ❻ **A Coruña (La Coruña)**, picking up the NVI on the outskirts of A Coruña towards Lugo, where the N640 heads northeast towards the coast. At Ribadeo, turn east on to the N634.

Afternoon/Evening
Once on the **2 Costa Verde** (➤ 97–98), head for **Luarca** (➤ 97) and spend a couple of hours pottering about enjoying the resort's relaxed atmosphere (left), then head further along the Costa Verde to **Llanes** (➤ 98), where you could spend one or more nights.

Day Three

Head for **Cangas de Onís**, the starting point for a superbly scenic day's drive in the **Picos de Europa** (➤ 106–107). Return to Llanes for a second night or head further east and spend the night at the picturesque resort of **3 Santillana del Mar** (➤ 99–100).

Day Four

Morning
Leave Llanes early or, if you've spent the night at Santillana, head straight for the **3 Museo de Altamira** (➤ 99–100) to enjoy this superb attraction before the crowds arrive.

Afternoon
Spend the afternoon exploring the string of villages and beaches along the **Costa Verde**, popping into the 'dinosaur' museum if you have time (➤ 98), then return to Santillana for the evening.

Day Five

Morning
Head to **4 Bilbao** (right, ➤ 101–102) on the N634. As you come in, look out for the purple signs to the **Museo Guggenheim** (➤ 101–102). Spend the rest of the morning at the Guggenheim, then have lunch in the museum's restaurant.

Afternoon
Take in Bilbao's **Casco Viejo** and then hit the shops – Bilbao has some of the best in the region, and there's usually evening entertainment on offer.

❶Santiago de Compostela

Santiago de Compostela, one of the three great shrines of medieval Christendom, has attracted millions of pilgrims over the centuries. They have walked the Camino de Santiago (▶ 22–24) to worship at the shrine of St James, the patron saint of Spain. It is one of Spain's most perfect medieval cities, a glorious mix of religious and secular buildings, with an ancient and thriving university, and a unique atmosphere.

Catedral de Santiago

Santiago's star turn is indubitably the cathedral. It dates from the 11th–13th century, the simple Romanesque lines of the interior providing a superb contrast to the ornate 1750 façade, the main access. Behind, stands the original 12th-century entrance, the **Pórtico de la Gloria** (Doorway of Glory), one of the sculptural glories of Spain. This triple doorway shows prophets and apostles surrounding Christ the Saviour and the Four Evangelists, with St James below, all carved with exceptional imagination and fluidity. The pillar beneath St James is worn from the millions of pilgrims' hands which have touched it in thanksgiving for their safe arrival. The interior's huge proportions and the ambulatory behind the altar were specifically designed to accommodate as many pilgrims as possible, and give them room to move around. You'll notice a rope-pulley system high above the transept. This operates the ***botafumeiro***, a monster incense burner used on major feast days, which needs eight men to swing it through an immense arc above the transept.

In marked contrast to the plain granite spaces of the cathedral, the high altar glitters, the lights of the candelabra flashing off the embossed silverwork and gilded figures.

Reached from the cathedral, the **Museo y Tesoro de la Catedral** (Cathedral Museum and Treasury) is housed around the magnificent 16th-century cloisters, and includes the Romanesque old cathedral beneath the Pórtico de la Gloria and the chapel of San Fernando. Stairs lead up to the gallery, completed in 1590, a good vantage point over the square.

Above: Christ the Saviour dominates the Pórtico de la Gloria

Left: The floodlit façade of the cathedral at Santiago

Exploring Santiago

The cathedral, superbly set on the sweeping **Praza do Obradoiro**, lies at the heart of the old city. From here, the two main streets, Rúa do Franco and Rúa do Vilar, lined with shops, bars and restaurants, lead to the Porta Fexeira. All around lies the **Barrio Antiguo** (old quarter), its lovely arcaded streets lined with beautiful granite buildings in the traditional Galician style. Praza do Obradoiro is surrounded on its other sides by three harmonious buildings. The oldest, the **Hostal dos Reis Católicos** (Hostel of the Catholic Monarchs) was founded by Ferdinand and Isabella (▶ 9) as a lodging house for pilgrims. In the centre of its elegantly plain façade is a superb plateresque doorway. Opposite, the **Colegio de San Jéronimo**, with its charming balcony, dates mainly from the 17th century, while the **Ayuntamiento** was built in the 18th century. East of here, the spacious **Praza de Quintana** is surrounded by notable buildings – the lovely arcaded **Casa de la Canónica**, facing a gracious flight of steps leading up to the 17th-century **Casa de la Parra**; opposite is the austere façade of **San Pelayo de AnteaIltares** monastery. On the other side

of the cathedral you'll find the huge complex of the **Monasterio de San Martiño Pinario**, with its church and three cloisters.

Santiago's Museums

The first choice must be the pilgrimage museum, **Museo das Peregrinacións**, a few minutes' walk through the back streets to the north of the cathedral. The museum tells the story of pilgrimage in general, and the Santiago pilgrimage in particular. There's a copy of the fascinating *Codex Calixtinus*, a 12th-century guide to the route, full of tips about travel and information about Santiago; look out too for the collection of souvenirs – 14th-century pilgrims took home much the same keepsakes as people do today. East from here, the fascinating **Museo do Pobo Gallego** (Museum of the Galician People) concentrates on Galician history and culture. Its galleries are housed in the church of Santo Domingo outside the walls of the old city. Interesting rooms encircle the 17th-century cloister, in one corner of which a superb staircase, with three intertwining flights of steps, rises to the different floors of the building.

TAKING A BREAK

A few steps from the cathedral is **Sant-Yago** (Rúa da Raiña 12, tel: 981 58 24 44), housed in a traditional old stone building where Alfonso Fraga concentrates on ham dishes of superb quality, as well as a wide range of Galician specialities.

Santiago's arcaded streets give shelter from the Galician weather

✚ 198 A4

Tourist Information Office
✉ Rúa do Vilar 63 ☎ 981 55 51 29; www.santiagoturismo.com
🕐 Jun–Sep daily 9–9; Oct–May 9–2, 4–7

Cathedral
✉ Praza do Obradoiro ☎ 981 58 35 48 or 981 56 05 58 🕐 Daily 7:30–9; hourly rooftop tours Tue–Sat 10–1, 4–7; opening times may vary 🎟 Free

Museo y Tesoro de la Catedral
✉ Praza do Obradoiro ☎ 981 56 05 27
🕐 Summer Mon–Sat 10–2, 4–8, Sun 10–2; winter Mon–Sat 10–1:30, 4–6:30, Sun 10–1:30
🎟 Moderate

Museo das Peregrinacións
✉ Rúa San Miguel 4 ☎ 981 58 15 58
🕐 Tue–Fri 10–8, Sat 10:30–1:30, 5–8, Sun 10:30–1:30 🎟 Inexpensive

Museo do Pobo Gallego
✉ Rúa de San Domingos de Bonaval ☎ 981 58 36 20; www.museodopobo.es 🕐 Tue–Sat 10–2, 4–8, Sun 11–2 🎟 Free

---

SANTIAGO DE COMPOSTELA: INSIDE INFO

Top tips The **best time** to visit Santiago is around **25 July**, the feast of St James, which coincides with the two-week long Gallego folklore festival. **Reserve well in advance** as the city is packed at this time.

• To get a true taste of what the Santiago experience means to the pilgrims, look in on the **12 noon Pilgrim's Mass** in the cathedral.

• Be prepared for **heavy rain** in Santiago – the city's situated in one of the wettest corners of Galicia, the rainiest region in Spain.

• Try to see the Praza do Obradoiro **after dark** to witness the dramatic floodlighting and strolling musicians.

• For an **overall view** of Santiago, stroll along the **Paseo da Ferradura** in the pleasant public gardens southwest of the old town.

② Costa Verde

The Costa Verde – the Green Coast – is, as far as foreigners are concerned, one of Spain's best-kept secrets. Stretching right along the Asturian coastline into Cantabria, this chain of fishing villages and low-key resorts, golden beaches and tumbling cliffs has something for everyone. Pines, eucalyptus, springy turf and the clear green sea give it its name, while its natural beauty is enhanced by the wooded hinterland with mountains rising behind.

West of Gijón

Travelling along the coast from the west, make **Luarca** (Lluarca) your first stop. This lovely little town, set at the mouth of the River Negro, combines the charms of an old-fashioned resort with its true function as a working fishing port. Attractive houses line its streets and squares and encircle the harbour, which is sheltered by a rocky headland crowned with a church and lighthouse. East of here, **Cudillero** (Cuideiru) is another charmer, with colour-washed arcaded houses curving around its port and a plethora of excellent fish restaurants. Neighbouring **Salinas** is a more developed resort, its chief draw is its pinewoods and beach, one of the longest on the coast. You could take the AS328 out over the moorland to the **Cabo de Peñas**, the northernmost point of the Asturian coast.

Fishing boats fill the harbour at Luarca

Inset: Clean water and clear air are the trademarks of the Costa Verde

East of Gijón

Beyond Gijón (Xixon), it's worth pausing at **Lastres** (Llastres), huddled beneath steep cliffs. It is home to the **Museo del Jurásico de Asturias** which contains the most complete and representative collection of dinosaur remains in the world. **La Isla**, a small resort, has a great reputation for cider and seafood. **Ribadesella** (Ribesella), at the mouth of the River Sella, is much larger, a working port and holiday town with an excellent beach. East of here, **Llanes** is a delight, and one of the best bases for exploration. The old town stands at the river mouth, and there's a clifftop *paseo*, all green turf and tamarisk trees, with superb views.

Into Cantabria

Across the border into Cantabria, **San Vicente de la Barquera** is worth visiting for its situation alone. The old town perches above the sea and is approached by a causeway. **Comillas**, where pretty cobbled streets lead to two wonderful beaches, makes a good stop. There's a tiny nature reserve for wildfowl and seabirds, and El Capricho, a grandiose villa designed by Gaudí, which is now an expensive restaurant. From here, it's not far to **Santillana del Mar** (► 99, 100) and the charms of **Santander**, a stunningly sited, elegant resort, with some of the best beaches in Spain.

Gaudí's El Capricho

TAKING A BREAK

At **Playa de Comillas** try **La Caracola** (Playa de Comillas, tel: 942 72 07 41) bar-cum-restaurant.

Tourist Information Office, Llanes
⊞ 199 D4 ⊠ La Torre, Calle Alfonso IX
☎ 985 40 01 64; www.infoasturias.com;
www.ayto-llanes.es ⚙ Summer Mon–Sat
10–2, 5–9, Sun 10–3; winter Mon–Fri 10–2,
4–6:30, Sat 10:30–1:30

Tourist Information Office, Santander
⊞ 199 D4 ⊠ Jardines de Pereda s/n
☎ 942 20 30 00; www.turismo.cantabria.org

⚙ May–Sep daily 9–2, 4–9; Oct–Apr Mon–Fri
9:30–1:30, 4–7, Sat 10–1

Museo del Jurásico de Asturias, Lastres
⊞ 199 D4 ⊠ La Rassa de San Telmo
☎ 902 30 66 00 ⚙ Jul–Sep daily
10:30–2:30, 4–8; Oct–May Mon 10:30–2:30,
Wed–Sun 10:30–2:30, 4–7 ⚑ Moderate

COSTA VERDE: INSIDE INFO

Top tips Very few off-the-beaten-track beaches have any facilities, **so take a picnic** and **be prepared to walk** from where you leave the car.

• The **N632 and N634** are relatively fast roads but are **set back** from the coast; if you use them you'll get little sense of the Costa Verde. Instead **take side roads** wherever possible.

• The Costa Verde is **best explored outside** the peak holiday months of **July and August**, when it's busy with Spanish and French holidaymakers.

3 Museo de Altamira and Santillana del Mar

The winning combination of the stunning Altamira museum, which tells the story of one of Europe's greatest Paleolithic treasures, with the mellow charms of the tiny, picturesque village of Santillana del Mar, makes this little corner of Cantabria unmissable.

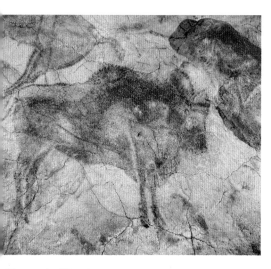

A bison at Altamira – art from the dawn of mankind

Museo de Altamira

In 1879, the archaeologist Marcelino de Sautuola discovered the extraordinary pictures and engravings at **Altamira** – the first **Paleolithic cave paintings** to be found. Astoundingly, some date back to 25,000 BC, art speaking to us from the dawn of mankind. The chamber depicting bison (15,000–12,000 BC) established Altamira's reputation and visitor numbers soared. Throughout the 20th century, concern grew at the effect the presence of the crowds was having on these fragile masterpieces, a concern balanced by the realisation that these extraordinary works should be accessible. The result was the admirable **Museo de Altamira**, opened in 2001, which incorporates a replica of the painted caves with a state-of-the-art exhibition space, museum and audiovisual facility.

The tour of the **Neocave**, as the replica is called, tells the entire story of man's habitation of the caves, the highlight being a superbly accurate duplicate of the painted rocks themselves. You'll see how these ancient artists used the rock

formations to suggest shape and movement –
bison galloping, curled in sleep and crouched
together. Look out too for deer, wild boar and a
primitive horse. The artists outlined the shapes,
as big as 1.5m (5 feet), with charcoal and
coloured them using natural pigments, mainly
ochre, mixed with animal fat.

Santillana del Mar
You have to see the chocolate-box-pretty village
of **Santillana del Mar**, just 3km (2 miles) from
Altamira, which, despite its name, is not on the
sea. This architecturally homogenous gem grew
up around the monastery of Santa Juliana,
waxing rich in the 15th century. The majority
of the balconied houses date from the
15th–18th centuries, while the *colegiata*
(collegiate church), with its Romanesque cloister, dates from the 12th–13th. Santillana is tiny,

*Farmland lies beyond the ochre roc[
Santillana del Mar*

and a real tourist hot spot – come early or late, when the bus tours have gone
and the returning cattle prove that this is still a functioning farming community.

TAKING A BREAK
The best place to stop is **the museum's own coffee shop** and restaurant –
light and airy with a wide choice of better-than-average snacks. Alternatively,
there is the hotel/restaurant **Altamira** (➤ 109) in the village.

Museo de Altamira
➕ 199 D4 ✉ Santillana del Mar ☎ 942 81
80 05; www.museoaltamira.mcu.es
🕐 Summer Tue–Sat 9:30–7:30, Sun 9:30–3;
winter 9:30–5, Sun 9:30–3 💰 Inexpensive

Tourist Information Office,
Santillana del Mar
➕ 199 D4 ✉ Jesús Otero 20
☎ 942 81 82 51; www.santillanadelmar.com
🕐 Daily 9:30–1:30, 4:30–7:30

MUSEO DE ALTAMIRA AND SANTILLANA DEL MAR: INSIDE INFO

Top tips If you have the chance, **spend time first in the exhibition before visiting
the Neocave** – it's the best way to get the most out of your visit.
• It is no longer possible to visit the original caves due to a protracted, ongoing
survey of contamination levels. Consult the website for further news.

Getting in Entry to the Neocave is **timed**; your time will be printed on your
ticket as it is issued. Be prepared for a **lengthy wait** at busy times.
• You can **pre-reserve** an entry time to visit the museum by faxing them on 942
84 01 57. If you're already in Spain, Banco Santander banks' cashpoint
network offers a reservation facility – follow the on-screen instructions.

In more detail The limestone caves at **Puente Viesgo**, 24km (14.5 miles)
from Santander, are also worth visiting, both for their rock formations and the
cave paintings, which are believed to be older than the ones at Altamira. The
visitor centre has an excellent interactive exhibition. Tours are in Spanish only.

4 Bilbao and Museo Guggenheim

In the early 1990s few people would have earmarked Bilbao (Bilbo), the run-down, ex-industrial Basque capital, as a potential major tourist draw. Today, it's precisely that, thanks to the vision of the Basque government and the Museo Guggenheim. This astonishing structure is the vanguard of a huge and imaginative urban renewal scheme, which has seen the regeneration of the whole of downtown Bilbao.

Museo Guggenheim

Designed by Canadian-born architect Frank O Gehry, the Guggenheim opened in 1997 as a European showcase for some of the Guggenheim Foundation's collection of 20th-century art. Standing on the banks of the River Nervión, this astounding building, all sinuous curves, glass and glittering titanium, dominates the city's heart. The building centres round a 55m (180-foot) high atrium with irregular-shaped galleries leading off – one over 130m (142-yards) long. Glass lifts whisk you up to higher levels, where curving walkways hang from the roof and give access to the upper exhibition spaces. Outside, a terrace overlooks a reflecting pool above the river, while on the other side of the building, a flight of shallow steps leads down to the main entrance. Inevitably, it's the building itself that attracts the crowds, but the permanent collection includes works by most major 20th-century artists and the temporary exhibitions staged here are among the most diverse and stimulating on show anywhere in Europe.

The titanium curves of the Guggenheim reflect the changing light

✚ 199 E4

Museo Guggenheim
✉ Abandoibarra Etorbidea 2
☎ 944 35 90 80; www.guggenheim-bilbao.es
🕐 Tue–Sun 10–8 💰 Expensive

Tourist Information Offices, Bilbao
✉ Abandoibarra Etorbidea 2 (near Museo Guggenheim) ☎ 944 79 57 60;
www.bilbao.net 🕐 Summer Mon–Sat 10–3, 4–7, Sun 10–3; winter Tue–Fri 11–2:30, 3:30–6, Sat 11–3, 4–7, Sun 11–2

✉ Plaza Ensanche 11
☎ 944 79 57 60; www.bilbao.net
🕐 Mon–Fri 9–2, 4–7:30

Museo Vasco
✉ Plaza Miguel de Unamuno 4 ☎ 944 15 54 23; www.euskal-museoa.org 🕐 Tue–Sat 11–5, Sun 11–2 💰 Moderate

Museo de Bellas Artes
✉ Plaza del Museo 2 ☎ 944 39 60 60; www.museobilbao.com 🕐 Tue–Sat 10–8, Sun 10–2 💰 Moderate

The City

Don't ignore the rest of Bilbao, a thriving, friendly city stretching along a river valley, from whose streets you can always glimpse green hills. The **Casco Viejo** (old quarter), across the river, is home to the Gothic cathedral, the elegant arcaded Plaza Nueva and the fascinating **Museo Vasco**. This is housed in a lovely old building surrounding a cloister and will fill you in on the history and culture of the Basques. The Casco Viejo is also home to Bilbao's best bars and restaurants. Back across the river, you might also want to take in the **Museo de Bellas Artes**, a few minutes' walk from the Guggenheim, set in a tranquil green park. Here, you'll find paintings by El Greco, Goya and Murillo, as well as a number by Basque artists. Nearby, the Palacio Euskalduna, a huge and imaginative structure built on the site of an old shipyard, is part of Bilbao's ongoing re-development.

TAKING A BREAK

Head for the streamlined **Guggenheim Bilbao Restaurant** (Anandoibarra Etorbidea 2, tel: 944 23 93 33). There is an excellent range of snacks or some of the lightest and most innovative "new Basque" cooking imaginable. You must book, however, and the restaurant is closed on Monday.

BILBAO AND MUSEO GUGGENHEIM: INSIDE INFO

Top tips You'll find a huge and excellent variety of books and gifts in the **museum shop**.
• **Bus Vision Bilbao** is a jump-on, jump-off **tourist bus** which loops round the main areas of the city throughout the day.
• Bilbao has an efficient **metro system** linking the Casco Viejo with the rest of the city.

In more depth Jeff Koons' *Puppy*, a 24m (79-foot) figure of a puppy made entirely of brightly coloured flowering plants, was installed as a temporary exhibition when the museum first opened. He's still there – the Bilbainos loved the figure so much they petitioned for it to stay. *Puppy* is re-planted every May.

Getting in The entry **ticket** to the Guggenheim is valid for the **whole day**, so you can come and go more than once.
• **Advance reservations** in Spain are available through the BBK Teleka system or La Caixa banks cashpoint system – follow the instructions on screen.

At Your Leisure

5 Rías Baixas (Rías Bajas)

Foreign visitors are starting to discover the delights of the Rías Baixas, the beautiful, fjord-like inlets running inland from the Atlantic on Galicia's western coast. There are four: Vigo, Pontevedra, Arousa and Muros e Noia. Vigo and Pontevedra, are the most developed, with an increasingly sophisticated tourist infrastructure. The northern *rías* (inlets) are more low-key, and fishing villages and agriculture still predominate. All four enjoy a mild climate and a stunning indented coastline, punctuated by white-sand beaches and backed by tree-clad hills. The resorts are friendly, the sailing and seafood superb, making this area ideal for a few days' relaxation.

Tourist Information Office, Vigo
➕ 198 A4 ✉ Rúa Teofilo Llorente 5
☎ 986 43 05 77;
www.turismodevigo.org 🕐 Jul–Aug
Mon–Fri 9:30–2, 4:30–7:30, Sat–Sun
10–2, 5–6:30; Sep–Jun Mon–Fri 9:30–2,
4:30–6:30, Sat 10:30–12:30

Tourist Information Office, Pontevedra
➕ 198 A4 ✉ General Gutiérrez
Mellado ☎ 986 85 08 14 🕐 Mon–Fri
9:30–2, 4:30–6:30, Sat 10–12:30

6 A Coruña (La Coruña)

The town of A Coruña sits on a defensive peninsula facing the *ría* on one side and the open sea on the other. The city saw Roman occupation – the lighthouse known as Torre de Hércules dates from the 2nd century – and was the departure point for the Armada in 1588. In 1809, during the Peninsular Wars, it was the site of a British retreat – the commander, Sir John Moore, was killed and buried here. Behind the medieval quarter is the lovely colonnaded Praza de María Pita. Cut through west to the Praia del Orzán, where Atlantic waves break on a beach in the heart of the city.
➕ 198 A4

Tourist Information Office
✉ Plaza de María Pita s/n ☎ 981 18
43 44; www.turismocoruna.es
🕐 May–Oct Mon–Fri 9–8:30, Sat 10–2,
4–8, Sun 10–3; Nov–Apr Mon–Fri
9–2:30, 4–8:30, Sat 10–2, 4–8, Sun
10–3

Galician Farming

Driving through Galicia you'll notice at once the tiny fields, a legacy of ancient inheritance laws which sub-divided the land for generations. Look out, too, for *hórreos* (granite-built granaries), complete with air vents and holy statues, standing on pillars to keep out the damp and rodents. Favourite crops are bizarre cabbages on stalks and allotments full of turnip tops, both of which feature prominently in local cooking. The *rías* are intensively farmed for shellfish of all sorts; the raised platforms of the *mejilloneiras* (mussel rafts) can be seen above the waterline.

7 San Sebastián (Donostia)

The Basques are rightly proud of lovely San Sebastián, an elegant, prosperous city, whose setting has to be one of the finest enjoyed by any resort. Two green headlands shelter a crescent-shaped beach, complete with off-shore island; while to the east, graceful bridges span the mouth of the River Urumea. The headland on the east of the main Bahía de la Concha is home to the medieval town. Its narrow streets packed with bars and restaurants are centred around the Plaza de la Constitución.

Monte Urgull dominates this old quarter; there are wonderful views from its summit, which is topped by a huge figure of Christ. The city has grown along the river, while at the other end of the bay rises Monte Igueldo. Ride up to the top on a funicular for more panoramas or enjoy the summer crowds and the four great beaches. San Sebastián rose to prominence during the 19th century, when it became a fashionable resort. Its arts festivals draw the crowds in summer, while its cuisine is revered nationwide.

✚ 199 F4

Tourist Information Office
✉ Calle Reina Regente 3 ☎ 943 48 11 66; www.sansebastianturismo.com
🕐 Jun–Sep Mon–Sat 8–8, Sun 10–2; Oct–May Mon–Sat 9–1:30, 3:30–7, Sun 10–2

A waterfront skirts San Sebastián's marina

Off the Beaten Track

If you love places on the edge, a sense of isolation and superb scenery, head for the **Costa da Morte**, (Costa de la Muerte), the stretch of wild, dangerous coast west of A Coruña and Santiago de Compostela. This is a place of legend, barren headlands and remote fishing communities; its name – Death Coast – comes from the hundreds of shipwrecks along its shores. Beautiful and deserted beaches are strewn along the coast, backed by sweeping sand dunes and granite hills beneath which huddle windswept fishing villages. **Fisterra** (Finisterre), the Romans' "end of the world" is as far west as you can go, a bleak cape with a lighthouse perched high above the roaring surf. Softer options are the small towns along this stretch; attractive **Camariñas**, with its glassed-in balconies, and **Noia** in its marvellous natural setting, are the pick of the bunch.

Further Afield

8 Puente la Reina

Few places in Navarra (Navarre) are as evocative of the age-old history of the Camino de Santiago (➤ 22–24) as Puente la Reina, a tiny town sited where the two trans-Pyrenean branches of the pilgrim route meet. A perfect example of how towns grew up along the Camino, it gets its name from the superb 11th-century bridge, built by royal decree to facilitate the pilgrims' passage.

There are two fine churches, the Iglesia del Crucifijo, once a Templar church, and another dedicated to St James himself. Just east of the town, the 12th-century octagonal Romanesque church of Eunate is one of the loveliest on the route. Come here in the late afternoon to see pilgrims arriving in the village, as they've done for over 800 years, with the Pyrenees safely behind them and over 600km (372 miles) still to go.

Tourist Information Office, Puente la Reina
➕ 199 F4 ✉ Calle Mayor 105 ☎ 948 34 13 01; www.turismo.navarra.es ◷ Jun–Aug Tue–Sat 10–2, 4–7, Sun 11–2

9 Pamplona (Iruñea)

Ernest Hemingway put Pamplona firmly on the international tourist map when he extolled the manic, exhilarating delights of the fiesta of San Fermín in his novel *The Sun Also Rises*. From 7–14 July the entire city gives itself over to 24-hour, non-stop mass celebration in honour of its patron saint with parades, fireworks, bands, funfairs, dancing in the streets and above all the *encierro*, the running of the bulls.

Each morning at 8 o'clock, six bulls are released from their corral to run through the narrow streets to the bullring. Ahead of them run hundreds of people, fleeing in excitement and fear, trying to escape the occasionally maddened animals yet staying as near them as possible, while the watching crowds cheer, yell and push would-be escapers firmly back into the bulls' path. It's dangerous, primitive and, for the runners, addictive. The bulls are killed each evening at the fight.

Outside San Fermín, Pamplona is a pleasant and historic city, filled with open green spaces, one of which contains the ruined Ciudadela (citadel). The Gothic cathedral boasts some lovely cloisters and a fine museum containing sacred art from all over Navarra. Behind it is the Judería, the only vestige of the once-large Jewish community, and the Navarrería, the oldest part of Pamplona, which gives access to the old city walls high above the River Arga.

Tourist Information Office, Pamplona
➕ 199 F4 ✉ Eslava 1 ☎ 848 42 04 20; www.sanfermin.com ◷ Summer daily 9–8; winter Mon–Sat 10–2, 4–7, Sun 10–2

Running the bulls at Pamplona during the Fiesta de San Fermín

THE PICOS DE EUROPA

Drive

This spectacular drive will give you the best idea possible, without actually trekking into the mountains, of the grandeur and magnificence of the Picos de Europa. The route is immensely varied, covering narrow gorges with precipitous rock walls, upland mountain meadows and woodland, and high plateaux. Along the route there are frequent stretches of narrow road with overhanging rocks and steep drops; nervous drivers who are unused to mountain roads should be prepared for testing driving in places.

1–2

Start in **Cangas de Onís** (easily reached from Oviedo) and bear right after the bridge onto the N625 (signposted Riaño 63) and follow the course of the **River Sella**, teeming with

DISTANCE 170km (105.5 miles) **TIME** Driving 4 hours, but allow all day to give yourself plenty of time to enjoy the mountains
START POINT Cangas de Onís 🚩 199 D4
END POINT Panes 🚩 199 D4

trout, past smallholdings and grazing cattle. The valley narrows to the impressive gorge of the **Desfiladero de los Beyos**, said to be the narrowest motorable gorge in Europe. As this eventually widens, the road climbs steeply to the mountain village of **Oseja de Sajambre**, with great views to the sharp peak of Niaja (1,732m/5,684 feet).

Taking a Break

The 1,000m (3,280-foot) high village of Riaño is the best place to stop – try the **Hotel Presa** (Avenida de Valcayo 12, tel: 987 74 06 37), where you can fill up on *tapas* or enjoy mountain home-cooking in the wood-panelled restaurant.

When

Choose a clear, dry day with high cloud – this drive would be very taxing and unenjoyable in bad weather.

Rocky peaks rise above upland farmland near the small town of Potes

2–3

After Oseja, the road continues upwards through a lovely stretch of high woodland and open alpine meadows to the pass at **Puerto del Pontón**, a height of 1,290m (4,231 feet).

3–4

Continue along the N625 to Riaño. This is high-plateau country and ahead of you opens out the immense stretch of **the Riaño reservoir** (Embalse de R año), built to irrigate the plains around León and Palencia. The village of Riaño was built to replace the villages lost when the dam was completed in the 1980s.

4–5

Take the N621 from Riaño towards **Portilla de la Reina**. At first little villages punctuate this gentler landscape, which soon becomes increasingly rocky and narrows until the road reaches the pass, with its bronze statue of a deer, at **Puerto de San Glorio** (1,609m/5,231 feet). From the pass there are superb views into Cantabria.

5–6

From here the twisting road descends very steeply through rapidly changing vegetation; at **La Vega** follow the N621 to the left towards **Potes**.

6–7

At the town of Potes, you could make a 20km (12.5-mile) detour into the heart of the mountains to the cable-car at **Fuente Dé**. This swoops up 900m (2,954 feet) to a viewpoint perched to the east of the massif of Torre Cerredo (Tesorero; 2,648m/8,691 feet), the Picos' highest peak. It's a popular excursion so be prepared to wait to ride both up and down. Otherwise, follow the road through the dramatic **Desfiladero de la Hermida** gorge, whose sides are so steep that no sunlight touches the tiny village of La Hermida for six months of the year. The road follows the course of the **River Deva**, another salmon and trout river, to arrive at **Panes**.

From here the AS114 skirts the northern edge of the Picos back to Cangas de Onís.

Mar Cantábrico

N621

N634

N632

① Cangas de Onís

Sames

Desfiladero de los Beyos

N625

Sella

635

② Oseja de Sajambre

1290m Puerto del Pontón

③

Embalse de Riaño

Riaño

④

N621

Boca de Huérgano

615

N621

Picos de Europa

2648m Torre Cerredo ▲

Espinama

Fuente Dé

Portilla de la Reina

⑤

1609m Puerto de San Glorio

Sierra de Cuera

AS114

Panes ⑦

La Hermida

Desfiladero de la Hermida

N621

⑥ Potes

Deva

La Vega

627

0   20 km

0   12 miles

Where to... Stay

Prices
Expect to pay per person per night
€ up to €50 €€ €50–€90 €€€ €91–€120 €€€€ = over €120

SANTIAGO DE COMPOSTELA

Casa Hotel As Artes €€

Hospitable owners run this sparkling inn near the cathedral, a delightful budget option with stone features and wooden shutters. Each of its seven rooms has a name, such as Vivaldi or Picasso, and an appropriately arty theme. All are stylishly decorated, with wooden floors and wrought-iron beds. Embroidered bed-linen adds a touch of luxury. Most rooms have showers. Breakfast, served in the small café, includes fruit salad and a range of tempting breads and cakes.

🚉 198 A4 ⊠ Travesia Dúas Portas 2
☎ 981 55 52 54; www.asartes.com

Parador Hostal de los Reyes Católicos €€€€

The Catholic Monarchs, Ferdinand and Isabella (▶ 9), founded a hostel next to Santiago's cathedral for pilgrims at their journey's end; today, it is one of Spain's most famous *paradors*, still housed in the original magnificent 16th-century building: fronting on to the main square. Centred around four courtyards, this historic and supremely comfortable hotel, with its terrace, restaurant and splendid public rooms, has to be one of the finest places in Spain to stay.

🚉 198 A4 ⊠ Praza do Obradoiro 1
☎ 981 58 22 00;
www.parador.es

COSTA VERDE

Hotel Sablón €€

Situated beside the old city walls, and built on low cliffs overlooking a sandy beach, this hotel's position alone merits a stay here. Add comfortable rooms – many with sea views – plus an excellent restaurant, and it all adds up to one of the Costa Verde's most attractive places to stay.

🚉 199 D4 ⊠ Playa del Sablón 1,
Llanes ☎ 985 40 07 87;
www.hotelsablon.com

Posada del Rey €€€

There are six double rooms in this evocative, historic hotel frequented in 1517 by Carlos, first king of the united Spain. The rooms are imaginatively decorated with bold colours coupled with antiques, beams and terracotta tiles. Modern touches include fridges and microwaves.

🚉 199 D4 ⊠ Calle Mayor 11, Llanes
☎ 985 40 13 32;
www.llanesnet.com/posadadelrey

SANTILLANA DEL MAR

Parador Gil Blas €€€

In one of the quieter squares of Santillana, this pair of lovely old mansions has been transformed into a luxurious *parador*. The traditional beamed ceilings, antique furniture and supremely comfortable rooms make this a top choice.

🚉 199 D4 ⊠ Plaza Ramón Pelayo 8
☎ 942 81 80 00; www.parador.es

BILBAO

Hotel López de Haro €€€€

This luxury hotel is housed in a traditional-style building in a quiet area of Bilbao, opposite the old quarter and an easy walk from the Guggenheim. Rooms are individually decorated with chintz furnishings and marble bathrooms. The parking is a real bonus in this busy city.

🚉 199 E4 ⊠ Obispo Orueta 2
☎ 944 23 55 00;
www.hotellopezdeharo.com

Where to...
Eat and Drink

Prices

Expect to pay per person for a meal, including wine and service

€ up to €12   €€ €12–€30   €€€ over €30

Alameda €€

This popular restaurant, on the edge of Santiago's historic core, has a light, airy dining room and a terrace for summer eating. The accent here is on the full range of Galician cooking, so there's a chance to sample much else besides fish and shellfish. Try ham for a starter, followed *lacon con grelos* (pork shoulder with turnip tops), before moving on to the choice of imaginative puddings.

🕂 198 A4 ⊠ Porta Faxeira 15
☎ 981 58 66 57 🕐 Daily 1–4,
8–11:30

Don Gaiferos €€

This long-established place beside the church of Santa Maria Salome (not far from the cathedral) is popular with visitors and locals alike. Its cellar-like dining room has a classy but unpretentious feel, and is renowned for its excellent seafood. Hake, prawns and scallops are all included on the menu, along with a fine fish casserole. Steaks are good too, as are the desserts. Seafood prices are on the high side, but the quality amply justifies the expense.

🕂 198 A4 ⊠ Rúa Nova 23 ☎ 981
58 38 94 🕐 Tue–Sat 1:30–3,45,
8:15–11:30

Casa Eutimio €€

Tucked down by the port, and part of the hotel of the same name, this friendly restaurant serves up fish straight off the boats. Hake cooked with local cider, grilled fish and shellfish, and a splendid pudding selection are the house specialities – wash it down with a young Rioja.

🕂 198 C4 ⊠ San Antonio s/n, Lastres
☎ 585 85 00 12 🕐 Tue–Sun 1–4,
9–midnight

El Barómetro €€

The decor may be plain and functional, but this is the real thing, a waterfront restaurant where the fish menu is dictated by the seasons and what comes off the boats. The huge range of fish landed here includes everything from octopus to sardines, hake to lobster – choose what's recommended by the friendly staff.

🕂 198 C4 ⊠ Paseo del Muelle 5,
Luarca ☎ 985 47 06 62 🕐 Thu–Tue
1–4.30, 9–midnight, Wed 1–4.30

Altamira €€

A lovely 16th-century townhouse, also home to an hotel, is the setting for this classily simple restaurant. Cooking here is firmly Cantabrian, with local specialities such as game and plenty of fish on the menu. The summer terrace is an added bonus.

🕂 199 D4 ⊠ Calle Cantón 1
☎ 942 81 80 25 🕐 Daily 1–4,
8–11

Víctor €€–€€€

If you've been exploring the old quarter of Bilbao, head for Plaza Nueva, home to one of Bilbao's great traditional restaurants. Victor specialises in true Basque cooking; here you'll find dishes like *bacalao* (cod) served in different ways, superb hake and shellfish and traditional potato and pepper dishes.

🕂 199 E4 ⊠ Plaza Nueva 2 ☎ 944
15 16 78 🕐 Mon–Sat 1–4, 9–midnight

Where to...
Shop

If you're looking for holiday souvenirs, the best bet in the Northern coastal regions are traditional goods such as **pottery and ceramics** – you'll find local styles differ throughout the region, with a variety of shapes and glazes. A Coruña and Santiago de Compostela both have shops with a good selection from all over the region, and it's worth looking in smaller local potteries wherever you see them.

Galicia is big on **basketware,** woven from chestnut and wicker – look out for *olas,* narrow-necked jugs, lined with plastic, which are used for serving wine. You can still pick these up sometimes in markets, along with a wonderful selection of useful kitchen gadgets – look out in particular for the cheap and practical wooden fish scapers.

Jet has been used for centuries for jewellery-making; the best place for this is Santiago de Compostela, where you'll also find religious souvenirs, all carrying the scallop shell symbol of St James. Santiago is also a good place for bookshop browsing – if you're interested in the Camino (▶ 22–24), there's a good choice of English-language bookshops here. Moving east along the coast into the Asturias, you'll start to see traditional **clogs** (*madreñas*) in the shoe shops – they're wonderfully comfortable. Basques really do wear **berets,** they also favour cheerful blue-and-red checked handkerchiefs and cosy knitted jackets decorated with tassels. Head for good food-shops to track down **local specialities** – cheeses, cakes and biscuits and aromatic mountain honey.
If you're intent on less ethnic shopping, Bilbao and San Sebastián are the best bets – huge shopping malls on the outskirts, department stores and a full range of fashion boutiques in the downtown areas.

Where to...
Be Entertained

Local tourist offices are the first stop to find out what's happening in the way of entertainment. Summer sees festivals throughout the region, and even the smallest resorts will have lots on and discos throbbing all night.

GALICIAN CULTURE

The big time in Santiago is late July, when the **feast of St James** coincides with a two-week celebration of Galician culture, with concerts, parades, street music and markets.

OPERA, THEATRE AND CONCERTS

To the east, things are considerably more sophisticated in **Bilbao** and

San Sebastián. Bilbao has a good cultural scene with opera, theatre and concerts – pick up a copy of the bi-monthly *Bilbao Guide* from the tourist office, or look in the local newspaper, *El Correo*.

July sees **San Sebastián's Jazz Festival,** followed in August by the **Semana Grande,** a week of special events and fireworks, while, come September, the city is packed again for the **International Film Festival**. Full information is available from the tourist offices.

BULL-RUNNING

The biggest and most famous festival of the lot is **Pamplona's San Fermín,** a riotous week of bull-running and much more besides, which runs from 7–14 July.

Barcelona

Getting Your Bearings

Dazzling, self-confident Barcelona has all a big city needs – and more. Thriving, prosperous and beautifully situated, it boasts some of Spain's finest museums and superb architecture. Fully deserving its avant-garde reputation, Barcelona is energetic, affluent and hedonistic, a city that seduces and charms.

Stretching back from the redeveloped waterfront runs the world-famous Ramblas, a magnetic thoroughfare choked with crowds, vendors and street performers. Eastwards lies the heart of the ancient city, the Barri Gòtic (Gothic quarter), home to the cathedral. Here, fine medieval churches and mansions line a warren of narrow, historic streets, and several of the city's best museums are sited. To the north stretchs the newer, late 19th-century city areas, stunning examples of Barcelona's famous *Modernista* architecture. This grid-pattern of elegant streets is known as the Eixample, and includes the high point of *Modernisme*, Gaudí's great church, the Sagrada Família. Art lovers will find the best of the rest museum-wise at Montjuïc to the west of the harbour area; this is also home to the Olympic sports complex.

Around the city stretches the autonomous region of Catalonia (Cataluña), of which Barcelona is the capital. Northeast, the coast extends from the city to the lovely cliffs, beaches and villages of the Costa Brava; the main inland centre in this area is Girona, an ancient walled city set high above a river. Catalonia's other famous holiday area is the Costa Daurada to the southwest. Here good beaches are centred around Tarragona, an attractive small city rich in Roman remains. Inland, the scenery is mountainous, its drama typified by the spectacular rocky massif on which stands the monastery of Montserrat.

★ Don't Miss

10 C DEL BISBE CATALÀ
Monestir de Pedralbes

VIA AUGUS

PG DE M GIRONA
AV DE PEDRALBES
Maria Cristina
Palau Reial
AVINGUDA

JOAN XXIII
Camp Nou
Les Corts
DE
AV D
MA
TRAV

9
Museu del Futbol Club Barcelona

Cadaqués
Figueres
Roses
Ripoll
L'Escala
N152
A7/E15
Girona 12
(Gerona)
Cost Brav
11
Monestir de Montserrat
Tossa de Ma
Lloret de Mar
N11
Blanes
A19
13
Santes Creus
□ **BARCELONA**
Poblet
14
Sitges & Costa Daurada
Tarragona 15
Salou
Port Aventura
A7/E15

0 _____ 50 km
0 _____ 30 miles

Deltebre
Parc Natural del Delta de l'Ebre

At Your Leisure

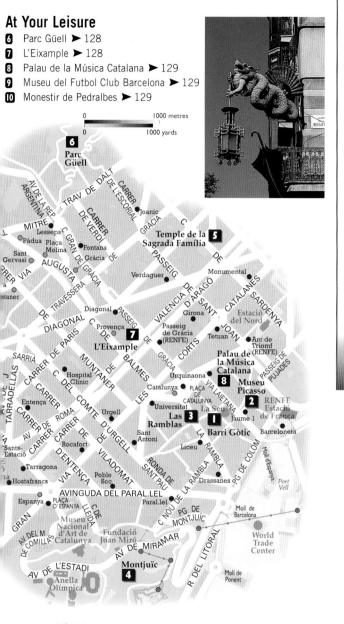

Further Afield

It's perfectly possible to see the best of Barcelona in three days – one of the reasons it's such a popular place for weekends away. The city splits neatly into different areas, each a little entity within itself, each with its own interest and character. Use public transport to start your explorations, then aim to walk, one of Barcelona's great pleasures, to get the best out of the city and its star outlying attraction, the great monastery of Montserrat.

Barcelona in Three Days

Day One

Morning

Spend the morning soaking up the atmosphere and taking in the sights of the ❶ **Barri Gòtic** (right, ➤ 116–118). After you've visited **Plaça de Sant Jaume** (➤ 116) and **La Seu** (➤ 116–117), the city's 13th-century cathedral, a visit to the **Museu d'Història de la Ciutat** (➤ 117) will help put what you've seen into perspective. Have lunch at one of the bars in the squares around **Santa Maria del Pí** (➤ 118).

Afternoon

Spend a couple of hours at the ❷ **Museu Picasso** (➤ 119–120) before heading for ❸ **Las Ramblas** (➤ 121–122), the heart of Barcelona, with its vibrant street life. Pause for a break and a drink in the elegant **Plaça Reial** (➤ 122).

Evening

Have dinner near the **Ramblas** before a late-night stroll and a nightcap overlooking the waterfront in the **Port Vell** (➤ 133–134).

Day Two

Morning

Head for ❹ **Montjuïc** (➤ 123–124) to immerse yourself for a couple of hours in the **Museu Nacional d'Art de Catalunya** (➤ 123), one of Barcelona's top attractions. For a change of pace, take a stroll through

Montjuïc's leafy spaces and pause for a drink at a shady café – you could even climb to the top for superb city views or inspect the impressive Olympic facilties (➤ 138). True art aficionados might prefer to tackle the collection at the **Fundació Joan Miró** (➤ 123–124).

Afternoon

Take the funicular down Montjuïc and hop on the metro at Parel·lel to head for Gaudí's spectacular **5 Temple de la Sagrada Família** (➤ 125–127). For a taste of Gaudí's secular style, you could then head for the **6 Parc Güell** (left, ➤ 128), from where there are fabulous views over the city.

Evening

Spend the evening in the **7 L'Eixample** district (➤ 128–129). There are excellent shops, laid-back bars, many restaurants and more Modernist architecture.

Day Three

Morning

For a taste of Catalonia outside Barcelona, take a trip to the great **13 Monestir de Montserrat** (below, ➤ 131) in its spectacular mountain setting. If the day's fine, you could pick up a picnic on your way to enjoy along one of the paths that wind around the mountainside.

Afternoon

Return to Barcelona and spend the rest of the day in and around the **Port Vell** (➤ 133–134) waterfront district, finishing up with a fish dinner in **La Barceloneta** (➤ 134).

❶ Barri Gòtic

Redolent of Barcelona's long history and still the spiritual heart of Catalonia, the Barri Gòtic is a maze of narrow streets, sun-dappled squares and ancient monuments to Barcelona's golden age. Here you'll find grand buildings housing wonderful treasures, local markets, antiques shops, bars and restaurants in an area that's as much a draw for the natives as it is for visitors.

The present Barri Gòtic dates principally from the 14th and 15th centuries, the years that marked the city's commercial zenith as one of the Mediterranean's prime maritime and merchant powers. This tightly packed, labyrinthine quarter was built inside the old Roman walls, and the Barri's main open space, the **Plaça de Sant Jaume**, lies on the site of the Roman forum and market-place. On its south side stands the **Ajuntament** (Town Hall), a wonderful 14th-century Catalan-Gothic building, which is home to the city's government.

The first floor contains the splendid old council chamber, the Saló de Cent. Across the square is the **Palau de la Generalitat** (Generalitat Palace), the seat of the government of Catalonia. Begun in 1403, it has an elegant Renaissance doorway facing the square, while round the corner you can see its 15th-century façade – look out for the statue showing St George (Sant Jordi), the patron saint of Catalonia, and the Dragon.

From the square you can walk up Carrer del Bisbe, with its overhanging, intricate bridge and down the side of the cathedral, **La Seu**, to the

Plaça de la Seu in front of this great Gothic building. The cathedral is dedicated to St Eulàlia, martyred for her Christian beliefs by the Romans in the 4th century, whose tomb lies in the crypt below the high altar. La Seu was begun in 1298 on the foundations of an earlier church, and more or less finished by 1448 – though the façade took a further 500 years to complete. The interior, with its carved choir and 28 side chapels, is ablaze with dazzling lighting which illuminates the soaring splendours of the columns and flashes off the gold and silver, while myriad twinkling candles punctuate the darker corners. Don't miss the beautiful 14th-century **cloister**, which encircles a lush green space complete with palm trees, magnolias and a charming flock of white geese, said to symbolise St Eulàlia's virginal purity.

East of La Seu you'll find the **Plaça del Rei**, surrounded by a pleasing clutch of historic monuments. The square was originally the courtyard of the palace of the Counts of Barcelona, the **Palau Reial Major**, whose main hall, the spacious 14th-century Saló del Tinell, still survives. It was on the steps of the palace that King Ferdinand and Queen Isabella are said to have received Christopher Columbus on his return from his first voyage to America in 1493. The five-storeyed, arched structure is the Mirador del Rei Martí (King Martin's Tower), built during the Renaissance; you can also see the Capella de Santa Agata (St Agnes' Chapel), with its stained glass and single nave. The Saló del Tinell and the chapel are part of the wonderful **Museu d'Història de la Ciutat** (City History Museum), which tells Barcelona's story through 2,000 years of history. Perhaps the most fascinating parts of the museum are the Roman and Visigothic streets lying beneath the square itself, which were discovered during the 1930s.

Left: Evening crowds outside the floodlit cathedral, La Seu

Far left: The Plaça del Rei and the steps where Christopher Columbus was welcomed home

The glorious rose window at Santa Maria del Pí

A few minutes' walk will take you back past La Seu to the charming series of winding streets and linked squares surrounding the 14th-century Gothic church of **Santa Maria del Pí**, named for the pine trees that once grew here. The serene simplicity of the interior is offset by some glowing stained glass – the rose window is claimed to be the largest in the world. These squares comprise one of the nicest parts of the Barri Gòtic, an ideal place to enjoy the weekend artists' market or have an evening drink while you watch the street entertainers who frequently perform here.

TAKING A BREAK

Bar Bilbao-Berria (Plaça Nova 3, tel: 933 17 01 24). Grab a table outside and choose from the delicious array of *pintxos* lining the bar.

La Seu
✚ 197 E3 ✉ Plaça de la Seu ☎ 933 42 82 60; www.catedralbcn.org ⊙ Daily 8–12:45, 5:15–7:30 (access to all sections pm only) 💷 Moderate 🚇 Jaume I/Liceu

Museu d'Història de la Ciutat
✚ 197 E3 ✉ Calle Beguer s/n ☎ 933 15 30 53; www.museuhistoria.bcn.cat ⊙ Jun–Sep Tue–Sat 10–8, Sun 10–3; Oct–May Tue–Sat 10–2, 4–7, Sun 10–3 💷 Moderate 🚇 Jaume I/Liceu

---

BARRI GÒTIC: INSIDE INFO

Top tips Remember to **cover your arms**, shoulders and the tops of your legs before you visit the cathedral.
• Try to catch one of the **concerts** that are sometimes held in the Plaça del Rei. Check with the tourist office for details.
• There's often a display of the *sardana*, the **Catalan folk dance**, in the Plaça de La Seu at noon on Sunday.
• The narrow streets of the Barri Gòtic are best explored on foot. It's easy, though, to get **lost** in the warren of streets; remember, any street leading **downhill** will get you out of the area.

Hidden gems Don't miss the remnants of the **old Roman walls**; you'll find them between the east side of the cathedral and Via Laietana. Built between 270 and 310, they marked the confines of the city through to the 11th century.
• Check out the **Casa de l'Ardiaca** (Archdeacon's House) and the **Palau Episcopal** (Bishop's Palace) on Carrer del Bisbe next to the cathedral. You can't go into the buildings themselves, but both have lovely courtyards with outer stairways, a typical feature of old palaces in Barcelona. There are Romanesque frescoes in the patio at the top of the Palau's staircase.

❷ Museu Picasso

More people visit the Museu Picasso (Picasso Museum) than any other attraction in Barcelona, drawn here by the mystique of the most towering artistic figure of the 20th century. The museum is housed in a series of converted medieval buildings and, along with the newer Museo Picasso in Málaga (► 174), contains one of the most important collections of the artist's work globally.

An interesting point about the collection is that it isn't fully representative; don't come expecting to see any of Picasso's most famous works, or much in his Cubist style. What you will find here is the most marvellous opportunity to trace how he developed as a painter, from early pictures made when he was a young boy to canvases produced just a few years before his death.

The museum opened in 1963 based on the collection of Jaume Sabartés, friend and secretary to Picasso – you can see him in many of the portraits, including one splendid abstract. There's a wealth of early work, all still influenced by his father's naturalistic style, dating from before Picasso's first visit to Paris in 1900, including drawings, family portraits

Above: Picasso's menu for Els Quatre Gats café

Left: A medieval courtyard in the Museu Picasso

Pablo Picasso

The son of a drawing teacher, Pablo Ruiz Picasso was one of the most important figures of 20th-century art. He was born in Málaga in 1881 (➤ 174) and moved to Barcelona in 1895. Throughout his life he felt himself to be Catalan rather than Andalucian, and the years he spent in Barcelona were some of his most formative. In 1900 he first visited Paris, where the influence of Toulouse-Lautrec was the inspiration for the pictures of his Blue Period (1901–04). His work developed through different styles until his key work, *Les Demoiselles d'Avignon* (1909), marked a break with representational style. From 1910 he developed Cubism, a style which depicts objects as seen from different angles at the same time. By the early 1930s, he was combining Cubism with Surrealism, re-inventing the human anatomy, while spiritually he was becoming increasingly involved with art as a means of protest, a philosophy which reached its climax in *Guernica* (➤ 53). Prolific and innovative right to the end of his life, his work is full of astonishing power and beauty. He died in 1973.

(don't miss *Tía Pepa*, his aunt), and landscapes and seascapes. Look out for the menu he designed for the Els Quatre Gats café, very much in the style of Toulouse-Lautrec. He then moved into his Blue Period, beautifully typified by *Los Desemparados*, through the Rose Period towards Cubism, which was to dominate much of his mature style. Another of the museum's highlights is *Las Meninas*, a series of some 50 works inspired by Velázquez's famous 17th-century painting in the Prado (➤ 49–52), which Picasso painted in 1969 and donated to the museum.

TAKING A BREAK

Close to the museum, **Plaça de la Garsa** (Carrer Assaonadors 13, tel: 933 15 24 13) occupies a former 16th-century stables and dairy. There's a good lunch menu and cold food such as pâté and cheese is served at other times. Classical music helps refresh both body and soul.

✚ 197 F3　✉ Carrer de Montcada 15–19　☎ 933 19 63 10; www.museupicasso.bcn.cat
🕙 Tue–Sun 10–8　💷 Moderate, free first Sun of month　🚇 Jaume I

MUSEU PICASSO: INSIDE INFO

Top tip The **best times to visit** are early morning and around lunch time; avoid Sundays, particularly the first Sunday of the month when entrance is free.

In more depth Take time to admire the building itself – two specially converted Gothic palaces, the Berenguer de Aguilar and the Baró de Castellet.

Must see In 1982 Jacqueline, Picasso's widow, donated over **40 ceramic vases, dishes and plates**, made by Picasso in the 1950s. Leave time to admire these stunningly vibrant works.

③ Las Ramblas

Las Ramblas is one of the Mediterranean's great streets – the heart of Barcelona for locals and visitors alike, a place to see and be seen, where you'll return time and again. Whether you're strolling its tree-lined length, sitting in its cafés, watching the crowds and street entertainers, or browsing the news-stands and flower stalls, the time spent here will be among your most unforgettable in Barcelona.

The Ramblas kicks off at the **Plaça de Catalunya**, which links medieval Barcelona with the 19th-century grid of L'Eixample (► 128) and runs south to the harbour, cutting through the Ciutat Vella (Old Town). The pedestrianised centre is overlooked by fine buildings and planted with plane trees; traffic is restricted to the outside strip. Each section of the Ramblas – it is divided into five – has a distinctive character, most marked by the subtle changes in what's sold at the kiosks.

There's always something to watch on the Ramblas

Start at the northern end, the **Rambla de Canaletes**. The big iron fountain is the focal point for post-match celebrations when Barça, the famous football team, triumphs and a drink here reputedly ensures you'll return to Barcelona. After the first cross-roads you enter the **Rambla dels Estudis**, known locally as the Rambla dels Ocells, a name it gets from the caged birds sold here. The church on the right is the Església de Betlem, built for the Jesuits in 1681.

Beyond here, lined with flower stalls, you're in the **Rambla de Sant Josep**. On the right is the wrought-iron entrance arch

Flower stalls add colour and scent to stretches of the Ramblas

to the glorious **Mercat de Sant Josep**. La Boquería, as it is known locally, has been here since the 1830s, a profusion of colour, scents and textures, and one of the Mediterranean's finest food markets.

Further down on the right, past the round pavement mosaic designed by Joan Miró, is the façade of the **Gran Teatre del Liceu**, Barcelona's opera house, first built in 1847 and re-opened for the second time (fire twice destroyed it) in 1999. Another 100m (110 yards) along on the left, where the street becomes the **Rambla dels Caputxins**, you'll find the arched entrance to the **Plaça Reial**, an elegant 19th-century arcaded square, complete with palm trees and quirky iron lamps designed by the young Gaudí.

The final stretch is the **Rambla de Santa Mònica**, which ends at Plaça del Portal de la Pau, with its slender monument to Colombus, erected in 1888.

TAKING A BREAK

Garduña (Jerusalén 18, tel: 933 02 43 23), a ramshackle restaurant within La Boquería, serves great seafood. You can either eat downstairs at the crowded bar or more formally upstairs. The atmosphere at lunchtime is best.

➕ 197 E3 🚇 Catalunya, Drassanes, Liceu

LAS RAMBLAS: INSIDE INFO

Top tips To experience the **Boquería market** in full swing, visit in the morning.
• Keep some **change** to hand to "activate" the living statues along the route.
• *Modernisme* fans should detour to Gaudí's **Palau Güell** (Carrer Nou de la Rambla 3–5, tel: 933 17 39 74; currently closed for renovation), just off the Ramblas. It's an astoundingly imaginative building, giving a taste of the architect's originality.
• Early evening is a good time for a drink in the **Plaça Reial**. Try to avoid it late at night, as it's a popular hangout for drug addicts and levels of crime are high.
• **Watch your valuables** at all times, particularly in crowds and late in the evening; petty theft is common.

④ Montjuïc

Rising to the west of the old city and the harbour area, the steep green hill of Montjuïc (The Hill of the Jews) is Barcelona's biggest open space, where you could easily spend an entire day. Site of the main area for the 1992 Olympic Games, Montjuïc is also home to two important museums, as well as verdant gardens with fabulous city views.

One of the magnificent Romanesque frescoes on view at MNAC

The main draw is the superb **Museu Nacional d'Art de Catalunya** (MNAC), housed in the Palau Nacional, which was constructed for the 1929 International Exhibition. It has undergone an extensive overhaul and is now one of the largest museums in Europe. Its highlight is the superb collection of **Romanesque art**, vibrant frescoes and sculpture brought from remote churches in the Pyrenees, dating from the 6th–13th centuries. The Gothic collection comes from all over Spain, including paintings and sculpture from the 1400s–1600s, and there are other treasures from all over Europe.

Nearby stands the striking white structure that's home to the **Fundació Joan Miró** (Joan Miró Foundation), opened in 1975 and expanded in 2001 as one of world's greatest collections of this famous Catalan artist's work. Miró was born in 1893 and his paintings and drawings, which link surrealism and abstract art, are instantly recognisable. Most of the works here were

Montjuïc is crowned by an historic castle

donated by the artist before his death in 1983 – more than 225 paintings, 150 sculptures and his whole graphic output. There are other works on display too, many donated by their creators, including Alexander Calder's *Mercury Fountain*, and pieces by Ernst, Balthus and Moore.

Further up the hill, on the topmost point of Montjuïc stands the 18th-century Castell de Montjuïc, still a military post and also housing the Museu Militar. It was here that Lluís Companys, first president of the Generalitat, was executed on Franco's orders in 1940. Before he was shot, he asked permission to remove his shoes and socks so he could die in contact with the soil of Catalonia.

For a change of pace, head downhill and take a lively crash course in Spanish regional architecture at the **Poble Espanyol**. Built for the 1929 International Exhibition, the streets and squares of this enclave are lined with replicas of famous or characteristic buildings from all over Spain – everything from white-washed Andalucian patios to the arcaded granite streets traditional in Galicia. The buildings contain shops, craft centres, bars and restaurants and the whole area, vibrating with life and noise, stays open late, late, late.

TAKING A BREAK

Stop at the Fundació Joan Miró's courtyard restaurant and café or check out the leafy terrace at **Bar Primavera** (➤ 136) which overlooks the city below.

Museu Nacional d'Art de Catalunya (MNAC)
✚ 196 C1 ✉ Palau Nacional, Montjuïc
☎ 936 22 03 76; www.mnac.es 🕐 Tue–Sat 10–7, Sun 10–2:30 💷 Moderate 🚇 Espanya
🚌 13, 50, 55

Fundació Joan Miró
✚ 197 D1 ✉ Parc de Montjuïc ☎ 934 43 94 70; www.bcn.fjmiro.es 🕐 Jul–Sep Tue–Sat 10–8 (also Thu 8–9:30pm), Sun 10–2:30; Oct–Jun Tue–Sat 10–7 (also Thu 7–9:30), Sun 10–2:30 💷 Moderate 🚌 50, 55

Poble Espanyol
✚ 196 B1 ✉ Avinguda del Marquès de Comillas ☎ 935 08 63 00; www.poble-espanyol.es 🕐 Mon 9–8, Tue–Thu 9am–2am, Fri 9am–4am, Sat 9am–5am, Sun 9–midnight 💷 Moderate 🚇 Espanya
🚌 13, 50

MONTJUÏC: INSIDE INFO

Top tips If time is short, the **one museum** you really should see is the Museu Nacional d'Art de Catalunya.
• Make for Montjuïc on weekend evenings to enjoy the **fabulous sound and light show** around the Font Màgica (Magic Fountain) below the Palau Nacional.

Getting in For **fabulous views**, take the **Transbordador Aeri cable-car** from Barceloneta or the Moll de Barcelona up Montjuïc to the Jardins de Miramar.
• A **funicular** runs from Paral·lel metro to halfway up Montjuïc and connects with the **Telefèric cable-car** to the castle.

5 Temple de la Sagrada Família

Antoni Gaudí's great unfinished church of the Sagrada Família (Holy Family) is Barcelona's most famous building, a monument both to this visionary architect and to the Catalan spirit. Soaring, complex, ebullient, it towers above the surrounding buildings in the east of the Eixample area and attracts almost every visitor to Barcelona. Love it or hate it, the sheer scale and vibrancy of this unique building is unforgettable.

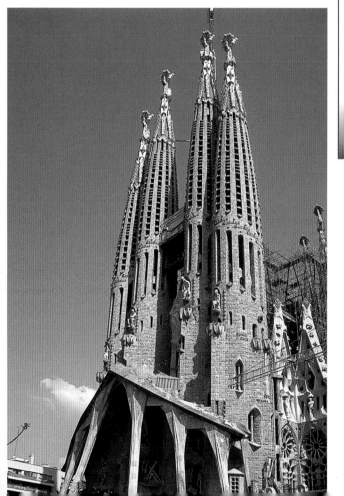

Conceived by a publisher, Josep Bocabella, in 1882 as an expiatory building to atone for Barcelona's increasingly left-wing ideas, the Sagrada Família was originally designed as a modest, traditional, neo-Gothic church. In 1884, the project was given to Gaudí, and remained in his hands until his death in 1926. His vision, inspired by his deep nationalist and religious fervour, was revolutionary. Rather than a simple church, he envisaged a vast cathedral, incorporating symbols of all the main tenets of Catholicism. His structure was to have three façades representing the birth, death, and Resurrection of Christ, above which would rise 18 organically inspired towers, glistening with mosaics. These would be reminders of the Twelve Apostles, the Four Evangelists, the Virgin Mary and Christ. The façades would be covered with scenes from the life of Christ, their porches dedicated to the cardinal virtues of Faith, Hope and Charity.

The east façade, the Nativity, has three richly

Visitors can climb amidst the soaring pinnacles

Emotionally charged sculpture on the Passion façade

carved and decorated doorways representing the three virtues. Above these, sculpted figures, all rendered with vivid naturalism, portray scenes from the Nativity and the Joyful Mysteries of the Rosary, the only real guidelines to Gaudí's ultimate vision. After his death, many argued that the Sagrada Família should be left unfinished as a memorial, some that Gaudí had always intended others to continue his project. Work started again in the 1950s and still continues; completion is as much as 30 years away, but eight spires now soar heavenwards and another façade is nearing completion. The new, and controversial, work on the Passion façade is that of Josep Maria Subirachs, who is also at work on the main entrance. Gaudí left no detailed plans of his intentions, and many critics feel that Subirachs' sculptures bear no resemblance to what the master envisaged. A Japanese sculptor, Etsuro Sotoo, is thought to be adhering better to Gaudí's original intentions.

Antoni Gaudí

The most famous architect of the *Modernista* movement was born in 1852, just before Barcelona's expansion in size and economic prosperity. Fuelled by growing Catalan nationalism, the time was ripe for an explosion of home-grown creativity which found its expression in *Modernisme*, with Gaudí as its most famous exponent. Heavily influenced by Moorish and Gothic architecture, he was also fascinated by the building potential of the new industrial technologies and the beauty of the natural world, fusing these elements in a unique style. Individual examples of his vision are found throughout Barcelona; the Sagrada Família is his mightiest monument. He died in 1926, run over by a tram, and was initially unrecognised. He was buried amid national Catalan grief.

TAKING A BREAK

There are splendid views of La Sagrada Família from **La Llimona** (Avinguda Gaudí 37, tel: 934 55 29 16), especially if you can find a free outdoor table.

🗺 197 E5 ✉ Plaça de la Sagrada Família ☎ 932 07 30 31; www.sagradafamilia.org
🕐 Apr–Sep daily 9–8; Oct–Mar 9–6 💰 Moderate, expensive with guided tour 🚇 Sagrada Família 🚌 19, 33, 34, 43, 44, 50, 51

TEMPLE DE LA SAGRADA FAMÍLIA: INSIDE INFO

Top tips Be prepared for crowds and plan your **visit early or around lunchtime.**
• Before you go in, walk to the end of the Plaça de la Sagrada Família and **examine the church from a distance** – it's the best way to get your first impression before you zoom in for a closer look.

In more depth If you want to examine things at close hand, **take the lift** up the tower near the rose window. You get great close-ups of the extraordinary stonework and ceramics, and can clamber around the walls and other towers – though it is not recommended for vertigo sufferers.
• To learn more about the history of the church, its place in Gaudí's architectural development, and its construction, leave time for the on-site **Museu de la Sagrada Família**, where photos, models and sketches will fill you in.

Getting in The main entrance is on the west of the building, fronting the Plaça de la Sagrada Família.

At Your Leisure

6 Parc Güell

Intended as a private housing estate, Parc Güell was Gaudí's largest secular project, commissioned by wealthy industrialist Eusebi Güell in 1900. Only two houses were eventually built, but the recreational areas, paths and ornamental monuments were all completed by 1914 when work stopped. You can wander the hillside setting, with its wonderful views over the city, and admire this extraordinary ensemble of riotously imaginative pavilions, stairways and mosaic benches – among the most light-hearted of all Gaudí's work.

➕ 196 off C5 ✉ Carrer d'Olat
☎ 934 13 24 00 🕐 Daily 10–sunset
🏠 Park free; Casa Museu Gaudí moderate 🚇 Vallcarca/Lesseps 🚌 24

7 L'Eixample

The Eixample area of Barcelona was designed in 1859 as an extension to the booming and growing city. It's laid out on a grid shape, intersected by long, straight streets, with the wide avenue of the Avinguda Diagonal slicing through the middle. Right from its inception, L'Eixample became the fashionable place to live, with the moneyed classes moving out from the old city into its spacious new buildings and wide avenues. Once here, the rich bourgeoisie commissioned the *Modernista* architects to build them ever more fantastic edifices, and today this legacy has turned the whole district into a sort of glorious urban museum.

The main thoroughfares are the **Passeig de Gràcia** and the **Rambla de Catalunya**, still the heart of Barcelona's main commercial and

Ruta del Modernisme

Modernista fans should purchase the Ruta del Modernisme ticket (valid for 30 days, moderate price) for discounts on admission to the main sites, including the Palau Güell, Casa Milà and the Sagrada Família. You'll find it at the Centre del Modernisme (Passeig de Gràcia 41, tel: 934 88 01 39, Mon–Sat 10–7, Sun 10–2).

shopping district. Visit the largely pedestrianised Rambla to enjoy the shops and café life; if you're after architecture, head for the Passeig de Gràcia. The stretch between the Plaça de Catalunya and the Diagonal metro contains some outstanding *Modernista* buildings, among them the **Mansana de la Discòrdia** (Block of Discord). The buildings that make up the block are wildly diverse in style, ranging from the step-gabled **Casa Amatller** to Gaudí's **Casa Batlló**, with its distinctive undulating rooftop and shimmering ceramic-clad walls. Wander a little further along the street and you'll come to **Casa Milà**

Sinuous curves trace the roofline of the Casa Milà

(No 92), another Gaudí masterpiece. With its sweeping stone work and cascading metal balconies, it's easy to see how this controversial building got its nickname La Pedrera (meaning "the quarry").

➕ 197 D4 ✉ Eixample

Casa Milà
✉ Passeig de Gràcia 92 ☎ 934 84 59 95 🕙 Daily 10–8 💷 Moderate 🚇 Diagonal 🚌 7, 16, 17, 22, 24, 28, 44

8 Palau de la Música Catalana

For a mind-blowing blast of *Modernisme* in all its most colourful exuberance, head for the Palau de la Música Catalana, perhaps the most quintessential *Modernista* building of all. Designed by Lluis Domènech i Montaner as a home for the city's famous choir, the Orfeo, it was built between 1905 and 1908. The façade, splendidly decorated with mosaics and busts, gives a taste of what's to come inside – a riot of stucco work, stained glass, mosaics, sculpture and reliefs, all different, all bursting with colour, light and energy. An excellent 20-minute film takes you through the building's history. The Palau also presents over 300 immensely varied concerts each year.

➕ 197 E3 ✉ Sant Francesc de Paula 2 ☎ 932 95 72 00; www.palaumusica.org 🕙 Guided tours in Spanish and English Jul–Aug daily 10–7; Sep–Jun 10–3:30 💷 Moderate 🚇 Urquinaona 🚌 17, 19, 40, 45, 120

9 Museu del Futbol Club Barcelona

Barcelona – affectionately known as Barça by its 107,000 worldwide fans – is one of Spain's most successful soccer clubs. During the Franco years, the club was a symbol of Catalan nationalism, and the lads in red and blue still inspire intense passion. Seating 98,000, Camp Nou stadium was built in 1957, a steeply raked, all-seated venue which is reckoned to be one of the world's great soccer stadia. Fans of the beautiful game should try to catch a match here, but failing that tune in to Canal Barça, the club's own TV channel, or visit the stadium. Even empty of fans, the huge space is impressive, while the museum is crammed with memorabilia of every kind.

➕ 196 off A3 ✉ FC Barcelona, Avenida Arístides Maillol s/n ☎ 934 96 36 08; www.fcbarcelona.com 🕙 Mon–Sat 10–6:30, Sun 10–2 💷 Moderate 🚇 Collblanc/Maria Cristina 🚌 15, 43, 59, 70, 72, 75, 113

10 Monestir de Pedralbes

The beautiful Gothic Monestir de Pedralbes (Pedralbes monastery), founded in 1326, lies on the outskirts of the city. A haven of peace and tranquillity, the monastic buildings lie around a harmonious cloister with an adjacent church. You can explore the buildings, which give a wonderful picture of monastic life. Numerous works of art are on display, especially in the Capella de Sant Miguel, which contains 14th-century murals executed by Ferrer Bassa on the Passion and the Life of the Virgin.

➕ 196 off A4 ✉ Baixada del Monestir 9 ☎ 932 03 92 82 🕙 Jun–Sep Tue–Sat 10–5, Sun 10–3; Oct–May Tue–Sun 10–2 💷 Moderate, free first Sun of month 🚉 RGC train to Reina Elisenda 🚇 Palau Reial 🚌 22

Further Afield

⑪ Costa Brava

South from the French border, mountain valleys running headlong to the sea have carved out the **Costa Brava**, the Rugged Coast, where pine tree-clad headlands shelter sandy coves and deep azure water. Such scenic beauty attracted the developers, and the southern reaches of the area is now a dense strip of mass-tourism hotels and apartment blocks. **Blanes**, **Lloret de Mar** and **Tossa de Mar** are the main resorts, brash and cheerful in character. Tossa is the pick of the bunch: enjoy the walled medieval quarter or embark on a cruise, the best way to appreciate the coastline. Northwards, the coast is less developed. **Roses** is the biggest resort, but nicer by far is **L'Escala** with its low-key local tourism and rocky coastline, or **Cadaqués**, a picturesque, if touristy, coastal village famous in the 1920s and 1930s as a literary-artistic colony. Salvador Dalí lived at neighbouring **Portlligat**, where you can visit his bizarre house. He later moved back to **Figueres** (**Figueras**), his birthplace; the **Dalí Theatre-Museum** is here and contains the broadest range of works spanning the artist's career.

Tourist Information Office, Tossa de Mar
🚩 202 C3 ✉ Avenida Pelegrí 25
☎ 972 34 01 08; www.infotossa.com
🕐 Jun–Sep Mon–Sat 9–9, Sun 10–2, 5–8; Apr, May and Oct Mon–Sat 10–2, 4–8, Sun 10:30–1:30; Nov–Mar Mon–Sat 10–1, 4–7

Tourist Information Office, Roses
🚩 202 C3 ✉ Avenida de Rhode 101
☎ 972 25 73 31; www.rosesweb.info
🕐 Mon–Fri 9–7, Sat 10–6, Sun 10–1

Tourist Information Office, Figueres
🚩 202 C3 ✉ Plaça del Sol ☎ 972 50 31 55; www.figueresciutat.com
🕐 Jul–Aug Mon–Fri 8:30–9, Sat 9–9, Sun 9–3; off season Mon–Fri 8:30–3, 4:30–8, Sat 9:30–1:30, 3:30–6:30; winter Mon–Fri 8:30–3

Dalí Theatre-Museum
🚩 202 C3 ✉ Plaça Gala-Salvador Dalí
☎ 972 67 75 09; www.dali-estate.org
🕐 Jul–Sep daily 9–8; Mar–Jun and Oct 9:30–6, Nov–Feb 10:30–6 💰 Expensive

Cadaqués on the Costa Brava

⑫ Girona (Gerona)

The inland city of Girona, its narrow stepped streets crammed with lovingly preserved old buildings, stands on the banks of the River Onyar. Its province is among Spain's richest, so you'll find plenty of expensive restaurants, shops, bars and galleries, making it one of Catalonia's most tempting towns. Culturally, it's Girona's Arab and Jewish influences that provide the main interest; the maze of narrow streets and superb **Banys Àrabs** (Arab Baths) attesting to its 200-year history as an Arab town, while its Jewish quarter, El Call, occupied for over six centuries, is a warren of tall thin houses and interconnecting alleys. The impressive Gothic **cathedral**, with its superb single-vaulted nave and lovely cloister, stands on the site of an earlier mosque. You can learn more in the **Museu Arqueològic**, from where you can also reach the walls and ramparts surrounding the old city.

➕ 202 C3

Tourist Information Office
✉ Rambla de la Llibertat 1 ☎ 972 22 65 75; www.girona-net.com
🕐 Apr–Sep Mon–Fri 8–8, Sat 8–2, Sun 9–2; Oct–Mar Mon–Sat 9–5, Sun 9–2

Banys Àrabs
✉ Portal de Sobreportas ☎ 972 21 32 62 🕐 Apr–Sep Mon–Sat 10–7, Sun 10–2; Oct–Mar Tue–Sun 10–2
💷 Inexpensive

Catedral
✉ Plaça Catedral ☎ 972 21 58 14
🕐 Cathedral: daily 10–8. Cloister and museum: Tue–Sun 10–8 💷 Moderate

Museu Arqueològic
✉ Sant Pere de Galligants ☎ 972 20 26 32 🕐 Jun–Sep Tue–Sat 10:30–1:30, 4–7, Sun 10–2; Oct–May Tue–Sat 10–2, 4–6, Sun 10–2 💷 Inexpensive

⑬ Monestir de Montserrat

Some 50km (31 miles) northwest of Barcelona, the craggy outcrop of Montserrat rises above the undulating landscape. A short train and cable-car hop from the city, it's both a natural park, criss-crossed with paths and walkways, and the most important pilgrimage centre in Spain after Santiago de Compostela (► 94–96). Geologically, Montserrat was formed around 25 million years ago; legend says its Virgin, La Moreneta (The Black Virgin), was brought here by St Peter. In the 9th century a powerful Benedictine monastery grew up around the shrine; with a brief break in the 19th century, the monks have been here ever since. Services are held throughout the day – you can hear the famous boys' choir at 1pm (noon on Sunday, except July) – and you can climb the steps behind the main altar of the basilica to see the lovely gilded 12th-century Madonna at close quarters. Don't miss the audiovisual show, **Montserrat Portes Endins**, which tells the story of the shrine and the life of the Benedictine community, and leave time to stroll along some of the wooded mountain paths away from the crowds. There is accommodation if you want to stay.

➕ 202 B3

Monestir de Montserrat
✉ Montserrat ☎ 938 77 77 01; www.abadiamontserrat.net 🕐 Late Jun–late Dec daily 7–8:30; late Dec–late Jun 7–7:30 🚊 Barcelona, Plaça d'Espanya– Montserrat–Manresa, hourly; cable-car Manresa–Monistir every 15 minutes Mar–Oct daily 9:30–7; Nov–Feb 10–6 💷 Church: free. Museum and audiovisual show: moderate

Montserrat Portes Endins
✉ Montserrat ☎ 938 77 77 01
🕐 Daily 9–6 💷 Moderate (joint ticket to the museum)

⑭ Sitges and the Costa Daurada

South of Barcelona a string of sandy beaches have given this stretch its name, the **Costa Daurada** (Costa Dorada), the golden coastline. **Sitges** is the main resort, a vibrant town with excellent beaches and some of the most outrageous nightlife in mainland Spain. Further south, **Salou** attracts thousands of holidaymakers looking for good beaches, cheap beer and the entertainment at nearby **Port Aventura**, (➤ panel, below).

Further south, the long open beaches give way to sheltered coves and the **Parque Natural del Delta de l'Ebre** (Ebro Delta), one of Spain's largest wetland areas, which shelters thousands of wintering birds. To visit it, head for Deltebre where you'll find boats running into the park. Inland, the two Gothic Cistercian monasteries of **Poblet** and **Santes Creus**, both founded in the 12th century, provide a complete contrast. Poblet is slighty older and far more evocative, a stunning ensemble cradled by massive walls and set in lovely open countryside. Its late Romanesque cloisters are the high spot, a delicious contrast with the Gothic style of those at Santes Creus.

✚ 202 B3

Tourist Information Office, Sitges
✉ Sínea Morera 1, Sitges ☎ 93 894 50 04; www.sitges.org ◷ Mid-Jun to mid-Sep daily 9–9; mid-Sep to mid-Jun Mon–Fri 9–2, 4–6:30

🄸 Tarragona

Tarragona, Roman Tarraco, with its splendid Roman monuments,

The fine medieval cathedral at Tarragona dates from the 12th century

medieval quarter, and pleasant *ramblas*, is beautifully – and strategically – sited high above the sea. It was the capital of Roman Spain, a grand and rich city, and its surviving Roman buildings reflect the city's ancient power and prestige. The pick of these include the necropolis, the circus, two forums and a magnificent amphitheatre backing on to the sea – Tarragona's excellent museums will give you more information. Further out the remarkable Roman aqueduct is among Spain's finest Roman relics. A wander throught the narrow streets of the medieval old town, with its serene 12th–14th-century cathedral, is a must. Stroll down the Rambla Nova and see the lovely view from the Balcón del Mediterraneo at the seaward end. You could round off your visit with some wonderfully fresh fish – Tarragona is Catalonia's second largest port.

✚ 202 B3

Tourist Information Office
✉ Carrer Mayor 39 ☎ 977 25 07 95; www.tarragonaturisme.es ◷ Jul–Sep Mon–Sat 9–9, Sun 10–3; Oct–Jun Mon–Sat 10–2, 4–7, Sun 10–2

For Kids

• If you're on the Costa Daurada, the rides and attractions at **Port Aventura** will be top of every child's list (tel: 902 20 22 20 for information, open mid-Sep to Nov, late Mar to mid-Jun daily 10–midnight; mid-Jun to mid-Sep, 10–7).

• **Sand and sea** will keep most kids happy – choose beaches with **high clean water standards**, which are rated on boards displayed at the top of the beaches. **Fresh-water showers** and toilets should also be available.

• The **coastal cruises** on the Costa Brava appeal to children of all ages.

• Most children will enjoy exploring **medieval towns** – the **Roman circus** at Tarragona is a sure hit.

Port Vell to La Barceloneta *Walk*

This walk combines some lovely waterside stretches around Port Vell, one of Barcelona's prime recreational areas, with a glimpse of some interesting older neighbourhoods and the city's loveliest park. There are some fascinating, Catalan-slanted museums en route and the chance to admire one of the city's oldest and most atmospheric churches.

1–2

With the **Monument a Colom** (▶ 122) behind you, cross the busy road and take the Rambla de Mar walkway across the water towards the Maremàgnum centre. Along the waterfront to your left stretches the Moll de la Fusta, the old wharf, now a harbourside promenade. Before you start, you could detour the few steps west to the **Drassanes**, once the the hub of Barcelona's ship industry. These 13th-century shipyards functioned through to the 18th century but now house the **Museu Marítim** (Maritime Museum), a fascinating collection of all things nautical, including a

DISTANCE 2.5km (1.5 miles) **TIME** 1.5 hours without stops
START POINT Monument a Colom Ⓜ Drassanes ✚ 197 E2
END POINT Palau de Mar Ⓜ Barceloneta ✚ 197 F3

lavish replica of the 16th-century Royal Galley.

2–3

The hub of the **Port Vell** is **Maremàgnum**, a leisure and entertainment complex on the old wharves, which includes shops, bars, restaurants and the **IMAX**, which shows wildlife and adventure documentaries on a giant screen. Also here is the **Aquàrium de Barcelona**, a state-of-the-art exhibition focusing on Mediterranean sea life. Leave this area and cross the road at the east end of the Moll de la Fusta to head up the wide Via Laietana. Here you're on the fringes of the Barri Gòtic (▶ 116–118). Continue to Plaça Jaume I.

3–4

Branch diagonally right down Carrer de l'Argenteria to the superb Catalan-Gothic church of **Santa Maria del Mar**. Built between 1324 and 1329 on the orders of Jaume II, it originally stood on the seashore, hence the name, Our Lady of the Sea. A tribute to

medieval Catalan maritime power, the soaring columns rise above a wide nave, drawing the eye up to the beautiful vaulting.

4–5

Leave the church and walk north up Carrer de Montcada, a 14th-century street lined with mansions built around central courtyards, which is home to the **Museu Picasso** (▶ 119–120). This area is called **La Ribera** (the waterfront), once medieval Barcelona's trading and maritime district and now buzzing with bars, cafés and galleries. At the top, turn right along Carrer de la Princesa, then cross the Passeig de Picasso to enter the **Parc de la Ciutadella**.

5–6

The Ciutadella park gets its name from the Bourbon fortress, built in 1715 and mostly demolished in 1869. The surviving star-shaped portion is home to the Catalan parliament. Amid the tranquil formal greenery, you'll find the **Cascada**, an ebullient baroque

displaced by the construction of the Ciutadella fortress. It's an attractive corner, with its long narrow streets and small squares, but the main draw is the plethora of excellent **fish and seafood restaurants.** Turn right towards the sea to emerge on the Passeig Joan de Borbó.

7–8

Turn right and walk along the landscaped waterfront towards the old warehouse called the **Palau de Mar.** Beautifully renovated, this now houses bars, restaurants and the **Museu d'Història de Catalunya** (Catalan History Museum) which tells the story of the region and the city from neolithic to modern times.

fountain, and, in the southeast corner, the city's **zoo.**

6–7

Leave the park, cross the road and walk down Avinguda del Marquès de l'Argentera before turning left by the station and crossing the road into **La Barceloneta.** This classic 18th-century grid-pattern development was laid out in 1755 to house the people

---

Places to Visit

Museu Marítim
✚ 197 E2 ⊠ Avinguda de les Drassanes 1 ☎ 933 42 99 20 ⓖ Daily 10–8 ⓔ Drassanes 🚌 14, 18, 36, 57, 59, 64, 91 ⓦ Moderate

Aquàrium de Barcelona
✚ 197 F2 ⊠ Moll d'Espanya, Port Vell ☎ 932 21 74 74 ⓖ Jul–Aug daily 9:30–11; Sep–Jun 9:30–9 ⓔ Drassanes 🚌 19, 40 ⓦ Expensive

Santa Maria del Mar
✚ 197 F3 ⊠ Plaça de Santa María 1 ☎ 933 10 23 90 ⓖ Daily 9–1:30, 4:30–8 ⓔ Jaume I 🚌 14, 17, 40, 51, 57, 59 ⓦ Free

Parc Zoològic
✚ 197 F3 ⊠ Parc de la Ciutadella ☎ 932 25 67 80 ⓖ Mar–May daily 10–6; Jun–Sep 10–7; Oct–Feb 10–5 ⓔ Ciutadella 🚌 14, 17, 39, 41 ⓦ Expensive

Museu d'Història de Catalunya
✚ 197 F3 ⊠ Plaça de Pau Vila 3 ☎ 932 25 47 00; www.mhcat.net ⓖ Tue and Thu–Sat 10–7, Wed 10–8, Sun 10–2:30 ⓔ Barceloneta 🚌 14, 17, 36, 40, 45, 51, 57, 59 ⓦ Moderate

---

Cascada

Parlament de Catalunya

Parc Zoològic

Parc de la Ciutadella

PASSEIG DE PICASSO

5

AV DE MARQUÈS DE L'ARGENTERA

6

RENFE Estació de França

LA BARCELONETA

7

Museu Picasso **4**

RIBERA

CARRER DE MONTCADA

Jaume I
C DE L'ARGENTERIA

Santa Maria del Mar

Barceloneta

PLAÇA DE PAU VILA

Palau de Mar **8**

PASSEIG JOAN DE BORBÓ

VIA LAIETANA

PLAÇA JAUME I **3**

BARRI GÒTIC

400 metres

400 yards

Moll d'Espanya

IMAX

Aquàrium de Barcelona **2**

RAMBLA DE MAR

Port Vell

0

Drassanes

Monument a Colom **I**

Museu Marítim

AV DE LES DRASSANES

Moll de la Fusta

Where to... Stay

Prices

Expect to pay per person per night

€ up to €50 €€ €50–€90 €€€ €91–€120 €€€€ over €120

Hostal Jardí €€

Some of the rooms here overlook one of the old town's prettiest squares and you need to book well ahead to have one. Not only do these rooms have the view, they also tend to be better furnished than interior ones. Those without a balcony, however, are cheaper. All rooms have a bathroom and there's a sunny breakfast room.

➕ 197 E3 ⊠ Plaça de Sant Josep Oriol 1 ☎ 933 01 59 00; fax: 933 42 57 33 Ⓜ Liceu

Hostal Opera €€

Reasonably priced accommodation beside the Liceu opera house, just off the Rambla. The rooms are spacious and simply furnished with plenty of natural light. The comfortable lounge has satellite TV and free internet access for guests.

➕ 197 E2 ⊠ Carrer de Sant Pau 20 ☎ 933 18 82 01; www.hostalopera.com Ⓜ Liceu

Hotel Arts €€€€

This towering hotel, set in palm-filled gardens by the beach, was built to accommodate VIPs during the 1992 Olympic Games. It boasts the only seafront pool in Barcelona, as well as fabulous interiors and views that stretch practically across the Mediterranean. The upper floors are reserved for "The Club", those guests requiring an extra degree of privacy and privilege, and the top floors also have duplex apartments decorated by leading Catalan designer Jaume Tresserra.

➕ 197 off F3 ⊠ Carrer de la Marina 19–21 ☎ 932 21 10 00; www.ritzcarlton.com Ⓜ Ciutadella-Vila Olímpica

Hotel España €€

This popular hotel in El Raval, west of the Ramblas, has public rooms which are a showcase of Modernist design; the restaurant, in particular, has wonderful floral tiles and wood-work. The bedrooms, many of which overlook an interior patio, have a more modern appearance, and are comfortable and spacious.

➕ 197 E2 ⊠ Carrer de Sant Pau 9–11 ☎ 933 18 17 58; www.hotelespanya.com Ⓜ Liceu

Paseo de Gràcia €€

If you want to explore the Modernist buildings in L'Eixample, this modest hotel on the Passeig de Gràcia, one of the city's central boulevards, makes an excellent base. Rooms are pleasingly decorated in soft pastel colours and are well furnished. There are views of Plaça de Catalunya.

➕ 197 D4 ⊠ Passeig de Gràcia 102 ☎ 932 15 58 28; www.hotelpaseodegracia.com Ⓜ Passeig de Gràcia

Ritz Hotel €€€€

When the Ritz was founded in 1919, it was immediately dubbed "the grande dame" of Barcelona hotels. The interior is sumptuous and the multilingual staff are discreetly omnipresent. The list of rich and famous patrons includes Salvador Dalí, who stayed here for months on end. Rooms range from excellent doubles to suites. Dining options include a brasserie for light meals and snacks, and the renowned Caelis restaurant.

➕ 197 E4 ⊠ Gran Via de les Corts Catalanes 668 ☎ 935 10 11 30; www.ritzbcn.com Ⓜ Passeig de Gràcia

Where to...
Eat and Drink

Prices

Expect to pay per person for a meal, including wine and service

€ up to €12　　€€ €12–€30　　€€€ over €30

Agut d'Avignon €€€

The approach, via an unprepossessing alleyway near Plaça Reial, disguises the fact that this is one of Barcelona's best restaurants. A small hallway leads to a multi-level dining room with two balconies. The menu is rooted in classic Catalan cooking, but also takes inspiration from other Spanish regional cuisines and from contemporary trends in European cooking. The service, as you might expect, is impeccable.

➕ 197 E3 ⊠ Carrer de la Trinitat, 3/1 d'Avinyó 8, off Carrer d'Avinyo ☎ 933 02 60 34 ⓦ Daily 1–3.30, 9–11:30 Ⓜ Liceu

Bar Primavera €

This shady, outdoor bar, halfway up Montjuïc, provides a convenient recuperation point for a drink or sandwich for those who have chosen to make the climb on foot.

➕ 197 E2 ⊠ Carrer Nou de la Rambla 192 ☎ 933 29 30 62 ⓦ Apr–Oct daily 8am–10pm; Nov–Mar 8am–7pm Ⓜ Paral-lel

Els Quatre Gats €€

The walls of "The Four Cats" were once hung with works by Picasso and other great artists of the day, and this legendary restaurant and meeting place has preserved its art nouveau look well. As you eat unpretentious Catalan cooking in the large dining room, imagine this as the setting for poetry readings, piano recitals and lively debates.

➕ 197 E3 ⊠ Carrer de Montsió 3 ☎ 933 02 41 40 ⓦ Daily 8am–2am Ⓜ Catalunya

La Parra €€

Few restaurants have as much atmosphere as this former coaching inn. It serves country cooking at its most exuberant; huge chunks of lamb, rabbit or pork cooked on the wood-fired grill are then served on wooden boards along with *alioli* (garlic mayonnaise) and excellent *escalivades* (grilled peppers with onion and aubergine). There are tables outdoors in summer, but reservations are always advisable as this is a favourite family restaurant.

➕ 196 B2 ⊠ Carrer de Joanot Martorell 3 ☎ 933 32 51 34 ⓦ Tue–Fri 8:30–midnight, Sat 2–4.30, 8:30–midnight, Sun 2–4.30 Ⓜ Hostafrancs

Mama Café €–€€

A hip young restaurant that was feng-shui-designed for harmonious dining. The tables are set around a central brightly painted kitchen, and the menu provides a creative twist to Mediterranean cuisine with dishes such as chicken and wild mushroom brochettes and grilled cuttlefish wih basmati rice.

➕ 197 D3 ⊠ Carrer Doctor Dou 10 ☎ 933 01 29 40 ⓦ Mon–Sat 1–1 Ⓜ Catalunya

Nou Can Tipa €–€€

This noisy bar is a local classic. It serves steamed mussels, fresh fish, and shellfish, plus delicious tapas. The portions are generous and the barstaff convivial. The bar is easy to find in Barceloneta's main street, but booking is advisable.

➕ 197 F2 ⊠ Passeig de Joan de Borbó 6 ☎ 933 10 13 62 ⓦ Summer daily 1–4, 2–midnight; winter Tue–Sat 1–4, 8–midnight, Sun 1–4 Ⓜ Barceloneta

Where to...
Shop

Shops in the city range from little old-fashioned businesses and trendy boutiques to glitzy shopping centres and large department stores selling just about anything you might want.

DESIGNER GOODS

The Eixample harbours the city's densest concentration of fashion emporia. Lining the Passeig de Gràcia are the more exclusive establishments. **Armand Basi**, at No 49 (tel: 932 15 14 21, metro: Passeig de Gràcia) is an exciting Spanish designer whose collections often have a strong Latin-American influence. Galician designer, **Adolfo Domínguez** has his smart flagship outlet at Passeig de Gràcia 32 (tel: 934 87 41 70, metro: Passeig de Gràcia). **Antoni Miró** is one of the city's fashion gurus and you can find his beautiful shirts and dresses in his own shop at Carrer del Consell de Cent 349 (tel: 934 87 06 70, metro: Passeig de Gràcia).

Bd Ediciones de Diseño (Carrer de Mallorca 291, tel: 934 58 69 09, metro: Passeig de Gràcia, Diagonal), suitably housed in a fabulous *Modernista* building, sells upmarket designer furniture and household goods.

DEPARTMENT STORES/MALLS

El Corte Inglés (Plaça de Catalunya 14, tel: 933 06 38 00, metro: Catalunya) is Barcelona's largest store. Across from here is the impressive new **El Triangle complex** where you find the perfume temple, Sephora, as well as Camper (shoes), Zara, Massimi Duti and a massive FNAC outlet.

In the upper reaches of **Avinguda Diagonal** are several large shopping malls, housing international chains, plus Spanish big names. **L'Illa** (Avinguda Diagonal 545–557, tel: 934 44 00 00) is vast, with international stores such as FNAC (books, records) and Camper, a trendy shoe boutique. Its main rival is the **Pedralbes Centre** (Diagonal 609, tel: 934 10 68 21, metro: Maria Cristina).

ARTS AND CRAFTS

If you're looking for jewellery, glassware, textiles, prints and paintings, the labyrinthine streets of La Ribera and El Raval, west of the Ramblas, should come up trumps. **Galeria Maeght** (Calle Montcada 25, tel: 933 10 42 45, metro: Jaume I), housed in a Renaissance palace, is perhaps the city's most exclusive art gallery, while **Gothsland Galeria d'Art** (Carrer Consell de Cent 331, tel: 934 88 19 22, metro: Passeig de Gràcia) is a specialist in original Catalan Modernista furniture, art and home décor.

FOOD AND DRINK

There are plenty of specialist food shops throughout the city. **Tot Formatge** (Passeig del Born 13, tel: 933 19 53 75, metro: Jaume I) sells a vast selection of cheese, including all the best Catalan goats' cheeses. Complement your purchase with a bottle of something from **Vila Viniteca** (Carrer Agullers 7–9, tel: 933 10 19 56, metro: Jaume I), one of the city's leading wine-sellers.

In the Ramblas, **Escribà** (La Rambla 83, tel: 933 01 60 27, metro: Liceu) is one of the finest cake-and chocolate-makers in town. Don't miss the florentines. **La Botifarreria de Santa Maria** (Carrer Santa Maria 4, tel: 933 19 91 23, metro: Jaume I) is a gourmet delicatessen, while the **Casa del Bacalao** (Carrer de Comtal 8, tel: 933 01 65 39, metro: Catalunya) somehow dresses lumps of salt cod to look like jewels.

For the best selection of fresh produce, try **Mercat de Sant Josep** (la Boquería ▶ 122).

Where to...
Be Entertained

To see what's on in Barcelona, pick up the weekly *Guía del Ocio* listings magazine at a kiosk or consult its website, www.guiadelociobcn.es. *La Vanguardia*, the best local paper, also has an informative arts and entertainment page. Other websites worth visiting are www.red2000.com/spain/barcelon and www.spain-barcelona.com

CLUBS

The places to be seen after dark are **Port Vell** (▶ 133) and **Port Olímpic**, the smart marina created for the 1992 Olympiad, now the focus of Barcelona's vibrant club culture. There are, however, sophisticated clubs in the **Eixample** and **Gràcia**. This is also where you'll find the city's gay nightlife – there are so many gay venues that the area has been dubbed "Gayxample".

For a unique Barcelona clubbing experience, try the celebrated **La Terrazza** (Avinguda del Marqués de Comillas, tel: 934 23 12 85, metro: Espanya), just behind the Poble Espanyol (▶ 124). To see it at its best don't turn up before 3am. **Torres de Ávila** (Avinguda del Marqués de Comillas, tel: 934 24 93 09 metro: Espanya), at the main gates to the Poble Espanyol, is another city institution. Designed by Javier Mariscal during the spending spree prior to the 1992 Olympics, it is possibly Barcelona's most beautiful club, with seven bars, a techno dance floor and spectacular rooftop terrace.

OPERA AND MUSIC

The **Gran Teatre del Liceu** (La Rambla 51–59, tel: 934 85 99 13, metro: Liceu) is one of the world's biggest and most celebrated opera houses and a night out there always smacks of a gala event. The **Palau de la Música Catalana** (▶ 129) offers spectacular *Modernista* architecture, as well as high-quality music, while **L'Auditori** (Carrer de Lepant 150, tel: 932 47 93 00, metro: Marina) is now home to the **OBC** (National Catalan Orchestra).

THEATRE AND DANCE

Unless you speak Catalan or Spanish, your chances of finding drama to your tastes are limited. However, ballet, dance and mime are all well represented. If you visit the city in late June or early August, try to catch one of the productions put on as part of the annual **Festival del Grec** (contact the tourist office for more information).

SPORT

It's worth taking a look at the **Anella Olímpica** on the west of Montjuïc (▶ 123–124). The sports complexes and swimming pools were purpose-built for the 1992 Olympic games, though the Estadi Olímpic dates from the 1929 Exhibition. **Piscines Bernat Picornell** leisure complex (Avinguda de l'Estadi, tel: 934 23 40 41) has a pool and gymnasium.

Watersports are a major activity in the port area, though you're better off at Sitges, Castelldefels and the Costa Brava for windsurfing, yachting and kayaking. At the **Base Náutica de la Mar Bella** (tel: 932 21 04 32) along the Avinguda Litoral, you can rent windsurfing and snorkelling equipment and small craft, and even learn to sail. The nearby beaches offer some of the cleanest city seabathing anywhere in Europe. There is an official nudist beach here and a beach popular with gay couples.

Southern Central Spain

Getting Your Bearings

South of Madrid, the great empty landscapes of Extremadura and Castilla-La Mancha roll on for mile after mile. This is classic Spain, the land of the high *meseta* (plateau) of windmills, Don Quixote and castles. It's easy here to visualise the great early battles to expel the Moors, to get a sense of the stark beauty and loneliness of the land, to understand the sheer scale of the country. Nearer the Mediterranean, in Valencia, the contrast is sharp, the coastal mountain ranges sheltering lush valleys and the sea lapping along the shores of one of Europe's major holiday areas.

Talavera de la Reina
Navalmoral de la Mata
NV/E90
Tajo
Ara
Alcántara
Embalse de Alcántara
Embalse de Valdecañas
Tole
Arroyo de la Luz
4 N521 **6**
Trujillo
Montes de Toledo
Los Yébenes
Alburquerque
Cáceres
Sierra de Guadalupe
7 Guadalupe
CASTILI
EXTREMADURA
Embalse de García de Sola
Embalse de Cijara
LA MANC
Herrera del Duque
Porzuna
Mérida
Miajadas
Embalse de Orellana
5
□ **Badajoz**
NV/E90
Don Benito
Embalse del Zújar
Guadiana
Ci Re
N630
Castuera
Almadén
Puerto
N432
Almendralejo
Cabeza del Buey
Barcarrota
Sierra de Alcudia
Zafra
ANDALUCÍA
Pozoblanco
Cardeña

Similarly, there could hardly be a greater contrast between the region's major cities; Toledo, the epitome of the Spanish fusion of Moorish, Jewish and Christian cultures; Cuenca, an extraordinary cliff-hanging town set in some of Castile's most dramatic scenery; and prosperous, big-city Valencia. The gem-like towns of Cáceres and Trujillo in Extremadura, monuments to the days of the *conquistadores*, contrast with the Roman splendours of Mérida and the

Left: Sun, sand, sea and high-rise hotels at Benidorm on the Costa Blanca
Previous page: Windmills are a quintessential part of La Mancha's scenery

Above: The historic castle at Belmonte

religious fervour embodied in the great monastery of Guadalupe, making this remote area well worth exploring. To the east, the resorts of the Costa Blanca are the perfect antidote, offering international-standard resorts with all that that implies.

The landscape is on a grand scale, its appeal lying mainly in its subdued tones and harsh beauty. Towards the coast, the mountains shelter lush valleys, while Valencia's *huerta* is one of Europe's most productive market garden areas. This fronts on to the coast, where the golden beaches and rocky coastline have helped make the Costa Blanca popular year-round.

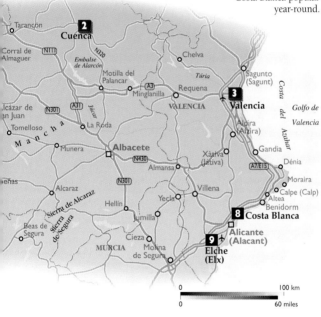

★ **Don't Miss**

At Your Leisure

For most visitors, exploring the whole of the great swathe of land that makes up Spain's southern central area would be too much in five days. Better, therefore, to see the major draws at a leisurely pace, before giving yourself a couple of relaxing days on the light-drenched Mediterranean coast. If you are determined to take in the lovely, remote towns of Extremadura, it makes sense to visit the west of the region first, before tackling Toledo.

Southern Central Spain in Five Days

Day One

Morning
Start your exploration of ❶ **Toledo** (➤ 144–146) at the **cathedral** (➤ 144), then head west to marvel at El Greco's *Burial of the Count of Orgaz* in **Santo Tomé** (below right, ➤ 144), before visiting the **Taller del Moro** (➤ 145).

Afternoon
After lunch, you could concentrate on the **Judería** area (➤ 144), visiting the **Casa del Greco** (➤ 144), the two synagogues (➤ 145), and **San Juan de los Reyes** (➤ 145). If you're up to it, late afternoon is the time to admire more great paintings in the **Museo de Santa Cruz** (➤ 145).

Evening
Take an evening stroll before dinner, then a walk or drive along the **Carretera de Circunvalación** (➤ Inside Info, page 146) to admire the **floodlit city** from afar.

Day Two

Morning
Leave Toledo and head east on the N400 to ❷ **Cuenca** (left, ➤ 147–148), a drive of 185km (115 miles). Get your bearings and have lunch in or around the **Plaza Mayor** (➤ 147).

Afternoon
The afternoon should give you enough time to enjoy Cuenca, including visiting the historic **cathedral**, the **museums** and **Museo de Arte Abstracto Español** (➤ 148).

Evening
Soaking up the atmosphere, while enjoying a drink and dinner, should round off your day.

Day Three

Morning
From Cuenca take the N320 south to join the A3 motorway to **Valencia** (left, ➤ 149–151), a distance of approximately 190km (118 miles).

Afternoon
Spend the afternoon taking in Valencia's main central sights – the area running from **Plaza Ajuntament** to the **cathedral** and the **Barrio del Carmen**. It's worth remembering that both the **IVAM** and **Bellas Artes** museums are open till 8pm – and there'll still be time to shop.

Day Four

Morning
Don't miss Valencia's superb **Mercado Central** (➤ 149) before taking in **La Lonja** (➤ 150), just across the street. Then head out from the centre to the **Ciutat de les Arts i les Ciències** (➤ 150).

Afternoon
Take the A7 motorway south towards the **Costa Blanca** (➤ 154–155). Stay on the coast; either the resort of **Dénia** or **Calp** would be a good bet, leaving you poised for the next day.

Day Five

Morning
Spend the morning exploring some of the **Costa Blanca**, or take a drive inland to the mountains of the **Sierra de Aitana**, before hitting **Alicante** (right, ➤ 154–155) in time for a typically Spanish late lunch.

Afternoon
Drive the 18km to **Elche (Elx)** (➤ 155) and spend the afternoon wandering in Europe's biggest palm forest.

Toledo

Toledo's got a great deal going for it – historical richness, superb architecture, a dramatic situation, all of which contribute to making it one of Spain's most evocative and visited cities. This golden city perches dramatically on a granite crag above the encircling gorge of the River Tajo (Tagus), its skyline little changed in more than three centuries. Moors and Jews left their mark on the bones of the earlier Roman and Visigothic settlements, contributing to a unique and fascinating cityscape.

Once a Roman town, Toledo became the Visigothic capital, an important trading and cultural centre, which was taken by the Moors in 712. From then on, Mozárabes (Christians subject to Moorish rule), Moors and Jews lived amicably together, a situation which remained unchanged even after the city was re-taken by the Christians in 1085. This fusion of cultures, which made Toledo unique, came to an end in the 16th century with the expulsion of the Moors and Jews and the establishment of Madrid as the Spanish capital.

From the Cathedral to San Juan de los Reyes

Mind-blowingly ornate, Toledo's **cathedral** was built between 1227 and 1493, and thus combines Gothic, Renaissance and baroque elements. Four aisles flank the **central nave**, running down to the *coro* (choir), which stands opposite the **Capilla Mayor**. Its huge altarpiece tells the story of the entire New Testament and is backed by the exuberant **Transparente**. Round the walls are over **20 chapels** and the cathedral's treasures include stunning stained glass and pictures by El Greco, Velázquez and Goya.

Santo Tomé contains El Greco's greatest masterpiece, The *Burial of the Count of Orgaz*, a perfect illustration of the artist's ability to combine the spiritual with drama and technical mastery. The church stands on the edge of the **Judería**, the old Jewish quarter, where you'll find the **Casa-Museo del Greco**, home to some superb paintings by the artist, including his *View*

El Greco (the Greek) 1541–1614

El Greco – real name Domenicos Theotocopoulos – arrived in Spain from his native Crete via Italy, where he had indubitably been influenced by the angular forms, sinuous composition and virulent colours of Mannerism. He arrived in Toledo in 1575, having failed to find work, as he had hoped, at the Escorial. Here he remained, painting religious works for the city's churches and portraits of the nobility. His fusion of Mannerist forms with an intense and Byzantine spiritualism was perfectly attuned to the contemporary Spanish mood, to the extent that, despite his foreign birth, he is thought of as a quintessentially Spanish painter. His work became increasingly abstract and idiosyncratic, aspects which more than anything else make his pictures fresh and relevant for modern viewers.

and Map of Toledo. Nearby is the 14th-century **Taller del Moro**, worth seeing for the doorways and decoration. Both the Casa Museo del Greco and the Taller del Moro are closed for renovation. Toledo's two remaining **synagogues**, the **Tránsito**, a simple galleried 14th-century building housing the Jewish museum, and **Santa María la Blanca**, should not be missed. The horseshoe arches and tiled floor of 14th-century La Blanca are a good example of cultural fusion, as much reminiscent of a mosque as a synagogue or church. Further on, **San Juan de los Reyes**, built in 1476, is typically Isabelline; the chains on the exterior are those taken from the Christian prisoners freed from the Moors in Andalucía.

Other Sights

To the east of San Juan, and almost right across town, is Toledo's main square, the **Plaza de Zocódover** – its name, intriguingly, comes from the Arabic word *souk* – which is dominated by the bulk of the **Alcázar**, built and rebuilt over

Toledo's cityscape has changed little over the centuries

the centuries. In 1936 it was held by Colonel José Moscardó against the Republicans, who threatened to shoot his son, their prisoner, if he did not surrender. Moscardó told his son "If it be true, commend your soul to God, shout *Viva España*, and die like a hero". The threat was carried out. Just two months later the Alcázar was relieved by Nationalist troops. Nearby is the superb **Museo de Santa Cruz**, a collection of some of Toledo's greatest El Grecos and other masterpieces, housed in a former 16th-century hospice with an exquisite plateresque façade. Outstanding here is El Greco's febrile *Assumption*, his *Crucifixion* featuring a backdrop of Toledo, and a vast collection of tapestries and carpets.

Tourist Information Office
✉ Puerta de Bisagra ☎ 925 22 08 43;
www.toledo.es 🕐 Summer Mon–Sat 9–7,
Sun 9–3; winter Mon–Sat 9–6, Sun 9–3

Cathedral
✉ Plaza Mayor ☎ 925 22 22 41
🕐 Cathedral: daily 10–12, 3:30–6:30;
Museum: Mon–Sat 10–6:30, Sun 2–6:30
💶 Moderate, free Wed pm

Santo Tomé
✉ Plaza de Conde ☎ 925 25 60 98
🕐 Daily 10–6:45 💶 Inexpensive

Sinagoga del Transíto
✉ Calle de los Reyes Católicos ☎ 925 22
36 65 🕐 Summer Tue–Sat 10–2, 4–9, Sun
10–2; winter 10–2, 4–6, Sun 10–2
💶 Inexpensive

Santa María la Blanca
✉ Calle de los Reyes Católicos ☎ 925 22
72 57 🕐 May–Sep daily 10–2, 3:30–7;
Oct–Apr 10–2, 3:30–6 💶 Inexpensive

San Juan de los Reyes
✉ Plaza de San Juan de los Reyes ☎ 925
22 38 02 🕐 Summer daily 10–7; winter
10–6 💶 Inexpensive

Museo Santa Cruz
✉ Calle Cervantes 3 ☎ 925 22 14 02
🕐 Mon–Sat 10–6:30, Sun 10–2
💶 Inexpensive

Casa-Museo del Greco
✉ Calle Samuel Leví 3 ☎ 925 22 40 46
🕐 Closed for renovation

Museo de Arte Visigótico
✉ Calle San Clemente 4 ☎ 925 22 78 72
🕐 Tue–Sat 10–2, 4–6:30, Sun 10–2
💶 Inexpensive, free Sat pm and Sun

Taller del Moro
✉ Calle Taller del Moro ☎ 925 22 71 15
🕐 Tue–Sat 10–2, 4–6:30, Sun 10–2
🕐 Closed for renovation

Alcázar
✉ Cuesta del Alcázar ☎ 925 22 16 73
🕐 Closed for renovation of the military
museum, due to reopen in 2008

TAKING A BREAK
Sip an ice-cold creamy *horchata* and watch the world go by at the **Toledo Café Bar** in the Plaza de Zocodover, right across from one of the best marzipan shops in town.

TOLEDO: INSIDE INFO

Top tips To see Toledo at its best you should **spend the night** there – with the day trippers gone and the city **floodlit**, it gets back its soul.
• Parking is a nightmare; head straight for the **underground car park** near the Alcázar.

Must see You'll get the **best views** of Toledo by walking along the south bank of the Tajo on the Carretera de Circunvalación – it's amazing how little the skyline has altered from that shown in so many paintings by El Greco. The **classic view** depicted in his *Storm over Toledo* was painted from roughly where the Parador stands today.

② Cuenca

Cuenca's setting is extraordinary, perched on a crowded ridge enclosed by the deep gorges of two rivers, the Huécar and the Júcar. Ancient houses teeter on the gorges' edges, steeply stepped streets, lined with tall, narrow houses, meander ever upwards, while around the city spreads a mountainous landscape. Exploring the maze of lanes is a delight, the views are stupendous, and there's the bonus of one of Spain's leading modern art museums.

The Ciudad Antigua

Everything you'll want to see lies in the **Ciudad Antigua** (old city), a densely packed warren, mainly dating from the city's 14th–16th-century heyday, high above the river gorges. Start in the **Plaza Mayor**, the main square, with its 17th-century arcaded Ayuntamiento (Town Hall) and shady cafés. It's dominated by the **cathedral**, whose unfinished façade hides a 12th–13th-century building, Anglo-Norman in inspiration. Inside, there's a plethora of Renaissance and baroque monuments, modern stained glass and some extraordinary wrought iron grilles, an artisan speciality of Cuenca, examples of which you can see throughout the city. Nearby are two religious museums, the **Tesoro Catedralicio**, whose chief treasures are some ornate gold and silver plate, and the **Museo Diocesano**. This beautifully restored old building has two El Grecos and a moving 13th-century Byzantine diptych, encrusted with silver and gems, unique in Spain. There are more reminders of the past at the **Museo de Cuenca**, housed opposite in the city's old granary, ranging from local Roman finds to exhibits on geology and prehistory. There are other churches and lovely old mansions scattered throughout the streets and plazas – spend time simply wandering, walk along the gorge and soak up the atmosphere, for Cuenca is much more than the sum of its parts.

Cuenca's many houses cling to the edge of the two gorges

The Casas Colgadas and the Museo de Arte Abstracto Español

In the 14th century the rim of the gorge was lined with **Casas Colgadas** (Hanging Houses), wood and plaster houses whose balconies were cantilevered dizzyingly out into space. Today only three remain, one of which has been beautifully restored and converted to house the **Museo de Arte Abstracto Español** (Museum of Spanish Abstract Art). The gallery was established in the 1960s by Fernando Zóbel, a leading light among Spanish abstract artists, and acquired in 1980 by the Juan March Foundation, an institution devoted to 20th-century art. The museum has a core selection of paintings and sculpture by artists such as José Guerrer, Antonio Saura and Lucio Muñoz, and also stages temporary exhibitions.

TAKING A BREAK

Grab an outside table at the **Taberna El Botijo** in the medieval Plaza Mayor and enjoy a glass of local wine and a plate of crumbly Manchego cheese.

Casas Colgadas – home of the Museo de Arte Abstracto Español

🚹 199 F2

Tourist Information Office
✉ Plaza Mayor ☎ 969 23 21 19;
www.cuenca.org 🕐 Summer Mon–Sat 9–9,
Sun 9–2:30; winter Mon–Sat 9–2, 5–8, Sun 9–2

Museo de Arte Abstracto Español
✉ Casas Colgadas, Calle Canónigos s/n
☎ 969 21 29 83 🕐 Tue–Fri 11–2, 4–6,
Sat 11–2, 4–8, Sun 11–2:30 💶 Moderate

Cathedral
✉ Plaza Mayor ☎ 969 22 46 26 🕐 Daily
9–1:30, 4:30–7:30 💶 Free

Tesoro Catedralicio
✉ Plaza Mayor 🕐 Tue–Sat 11–2, 4–6,
Sun 11–2 💶 Inexpensive

Museo Diocesano
✉ Palacio Episcopal, Calle Obispo Valero
☎ 969 22 42 10 🕐 Summer Tue–Sat
11–1:30, 4:30–6:30, Sun 11–1:30; winter
Tue–Sat 11–1:30, 4–6, Sun 11–1:30
💶 Inexpensive

Museo de Cuenca
✉ Calle Obispo Valero ☎ 969 21 30 29
🕐 Tue–Sat 10–2, 4–7, Sun 10–2
💶 Inexpensive

CUENCA: INSIDE INFO

Top tips Don't miss the view of the **floodlit Casas Colgadas** from the Puente de San Pablo at night.
• Even if abstract art leaves you cold, you should **visit the Museum of Abstract Art** for the beauty of the building alone.
• Try to **visit during the week** – Cuenca is a popular weekend outing from Madrid and can get very busy.

❸ Valencia

Rich, stylish Valencia, Spain's third largest city, has to be one of the great party towns, with a year-round series of festivals, culminating in the Fallas, and some of the country's best nightlife. Add to this a balmy climate, fine buildings, excellent museums and elegant shops, and you've got the recipe for a city with plenty going for it.

The Plaza Ajuntament and Around the Cathedral

The old part of Valencia is encircled by the dry river-bed of the Turia, diverted in 1956 after some catastrophic flooding. Within this area you'll find the atmospheric **Barrio del Carmen**, the oldest part of the city, and most of the interesting sights. Start exploring at the **Plaza Ajuntament**, the main square, a large open space complete with a spectacular fountain (catch it at night), palm trees and flower stalls. It's dominated by the solid mass of the Ajuntament (City Hall), which is home to the **Museu Histórico Municipal**. From here head northwest to take in the *Modernista* **Mercado Central** (Central Market), one of the biggest in Europe, where you can buy seemingly every type of fish, fruit, meat and vegetable that's available. Opposite is one of Valencia's greatest

The Fallas

Huge satirical *fallas* (models), works of art in themselves, flowers and fireworks, wonderful costumes and music, dancing, bullfights and street parties – this is Fallas week, held in Valencia from 12–19 March in honour of San José. The festival's origins lie in a simple spring rite, when carpenters would burn their spare wood, and it's grown to become an international tourist attraction. Each *barrio* (neighbourhood) commissions its own *falla*, a giant figure which is judged and is the centre of neighbourhood celebrations throughout the week. There are floral processions to a huge image of the Virgin outside the cathedral, a *fallas* queen, and deafening daily firecracker displays in the Plaza Ajuntament. The week's riotous celebration culminates on 19 March, the *Nit de Foc*, when the giant *fallas* are set on fire and it's all over for another year. You can learn more at the Museu Fallero.

treasures, the beautiful late 15th-century Gothic **Lonja** (Exchange) and its lovely cloister, with soaring vaults and serene space, which was once the city's silk exchange. It still acts as a commercial exchange and comes to life when Sunday stamp and book markets are held here. East from here is the **cathedral complex**, which includes, besides the 13th–15th-century cathedral, an unfinished tower, the **Miguelete**, the cathedral museum and two plazas. The cathedral has been restored to its simple Gothic splendour, beautifully illuminated by the clear light filtering through the alabaster panels in the lantern above the crossing. The **Plaza de la Virgen** lies behind; here, every Thursday at noon since the Middle Ages, the Tribunal of the Waters meets to regulate grievances about the irrigation system in the outlying *huertas*.

Some City Museums

Museums are scattered all over the city, and if time is short it's hard to decide what to see. Try to take in the **Museo de Cerámica González Martí** (González Marti Ceramics Museum), worth seeing as much for the fabulously over-the-top 18th-century baroque façade and ornate interior as for the collection. There are ceramics here from all over Spain, and you'll see some stunning glazes, vibrant *azulejos* (tiles) and a reproduction of a traditional Valencian kitchen. Art lovers should head for the **Museo de Bellas Artes** (Fine Arts Museum), which presents an excellent overall view of Spanish painting, with works, among others, by El Greco, Goya and Velázquez. If modern art's more appealing, the **Instituto Valenciano de Arte Moderno (IVAM)** specialises in temporary exhibitions of 20th-century and contemporary art, while bullfighting is the focus of the **Museu Taurino**.

Ciutat de les Arts i les Ciències

Southeast of the city centre stands the ambitious **Ciutat de les Arts i les Ciències** (Arts and Science City), an architecturally stunning clutch of buildings designed by Valencian architect Santiago Calatrava. Funded by the Generalitat to encourage year-round tourism, these dazzling white buildings, all swooping curves and graceful arcs, are set around reflecting pools. **L'Hemisfèric** (Hemisphere) houses a giant screen, which acts as a planetarium, laser screen and Imax cinema. It's flanked by the **Museu de les Ciències Príncipe Felipe** (Prince Felipe Science Museum), an interactive science museum, and the **Parque Oceanográfico** (Ocean Park), a series of lakes, lagoons and aquariums replicating different ocean habitats

The impressive Ayuntamiento rises behind a fountain

Strawberry season in the Mercado Central

from around the world. The **Palacio de las Artes** (Arts Palace) hosts concerts, opera and theatre.

TAKING A BREAK

Indulge in a hot chocolate at **Valor** (Gran Via Marqués del Turia 79), one of Spain's famed *chocolatería* chains, across from the cathedral.

🔲 201 F4

Tourist Information Office
✉ Plaza de la Reina 19
☎ 963 15 39 31; www.turisvalencia.es
🕒 Mon–Sat 9–7, Sun 10–2

Museu Histórico Municipal
✉ Plaza Ajuntament 1 ☎ 963 52 54 78
🕒 Mon–Fri 9–2 💶 Inexpensive

Cathedral
✉ Plaza de la Reina ☎ 963 91 81 27
🕒 Daily 7:30–1, 4:30–8:30 💶 Moderate

La Lonja
✉ Plaza del Mercado ☎ 963 52 54 78
🕒 Tue–Sat 10–2, 4:30–8:30, Sun 10–3
💶 Free

Museo de Bellas Artes
✉ Calle San Pío s/n ☎ 963 87 03 00
🕒 Tue–Sun 10–8 💶 Free

Museo de Cerámica González Martí
✉ Calle Poeta Querol 2 ☎ 963 51 63 92
🕒 Tue–Sat 10–2, 4–8, Sun 10–2
💶 Inexpensive, free Sat pm, Sun

Instituto Valenciano de Arte Moderno (IVAM)
✉ Calle Guillem de Castro 118 ☎ 963 86 30 00; www.ivam.es 🕒 Jun–Sep Tue–Sun 10–10; Oct–May 10–8 💶 Inexpensive, free Sun

Museu Taurino
✉ Pasaje Doctor Serra 10 ☎ 963 88 37 38
🕒 Summer Tue–Sun 10–10; winter 10–8
💶 Free

Museu Fallero
✉ Plaza Monteolivete 4 ☎ 963 52 54 78; www.fallas.com 🕒 Tue–Sat 10–2, 4:30–8, Sun 10–3 💶 Inexpensive

L'Hemisfèric
✉ Avenida Autopista del Saler ☎ 902 10 00 31 🕒 Shows daily hourly from 11–6
💶 Moderate

Museu de les Ciències Príncipe Felipe
✉ Avenida Autopista del Saler 5 ☎ 902 10 00 31; www.cac.es 🕒 Summer Sun–Fri 10–10, Sat 10–8; winter Sun–Fri 10–6, Sat 10–8 💶 Moderate

---

VALENCIA: INSIDE INFO

Top tips There's a tourist bus, the **Bus Turistic**, which trundles round the **main tourist sights**. It leaves every half-hour from outside the cathedral and makes 17 stops on its circular route – a good way of avoiding hassle on the ordinary city transport system.
• Valencia is surprisingly big, so be prepared to do a **lot of walking**.
• **Watch bags and wallets at all times**; there's a high level of street crime and begging in the city.

In more depth Valencia is blessed with marvellous **city parks**, worth seeking out for green, shady peace. The whole **Turia river-bed** is planted and grassed, with trees, bicycle paths, children's playgrounds and a light and airy glass concert hall, the **Palau de la Música**. More traditional are the **Jardín Botánico**, with plants from all over the world, the lovely neo-classical **Jardines de Montforte** and the **Jardines del Real-Viveros**, all intricate design, palms and colourful planting.

At Your Leisure

4 Cáceres

Tucked away in the west of Extremadura, the provincial capital of Cáceres is an almost perfectly preserved walled town, a monument to the returning New World *conquistadores*, whose money funded its construction. Nearly everything you'll want to see lies within the mainly Moorish walls, best approached from the Plaza Mayor through the 18th-century Arco de la Estrella. Once inside, you can wander through streets lined with some of Spain's finest Gothic and Renaissance mansions. These are austere buildings, their appeal lying in their severe lines and beautiful ochre-coloured stonework. Star sights include the buildings around the Plaza de Santa Maria and the lovely Plaza de San Mateo. Keep an eye out for the family crests adorning the different mansions and the storks' nests perched on every available tower. Cáceres' provincial museum is worth a visit for the building alone; it's housed in the **Casa de las Veletas**, which, with its patio, well-proportioned rooms and horseshoe arches, is a perfect example of the local style.

➕ 200 B4

Tourist Information Office
✉ Plaza Mayor s/n ☎ 927 01 08 34; www.turismoextremadura.com
🕐 Summer Mon–Fri 9–2, 5–7, Sat 9:45–2; winter Mon–Fri 9–2, 4–6, Sat 9:45–2

Museo Provincial
✉ Plaza de las Veletas 1 ☎ 927 01 08 77 🕐 Mid-Apr to Sep Tue–Sat 9–2:30, 5–8:15; Oct to mid-Apr 9–2:30, 4–7:15 💶 Inexpensive, free for EU citizens

5 Mérida

If you're interested in Spain's Roman past, head for Mérida, which has more Roman remains than any other Spanish city. Once the tenth city in the Empire, Mérida was the capital of the Roman province of Lusitania, a rich centre, liberally endowed with superb public buildings. A 60-arched bridge, the Puente Romano, crosses the islet-scattered River Guadiana into the city, and is the best place to start your explorations. Just across the river to the left lie the Morerías archaeological excavations, where you can watch the digging. Ahead lies the heart of Mérida, with its great Arco Trajano (Trajan's Arch), while 10 minutes' walk northeast will bring you to the pick of the bunch, the Teatro Romano (Roman Theatre), Anfiteatro (Amphitheatre), Casa Romana del Anfiteatro (Amphitheatre Roman House) and the **Museo Nacional de Arte Romano** (National Museum of Roman Art). The Teatro Romano was built around 15 BC as a gift to the city from Agrippa, the right-hand man of Augustus, the first Roman emperor. With its two-tier colonnaded stage, it's one of the best

For Kids

If your children need entertaining, head straight for **Benidorm** where you can choose from:

• **Terra Mítica**, a huge park, crammed with stomach-churning rides and themed round the ancient Mediterranean civilisations.

• **Mundomar**, which has seal and dolphin shows, water features and woodland paths to explore.

• **Aqualandia**, the biggest and best-known aquapark on the coast, with a splendid variety of pools, slides, waves and rides.

preserved anywhere in the Roman empire, and is used during the summer for a classical theatre festival. Take a look at the Anfiteatro, built to seat 15,000, before admiring the wonderful mosaics in the Casa Romano. The fine collections in the nearby Museo Nacional de Arte Romano, housed in an airy structure reminiscent of a classical building, will help you make sense of all you've seen.

➕ 200 B3
www.merida.es

Tourist Information Office
✉ Paseo José Álvarez Sáenz de Buruaga s/n ☎ 924 00 97 30; www.turismoextremadura.com ⏰ May–Oct Mon–Fri 9–1:45, 5–7, Sat–Sun 9:30–2; Nov–Apr Mon–Fri 9–1:45, 4–6, Sat–Sun 9–1:45

Museo Nacional de Arte Romano
✉ Calle José Ramón Mélida 2 ☎ 924 31 16 90 ⏰ Mar–Nov Tue–Sat 10–2, 4–9, Sun 10–2; Dec–Feb Tue–Sat 10–2, 4–6, Sun 10–2 🖐 Inexpensive, free Sat pm, Sun

⑥ Trujillo

Trujillo is among Extremadura's most enticing towns, a tiny set-piece of narrow streets, tranquil squares, mansions, castle walls and towers complete with storks' nests. Like Cáceres (➤ 152) it's a *conquistador*

town, built with New World booty money. Francisco Pizarro, the conqueror of Peru, was born here, and his family built many of Trujillo's finest houses. Spend time exploring its streets, admiring its serene architecture, and sitting in the grandiose **Plaza Mayor**. If you climb up to the Moorish castle, there are wide views across the town and surrounding countryside.

➕ 200 B4
www.trujillo.es

Tourist Information Office
✉ Plaza Mayor s/n ☎ 927 32 26 77; www.trujillo.es ⏰ Daily 10–2, 4:30–7

⑦ Guadalupe

Picturesque Guadalupe, all russet-tiled roofs and flower-hung balconies, is dominated by the great mass of the **Real Monasterio de Guadalupe**, once one of Spain's most important pilgrimage centres. Established in 1340, the monastery stands on the site of the discovery by a cowherd of a miraculous Virgin, said to have been carved by St Luke. The vast complex, a fascinating mix of architectural styles, was richly endowed with artworks and treasures by returning *conquistadores*, who had taken their devotion to the Guadalupe Virgin to

The façade of the Real Monasterio de Guadalupe

the New World – the Caribbean island of Guadalupe is named after the monastery. The richly gloomy church interior, dimly glittering in the candlelight, is a mere foretaste of what's to come. There are two cloisters; the 14th–15th-century *mudéjar* cloister has a double storey of horseshoe arches and a bizarre central pavilion; the second cloister is pure 16th-century Gothic. Around these lie museums rich in paintings and sculptures, textiles and embroidery, jewels and relics. The finest room is the Sacristía, unaltered since its 17th-century construction and still hung with a magnificent series of paintings of scenes of the life of St Jerome by Zurburán. Right in the heart of the monastery, you reach the Camarín, a tiny, richly decorated room which contains the smoke-blackened, bejewelled figure of the Virgin herself.

➕ 200 B4

The Castillo de Santa Barbara dominates Alicante's waterfront

Tourist Information Office
✉ Plaza Mayor s/n ☎ 927 15 41 28;
www.turismoextremadura.com
🕐 Summer Tue–Fri 10–2, 5–7,
Sat–Sun 10–2; winter Tue–Fri 10–2,
4–6, Sat–Sun 10–2

Real Monasterio de Guadalupe
✉ Guadalupe ☎ 927 36 70 00
🕐 Daily 9:30–1, 3:30–6:30
💶 Moderate

🔘 Costa Blanca

Valencia's southern province is Alicante (Alacant), a wonderfully varied area with historic towns, fertile land and some impressive mountain scenery. It's best known though for its coastline, the Costa Blanca (White

Coast), a positive mecca for people from all over Europe seeking sun, sand, sea and good-value holidays. No resort is better equipped for mass-market tourism than **Benidorm**, a high-rise, brash and noisy resort with great beaches and non-stop entertainment. The coast's other resorts are lower key and have managed to retain some of their Spanish character, and you could do worse if you're looking for a few days by the sea. The stretch of coast from Dénia to Altea still has some unspoiled rocky shoreline, clean beaches and pretty towns – try **Dénia** itself, up-market, residential **Moraira**, or **Calpe (Calp)**, dominated by the looming mass of the rocky outcrop known as the Peñon d'Ifach. Old **Altea** is a picturesque, if much-visited village, while inland the mountains of the **Sierra de Aitana** rise above lush valleys dotted with fortress settlements like the much-visited **Guadalest**. South of Benidorm, **Alicante** has kept its Spanish soul and character – a dignified and pleasant city with palm-lined

ramblas (promenade-type streets), fine beaches and a magnificently sited castle. South again, the coastline is flatter, with rolling dunes, pine woods and resorts catering as much to Spaniards as foreigners.

Tourist Information Office, Alicante
➕ 201 F3 ✉ Avenida Rambla Méndez Nuñez 23 ☎ 965 20 00 00; www.alicante-turismo.com 🕐 Mon–Fri 9–8, Sat 10–2, 3–8

Tourist Information Office, Benidorm
➕ 201 F3 ✉ Avenida Martínez Alejos 16 ☎ 965 85 13 11; www.benidorm.org 🕐 Mon–Fri 9–8, Sat 10–1:30, 4:30–7:30, Sun 10–1:30

Tourist Information Office, Dénia
➕ 201 F3 ✉ Plaza Oculista Buigues 9 ☎ 966 42 23 67; www.costablanca.org; www.denia.net 🕐 Summer Mon–Sat 9:30–1:30, 5–8; winter 9:30–1:30, 4–7

9 Elche (Elx)

The ancient city of Elche, Roman Illici, stands on the Vinalopó river, surrounded and infiltrated by more than 300,000 palm trees, a veritable forest, unique in Europe. The groves probably date from Phoenician times and are protected by law. Many of the female trees bear dates, often on sale from street vendors, and the fronds of the male trees are sent all over Europe for use in Palm Sunday church

Palm trees in Elche's Huerto del Cura

The Big Black Bull

Throughout Spain the silhouette of a huge black bull looms proudly beside main roads. This is the Osborne bull, designed in 1956 by Manolo Prieto to advertise sherry and brandy made by the firm of Osborne. Universally loved, the bull faced a tricky moment in the mid-90s when Spain passed an act banning all roadside advertising. Public outcry won the day and the bull was exempt from the decree. It's said that Prieto, his designer, died a disappointed man – he would have preferred to be remembered for what he saw as his "real" art, not an advertising hoarding.

processions. The best way to get an idea of the scale of this exotic planting is to visit the Huerto del Cura, or hire a bicycle and explore the plantations around the city's edge.

Elche's main sights are clustered around the vast 16th to 17th-century baroque basilica of **Santa Maria**, whose blue-tiled dome dominates the centre. In August, this is the scene of Elche's Festa, the Misteri d'Elx. This medieval mystery play, celebrating in words and music the death and assumption of the Virgin, has been performed by the townspeople since the 1260s, soon after the *Reconquista* – there's a museum devoted to it.

Moorish civilisation is represented by a splendid watchtower, the **Calaforra**, and Arab baths. An archaeological museum is devoted to the ancient Iberian settlement of Illici, a few kilometres south, as well as classical and Islamic artefacts.
➕ 201 F3

Tourist Information Office
✉ Parque Municipal ☎ 965 45 27 47; www.turismedelx.com 🕐 Mon–Fri 10–7, Sat 10–2:30, Sun 10–2

Museu Municipal de la Festa
✉ Calle Major de la Vila 27 ☎ 965 45 34 64 🕐 Tue–Sat 10–1:30, 4:30–8 🎫 Moderate

Where to... Stay

Prices
Expect to pay per person per night

€ up to €50   €€ €50–€90   €€€ €91–€120   €€€€ over €120

TOLEDO

Hostal del Cardenal €€

This *hostal* is quintessentially Spanish. Built in the 18th century for the local archbishop, it is wonderfully peaceful with rambling gardens, interspersed with rose gardens, ponds and ancient walls covered with cascading vines. The rooms are decorated with antiques and there are lounges with oil paintings and *mudéjar* tiles. Feast your eyes, and then your stomach by dining in the excellent hotel restaurant.

➕ 199 D2 ⌖ Paseo de Recaredo 24
☎ 925 22 49 00;
www.hostaldelcardenal.com

Hotel Santa Isabel €

All the rooms in this small hotel in the old part of Toledo have small balconies – try for one that overlooks the convent opposite. The interior is fresh and modern with solid pine furniture, a large breakfast room and colourful tiling in the corridors The bathrooms are small but have all the essentials, while the basement garage is a definite plus.

➕ 199 D2 ⌖ Calle Santa Isabel 24
☎ 925 25 31 20; www.santa-isabel.com

CUENCA

Cueva del Fraile €€

For the facilities that it offers, which run to tennis courts and a swimming pool, this comfortable hotel some distance out of Cuenca is good value. Built around a patio, it occupies a 16th-century building in huge gardens and is furnished in traditional style.

➕ 189 F2 ⌖ Carretera
Cuenca–Buenache km7 ☎ 969 21
15 71; www.hotelcuevadelfraile.com

Posada de San José €€

A former 17th-century convent, this *posada* sits on the rim of the town's remarkable gorge and the view from the rooms is unforgettable. Ancient beams, uneven floors, low ceilings and an intriguing warren of rooms on different levels make this an evocative and romantic retreat. Every room is different, but all are furnished with decorative flair and most have a small terrace. The *tapas* bar is popular with locals and the restaurant welcoming and reliably good.

➕ 199 F2 ⌖ Calle Julián Romero 4
☎ 969 21 13 00;
www.posadasanjose.com

VALENCIA

Ad Hoc €€€

This hotel is right in the old quarter surrounded by some of the best bar life in Spain. The owner is an antiquarian and art enthusiast and this is reflected in the interior. Light brick work, vaulted ceilings and sensitive lighting against earthy toned paintwork create a welcoming environment.
Meals are available in a cosy dining room.

➕ 201 F4 ⌖ Boix 4 ☎ 963 91
91 40; www.adhocoteles.com

Reina Victoria €€€

The city's grande dame hotel had a makeover in 2004. Rooms, furnished with light wood and bright blue fabrics, have a contemporary look, and now have internet access. The spacious reception rooms have marble floors as does La Pergola, its much-touted restaurant.

➕ 201 F4 ⌖ Barcas 4–6 ☎ 963 52
04 87; www.husa.es

Where to...
Eat and Drink

Prices
Expect to pay per person for a meal, including wine and service
€ up to €12   €€ €12–€30   €€€ over €30

TOLEDO

Casón de los López de Toledo €€€

Prior to its conversion, this former private home was recognised as being one of the most beautiful buildings in Toledo. A vaulted foyer leads to a ground floor café which serves coffee and snacks, while upstairs there is a choice of dining rooms. There are magnificent antiques, paintings and artwork throughout and the market-based menu features fine Castilian and Continental cuisine, such as ravioli and garlic soup and baked cod with

Manchego cheese and onions. Diners can enjoy a post-dinner tot at the wood-panelled basement bar where more than 90 varieties of whisky are sold.

🏠 199 D2 ⊠ Sillería 3 ☎ 925 25 47 74 🕐 Mon–Sat 1:30–4, 8:30–11:30, Sun 1:30–4; closed Mon Jul–Aug

Hierbabuena €€–€€€

Dine on the sumptuous Moorish-style patio where there is plenty of natural light. Dishes change according to what is in season and include a year-round gourmet sampler menu. If you enjoy eating

meat, go for the game dishes such as boar, partridge or venison during the hunting season. Home-made desserts and quality wines accompany the meal.

🏠 199 D2 ⊠ Callejón de San José 17 ☎ 925 22 39 24 🕐 Mon–Sat 1:30–4, 8:30–11:30, Sun 1:30–4

CUENCA

El Figón de Pedro €€

Celebrated Spanish restaurateur Pedro Torres Pacheco owns this restaurant, which makes it worth seeking out despite being in the new part of town. With only a dozen or so tables, it's best to make advance reservations. The menu features modern interpretations of traditional fare, like gazpacho pastor, ajoarriero (cod cooked with eggs and garlic), followed by such Moorish-inspired desserts as alajú, made with honey, orange and almonds.

🏠 199 F2 ⊠ Cervantes 13, Cuenca ☎ 969 22 68 21 🕐 Tue–Sat 1:30–4, 9–11, Sun 1:30–4

VALENCIA

Casa Montaña €

This popular café-restaurant was founded in 1836. The seafood dishes are excellent as the starters, especially the jamón ibérico (Spanish ham) and tostada de queso la Serena (cheese on toast). The restaurant claims to have one of the longest wine lists in Valencia.

🏠 201 F4 ⊠ Calle José Benlliure 69 ☎ 963 67 23 14 🕐 Tue–Sun 1:30–4, 8:30–11:30, Sun 1:30–4

La Riuà €€

Decorated with ceramic tiles in the local style, this popular place just off Plaza de la Reina is well placed for exploring the old town. Classic local dishes ring the changes on fish in many guises, and there's plenty of home-made paella. Adventurous diners might go for the eels or baby octopus.

🏠 201 F4 ⊠ Calle del Mar 27 ☎ 963 91 45 71 🕐 Tue–Sat 2–4, 9–11, Mon 2–4; closed Easter and Aug

Where to... Shop

TOLEDO

The city's swashbuckling past means that you've found the right place if you happen to be looking for a sword or a suit of armour to take home as a memento of your stay in Toledo.

More conventional souvenirs include *damasquinado*, the Moorish art of inlaying gold thread against matte black steel, which you can buy in the form of jewellery, boxes and ornaments. You can see it being made at **Damasquinados Manuel Melendez** at Travesia del Conde 4, a long-established family business.

Toledo's other local speciality is marzipan. The quality varies but **Santo Tomé** at Calle Santo Tomé 5 claims to follow the original 13th-century recipe.

The town's main shopping street is **Calle Comercio** where you'll find most of the high street chains, including Zara, Mango, Benetton, Lacoste, Pull & Bear and Camper.

This area of central Spain is also renowned for its pottery with the best prices and variety at the roadside stores, although serious bulk buyers may consider a trip to **Talavera de la Reina**, 76km (47 miles) west of Toledo where most of the pottery is produced.

VALENCIA

The much sought-after **Lladró** porcelain originates in Valencia, and the city is also known for its glassware.

Valencia is famous for its *paella*, and one of the best buys here is a **paella pan**. They come in all sizes and can be found at several *ferreterias* (ironmongers) near the **Mercado Central** (▶ 149) – also worth a visit – on Plaza del Mercado, near the city centre.

Where to... Be Entertained

NIGHTLIFE

Toledo is a great city for taking an evening *paseo* stopping en route for *tapas* and a drink at one of the many bars. A good place to start is at **La Abadia** (Plaza de San Nicolas 3, tel: 925 25 11 40), a music bar that specialises in imported beers, while **Bar Camelot** (Calle Cristo de la Luz) doesn't get moving until quite late. For nightclubs, head to the northern end of town, which is where most of the students hang out.

The nightlife in **Cuenca** is concentrated around the Calle de San Miguel and Plaza de San Nicolas. More bars and clubs can be found around Calle Fray Luis de León off the Plaza de España in the new part of town.

Valencia's nightlife is renowned, along with its gay community, which is the third largest in Spain. Much of the action is centred around Barrio del Carmen. For something a little more sophisticated, head for **Café de las Horas** (Calle Conde de Almodovar 1, tel: 963 91 73 36), north of the Plaza de la Virgen.

THEATRE AND CLASSICAL MUSIC

Toledo's theatre, **Teatro Rojas** (Plaza Mayor, tel: 925 22 39 70), often has world-class theatre and dance productions.

In Valencia, check what's on at the **Teatro Principal** (Calle Barcas 15, tel: 963 53 92 00) or the **Palau de la Música** (Paseo Alameda 30, tel: 963 37 50 20) which has seasonal classical music recitals.

Andalucía

Getting Your Bearings

Andalucía is hot sun and deep shade, flamenco and fiestas, sweeping landscapes and great Moorish monuments – the epitome of the Spanish dream. No other region so perfectly encapsulates most peoples' vision of the country, whether you're looking for a hedonistic play area, unspoilt country-side or vibrant, beautiful cities. From its historic centres to its mountains, coast and holiday resorts, Andalucía has something for everyone.

The three major cities of Seville, Córdoba and Granada preserve a clutch of extraordinarily brilliant Moorish monuments, reminders of medieval Europe's most sophisticated civilisation. The region's smaller centres are equally fascinating: the little-known Renaissance gems of Baeza and Úbeda, Ronda with its spectacular gorge, and elegant Jerez, famed for its sherry, horses and orange trees. Off the beaten track you'll find white-washed hill towns, windswept fishing villages and quiet inland communities where strangers are rare.

Hotels at Marbella on the Costa del Sol, Europe's playground

Previous page: The Patio de los Naranjos fronts Córdoba's Mezquita

★ Don't Miss

At Your Leisure

Andalucía's towns are set in superb landscape, which ranges from the high peaks of the Sierra Nevada and the fertile upland valleys of Las Alpujarras, to the rolling olive-planted hills of the northeast and the cork forests and fertile plains of the west. The coastline

stretches from arid Almería through the Costa del Sol, Europe's most developed resort area, to the untouched beaches of the Costa de la Luz. West again is the wetland region of the Coto de Doñana. The surge in tourist development in the late 20th century resulted in some dire mistakes, but did have the benefit of creating good roads, hotels of an international standard and some of the best golf courses and sports facilities in Europe.

The Real Escuela Andaluz del Arte Ecuestre at Jerez – horsemanship at its finest

It's quite a challenge to see the best of Andalucía in five days, and you could use the trip as a taster for a return visit – getting the flavour of one of the loveliest, and most fascinating, parts of Spain. You'll need a day each for Seville (Sevilla) and Granada, but you could take in more of the region by making a briefer visit to Córdoba. This leaves time for exploring some of the coastal and mountain areas, essential for appreciating the diversity of this wonderful area, so rich in history, art, tradition and natural beauty.

Andalucía in Five Days

Day One

Morning
Start your day in ❶ **Seville** (➤ 164–167) by heading for the **cathedral** and its treasures, then be sure to climb up the **Giralda** (➤ 165) for a great view. Next visit the **Real Alcázar** (right, ➤ 165), where the tranquil gardens are the perfect climax to a hard morning's sightseeing.

Afternoon
Art enthusiasts could visit the **Museo de Bellas Artes** (➤ 167), one of the most important museums in Spain, before walking through the south and west areas of the city (➤ 176–177).

Evening
Head for the **Barrio de Santa Cruz** (➤ 166–167) for a drink and some *tapas* before dinner and a chance to experience some flamenco.

Day Two

Morning
Leave Seville on the fast NIV for the 143km (88-mile) drive to ❷ **Córdoba** (➤ 168–169), arriving around 11am. Head straight for the **Mezquita**.

Afternoon
Wander around the **Judería** (➤ 169), down to the **Alcázar de los Reyes Cristianos** (➤ 169), and along the **river bank** before leaving on the N432 to **5 Granada** (➤ 170–172) – the drive should take 2.5 hours.

Evening
Head for the Plaza de San Nicolás in the old Moorish quarter, the **Albaicín** (➤ 171) for your first view – perhaps at sunset – of the magnificent Alhambra palace.

Day Three

Morning
Be among the first at the **Alhambra** (left, ➤ 170–171) and spend the whole morning exploring one of Spain's greatest glories.

Afternoon/Evening
After a late lunch pass the afternoon visiting the **cathedral** and the **Capilla Real** (➤ 171), before joining the evening crowds downtown.

Day Four

Morning/Afternoon
Leave Granada and head south on the fast E902 to the coast. Drive along the **6 Costa del Sol** (➤ 174) on the N340/E15 as far as San Pedro de Alcántara. At San Pedro turn inland to Ronda on the A376.

Evening
Stroll through **7 Ronda** (➤ 174) to admire the gorge and spectacular Puente Nuevo (right), in the evening light before dinner.

Day Five

Morning
Spend the first part of the morning in Ronda before heading southwest on the A369 through the mountains of the Serranía de Ronda to reach the coast just east of Algeciras.

Afternoon
Drive along the **8 Costa de la Luz** (➤ 174–175), a beautiful, undeveloped strech of coastline, on the N340 then pick up the A4 at San Fernando and continue on to **9 Jerez de la Frontera** (➤ 175).

❶ Seville

Think "Andalucía" and you'll probably visualise whitewashed streets, Moorish architecture, flamenco dresses, orange trees and proud horsemen. Seville, the region's capital, has all this and more besides. Packed with diverse treasures, it's also renowned for its fiestas, relaxed and hedonistic lifestyle and the exuberance of its inhabitants. A truly seductive city, it encapsulates the spirit of the south and the essence of Andalucían allure.

Prosaically, Seville is Spain's fourth-largest city, the seat of a university, an important industrial centre and the heart of a rich agricultural region. In 1992 the World Fair was held in Seville, leaving the legacy of a radically modernised infrastructure and huge civic pride. First inhabited by Greeks, Phoenicians and Romans, Seville was among the most important of the Moorish city-states and, later, a favourite residence of the Christian monarchs. With the discovery of the New World in 1492, the city boomed, becoming one of the richest and most cosmopolitan in Europe. In the 17th century, despite economic and political decline, artists such as Velázquez, Murillo and Zurbarán worked here and by the 1800s the city was firmly on the European tourist map.

The Giralda tower is a triumph of Moorish architecture and engineering

The Big Three – the Catedral, Giralda and Real Alcázar

Seville's magnificent cathedral, built on the site of the Moorish mosque, is the third largest in Europe, only outsized by St Peter's in Rome and St Paul's in London. Vast, rich and, despite its size, harmoniously balanced, it was built between 1401 and 1519, a superb blend of Gothic austerity and Spanish flamboyance. Almost as wide as it is long, the interior is dominated by the **Capilla Mayor**, the chapel, its splendid, richly carved Flemish altarpiece glistening with gold leaf behind its immense grilles. Opposite lies the choir, with superb choir stalls and an ornate 17th-century marble and bronze screen. Stand between the two and look up at the transept roof, 56m (184 feet) above your head; this riot of stone filigree is supported by massive arches and columns, whose huge size is dwarfed by the scale of the cathedral. Other highlights include Christopher Columbus' grand tomb in the south transept, the treasury and sacristy, packed with paintings and precious altar-vessels, and the domed **Capilla Real** (Royal Chapel), the burial place of Alfonso X of Castile.

When the Christians destroyed the mosque to build the cathedral, they kept the minaret and transformed it into a

Cool arches and sunbaked space in the Real Alcázar

belltower. Nicknamed the **Giralda** – after the weathervane (*giradillo*) that crowns the structure – the 98m (321-foot) high tower was built in the 12th century during the caliphate of the Almohad dynasty. Inside, rather than steps, there is a ramp, wide enough for two horsemen to pass, which leads to the top, where you'll get wide views of the city. Directly below lies the lovely courtyard known as the **Patio de los Naranjos** (Courtyard of the Orange Trees), which once formed part of the mosque and now leads into the cathedral.

Seville's other great monument lies opposite the cathedral – the unforgettable **Real Alcázar** (Royal Palace). Slightly less swamped with tourists than its cousin in Granada, this palace epitomises the elegance and charm of *mudéjar* secular archi-tecture. Little remains of the original Moorish Alcázar, and most of what you see was built by Pedro the Cruel in 1362. His builders were Christianised Moors, the inventors of *mudéjar* style, and this Arabian Nights complex is one of the purest examples of their art still surviving. It's a labyrinth of courtyards, delicately stuccoed and tiled rooms, terraces and coffered chambers, fountains and arched patios. Later

Filigree-fine stuccowork in the Real Alcázar

Christian monarchs added their own touches. Charles V added some lavish, tapestry-hung rooms in the 16th century, but his great contribution was the Renaissance elements he incorporated into the existing **gardens**. Pergolas, terraces, pools and arcades, planted with magnolias and oranges, plumbago and jasmine, make this one of Spain's finest gardens.

Santa Cruz and the Bellas Artes

East of the cathedral lies the **Barrio de Santa Cruz** (Santa Cruz quarter), a maze of narrow white streets and sun-splashed squares shaded by orange trees. Originally the Jewish quarter, the area became popular with the 16th- and 17th-century nobility who added fine mansions along its alleyways. These are inward-looking houses, the windows of the plain walls facing the street barred with superb *rejas* (grilles), the interiors centring on green and shady patios. The finest of all, a little further north,

Festivals

Seville has two great annual festivals; **Semana Santa** (Holy Week), the last week of Lent, and the **Feria** (Spring Festival), usually held about two weeks after Easter. The **Semana Santa**, a deeply religious event when emotion and passion runs high, is celebrated by *pasos* (processions), held by confraternities from Seville's different districts. The processions consist of huge floats supporting religious statues, sumptuously decorated and carried by up to 60 men; they are accompanied by veiled and shrouded penitents, and extolled by improvised laments from the crowds. The **Feria** is completely secular, a week-long celebration of Andalucía's love-affair with horses, music and beautiful women. Carriages filled with laughing girls in flounced dresses, accompanied by horseback riders in traditional dress, parade the streets, gallons of sherry are drunk, and *sevillanas* are danced all night.

The sweep of the Plaza de España, a favourite with locals and visitors alike

is the **Casa de Pilatos**, built in 1519 and a splendidly unified mixture of *mudéjar*, Gothic and Renaissance elements. It's built around a succession of superb and lushly planted patios, has brilliant *azulejos* (tilework) and one of the city's most elegant interiors.

West from here, you'll find the **Museo de Bellas Artes** (Fine Arts Museum), housed in a 17th-century convent built around three graceful courtyards, which concentrates on the Golden Age of Spanish painting. The gallery in the former church is devoted to Murillo, and pride of place is given to his Immaculate Conception, a perfect example of his deeply religious, idealistic style. Zurbarán, another great master, is also well represented, his masterpiece being a stark, sculptural Christ on the Cross; look out too for his Carthusian Monks at Supper and Ribero's startling handling of light and dark in his pictures in the upstairs galleries.

South and west of the cathedral lie more delights, notably the buildings, gardens and museums surrounding the Plaza de España, the riverside area, and Triana which was once the gypsy quarter, across the Guadalquivir river. Explore them as part of a walk (► 176–177), or simply spend time wandering the streets and soaking up the atmosphere.

TAKING A BREAK

Right in the hub of town, **Bar Rincón San Eloy** (San Eloy 24, tel: 954 21 80 79) is a place to enjoy a breather from shopping – along with a glass of *fino* (sherry). There are *azulejo* (tile) steps for sitting on and a vast *tapas* menu.

✚ 200 B2
www.turismosevilla.org

Tourist Information Office
✉ Avenida de la Constitución 21
☎ 954 22 14 04; www.andalucia.org
🕐 Mon–Fri 9–7, Sat 10–2, 3–7, Sun 10–2

Catedral and Giralda
✉ Plaza Virgen de los Reyes
☎ 954 21 49 71 🕐 Jul–Aug Mon–Sat 11–6, Sun 2:30–6; Sep–Jun Mon–Sat 11–6, Sun 2:30–7; open for services 🎟 Moderate; free on Sun

Real Alcázar
✉ Plaza del Triunfo ☎ 954 50 23 23
🕐 Apr–Sep Tue–Sat 9:30–7, Sun 9:30–5; Oct–Mar Tue–Sat 9:30–5, Sun 9:30–1:30
🎟 Moderate

Casa de Pilatos
✉ Plaza de Pilatos ☎ 954 22 52 98
🕐 Mar–Sep daily 9–7; Oct–Feb 9–6
🎟 Moderate; free Tue pm

Museo de Bellas Artes
✉ Plaza del Museo 9 ☎ 954 22 07 90
🕐 Wed–Sat 9–8:30, Sun 9–2:30, Tue 2:30–8:30 🎟 Inexpensive, free to EU citizens

SEVILLE: INSIDE INFO

Top tips Avoid the cathedral on Sunday afternoons – the free entrance draws huge crowds.
• The **Alcázar** is very badly sign-posted; pick up an **English audio-guide** to help you find your way around.
• **Early afternoon** is a good time to visit the cathedral and the Real Alcázar during **high season**; it may be hot, but it won't be quite as crowded.
• **Watch your valuables** in Seville; the city has a bad reputation for mugging and petty theft.

Must see If you don't have a lot of time, head for the **Barrio de Santa Cruz** and the **Alcázar**.

② Córdoba

Córdoba had a great past, first as the largest Roman city in Spain and later as the capital of the Islamic empire in western Europe. From this era dates its most famous building, the Mezquita (Mosque), one of the world's most spiritual and powerful structures. Around this core, other lovely buildings and picturesque *barrios* are scattered, while the Guadalquivir waterfront is an added bonus.

The Mezquita

Córdoba's original 8th-century mosque was enlarged several times, attaining its present size at the beginning of the 11th century. For Spanish Muslims, Córdoba was an important place of pilgrimage, outshone only by Mecca and Jerusalem.

Sunlight filters through the myriad arches of the Mezquita

You enter through the **Patio de los Naranjos**, a symmetrical ablutions courtyard. Inside, you find yourself in a forest of pillars and arches. These form 19 aisles, made up of double arches supported by round and square columns. The arches alternate brick and stonework, creating a red-and-white striped pattern which acts as a unifying element to the whole. Through this shadowy maze, against the eastern wall, you can make out the mihrab (prayer niche). Right in the centre of this serene, rational building looms a flamboyant cathedral choir, built in 1523 as part of Charles V's scheme for "Christianising" Moorish places. When he realised what had been done in his name Charles was aghast, declaring "To build something ordinary, you have destroyed something unique in the world".

Around the Mezquita

West from the Mezquita, past the **Palacio Episcopal** (Bishops' Palace), stands the rebuilt **Alcázar** and some of Córdoba's most seductive **patios**, all white walls and brilliant flowers. Behind here lies the **Judería**, the old Jewish quarter, a tangle of narrow lanes and tiny squares, with the old **sinagoga** (synagogue) at its heart. This tiny 14th-century building is one of only three in Spain that survived the 1492 expulsion of the Jews. Nearby, there's the **Museo Taurino**, devoted to the art of bullfighting.

Across the River

Across the river is the **Torre de la Calahorra**, a Moorish fortress, now containing a museum, built in the 14th century to defend the **Roman bridge**, while along the river you'll see the ruins of the **mills** and **Moorish waterwheels**.

TAKING A BREAK

Begin your evening with a sherry in the bar or cool leafy patio of **El Caballo Rojo** (Calle Cardenal Herrero 28), reputed to be Córdoba's oldest restaurant.

✚ 200 C3
www.turismocordoba.org

Tourist Information Office
✉ Palacio de Congresos y Exposiciones, Torrijos 10 ☎ 957 47 12 35;
www.andalucia.org 🕐 Apr–Oct Mon–Fri 9:30–7, Sat 10–2, 5–7, Sun 10–2; Nov–Mar Mon–Sat 9:30–6, Sun 10–2

Mezquita-Catedral
✉ Torrijos ☎ 957 47 05 12 🕐 Summer Mon–Sat 10–7:30, Sun 2–7; winter Mon–Sat 10–7:30, Sun 2–6. Open Sun am for services
🎟 Moderate

Alcázar de los Reyes Cristianos
✉ Campo Santo de los Mártires
☎ 957 42 01 51 🕐 Tue–Sat 10–2, 4:30–6:30, Sun 9:30–2:30 🎟 Moderate

Torre de la Calahorra
✉ Calle Acera Arrecife ☎ 957 29 39 29
🕐 Closed for renovation

Museo Taurino
✉ Plaza Maimonides ☎ 957 20 10 56
🕐 Tue–Sat 10–2, 4:30–6:30 🎟 Moderate, free on Fri

Sinagoga
✉ Calle Judías 20 ☎ 957 20 29 28
🕐 Tue–Sat 9:30–2, 3:30–5:30, Sun 9:30–1:30
🎟 Inexpensive, EU citizens free

CÓRDOBA: INSIDE INFO

Top tips Arrive as **early as possible** at the Mezquita to beat the tour groups.
• **Stick to the south side** of the Mezquita as you enter and approach the mihrab – you'll get a better feel of the building as a mosque.
• **Opening times are changeable**; check at the tourist office for an update.

In more depth The mihrab in the Mezquita was erected in the 10th century by al-Hakam II to indicate the direction of Mecca and to amplify the words of the imam (priest). It was used as a model for numerous other mosques in Spain and North Africa. The design combines energy with stillness, a perfect illustration of the basic tenets of Moorish architecture.

Getting in Buy your **entrance ticket** to the Mezquita at the office underneath the Torre in the Patio de los Naranjos.

❸ Granada

Granada is home to the Alhambra, the most evocative, exciting and sensual of all Spain's monuments, beautifully preserved, lovingly tended, and set in superb natural surroundings. Nothing more perfectly reveals the sophistication and spirit of Moorish Spain, while the city's Christian monuments poignantly illustrate the transience of this, and every, great civilisation.

The Alhambra and Generalife

The **Alhambra** was the palace-fortress of the Nasrid Sultans, built around an existing Moorish 11th-century fortress between the 13th and 14th centuries. The complex, encircled by walls and towers, consists of the **Alcazaba**, the old fort; the **Palacios Nazaries**, the actual palace; and, beyond the walls, the **Generalife,** the summer palace and gardens of the sultans. Hard against the Nazaries looms the Renaissance bulk of Charles V's palace, built in the mid-16th century.

The **Alcazaba** is dominated by the Torre de la Vela, an imposing tower overlooking the city from where the Cross was first displayed when the city, the last Moorish strong-hold, fell to the Christians in 1492. The solid-ity of this military stronghold is a foil for the grace and delicacy of the **Palacios Nazaries**, the heart of the Alhambra. Council chambers, reception rooms, throne rooms and the harem are set about a series of patios and gardens. Originally crudely built, the chambers are principally a vehicle for ornamental stucco decoration, where Arabic inscriptions are used to form patterns and *trompe l'oeil* ceiling orna-mentation gives an illusion of staggering height. The **Sala de los Abencerrajes**, with its 16-sided honeycomb vault, is the finest of these, closely followed by the **Sala de los Reyes** and the **Sala de las Dos Hermanas.**

Marble arcades frame the fish pool in the **Patio de los Arrayanes**, the lions still stand guard around the central fountain in the **Patio de los Leones**, and the whole is encircled with flowering, shady gardens.

Nearby, a series of enclosed gardens, green and well-watered, surround the sultans' summer palace, the **Generalife**. The palace is little more than an elegant pavilion, it's the gardens that take star billing. A series of garden rooms, each opening out to another vista of verdant beauty, succeed one another. Each is beautifully planted to delight the senses – deep cool shade, bright clear colours, fragrance everywhere, and the constant trickle and tinkle of running water. Nowhere better illustrates the Moors' obsession with water – its sound, its movement – than the fountains, pools and cascades in this lovely spot, an earthly vision of the Koran's Paradise.

Above: The snow-capped Sierra Nevada rises behind the silhouetted Alhambra

Left: Moorish stucco work in the Alhambra glows golden in reflected light

The Catedral and Capilla Real

Granada's **Catedral** was begun in the 1520s and finished in the 1700s; it's big and impressive but easily outshone by the neighbouring **Capilla Real**, the burial place of the Christian Kings, Ferdinand and Isabel. Flamboyantly late Gothic in style, the interior contains a sumptuous marble monument, commissioned by Charles V in 1517. Ferdinand and Isabella lie in the crypt beneath their serene effigies and a candle burns continually at Isabella's dying request.

The Albaicín

The **Albaicín** spreads across the slopes of a hill opposite the Alhambra. It's the largest Moorish city quarter still in existence in Spain, a wonderfully atmospheric place to wander, whose narrow streets give a true sense of Granada as a Moorish city.

TAKING A BREAK

Stop for *tapas* or the excellent *menus del día* at the palm-shaded terrace at **Café au Lait** (Callejón de los Franceses 31), close to the cathedral.

➕ 200 C3

Tourist Information Offices
✉ Calle Santa Ana 2 ☎ 958 22 59 90; www.andalucia.org; www.granadatur.com
🕐 Mon–Fri 9–7, Sat 9–2, 4–7, Sun 10–2

✉ Plaza Mariana Pineda 10 ☎ 958 24 71 28; www.turismodegranada.org
🕐 Mon–Fri 9–8, Sat 10–7, Sun 10–3

Alhambra and Generalife
✉ Calle Real de la Alhambra ☎ 902 44 12 21; www.alhambra-patronato.es

🕐 Mar–Oct daily 8:30–8, 10–11:30; Nov–Feb 8:30–6 (also Fri–Sat 8–9:30pm) 💷 Expensive

Catedral
✉ Calle Gran Via de Colón ☎ 958 22 29 59
🕐 Apr–Sep Mon–Sat 10–1:30, 4–8, Sun 4–8; Oct–Mar Mon–Sat 10:45–1:30, 4–7, Sun 4–7
💷 Moderate

Capilla Real
✉ Calle Oficios ☎ 958 22 78 48
🕐 Apr–Sep Mon–Sat 10:30–1, 4–7, Sun 11–1, 4–7; Oct–Mar Mon–Sat 10:30–1, 3:30–6:30, Sun 11–6:30 💷 Moderate

---

GRANADA: INSIDE INFO

Top tips Try to **arrive as early as possible** at the Alhambra, before the crowds.
• An **audio-guide** will help you get the most out of your visit.
• The easiest way to reach the Alhambra is to take the **minibus service** that runs from the Plaza Nueva. If you do come by car, follow the purple signs from the ring road or city centre.
• The **best view** of the Alhambra is across the valley from the Plaza de San Nicolás in the Albaicín.
• Serious sightseers should purchase the **Bono Turístico**, a pass which gives access to the Alhambra, Generalife, Catedral, Capilla Real and other monuments plus 10 bus tickets. It's available from the Alhambra, the Capilla Real and the Caja General de Ahorros de Granada (Plaza de Isabel la Católica 6).
• **Watch your valuables** in the Albaicín; there's an escalating number of thefts.

Getting in For conservation purposes, only about 8,000 visitors are allowed daily into the Alhambra. To avoid queuing and probable disappointment, **advance reservation** to the Alhambra is highly recommended and imperative in the summer months. You can do this up to a year ahead:
• **Internet** www.alhambratickets.com
• **By telephone** In Spain 902 22 44 60, daily 9–6. From abroad 0034 915 37 91 78, daily 9–6.
• **At any BBVA bank** in Spain Mon–Fri 9–2; a small commission is charged.
• From many **hotels** within the province of Granada.
In all cases you will be issued with a **reference number** exchangeable for **tickets** at the "Advance Booking" window at the main entrance.
• Tickets are **valid** for either the **morning** or the **afternoon**. On your ticket a **half-hour period** will be specified during which you **must** enter the Palacios Nazaríes; if you fail to do so you cannot see this part of the complex, though, once inside, you can stay as long as you like.
• You can use the **different sections** of your ticket **in any order** as long as you visit the Palacios Nazaríes during your specified time slot. You will not be allowed into the Alhambra (even with a pre-booked ticket) less than one hour before closing time.

At Your Leisure

➍ Baeza and Úbeda

These elegant Renaissance towns, 9km (6 miles) apart, overlook a rolling landscape of olive trees in the upper valley of the Guadalquivir. They are crammed with stone churches and palaces set around attractive plazas.

Baeza is the smaller – here you'll find a cluster of Isabelline palaces (➤ 15), a Romanesque church, a fine cathedral, and some superb views. Úbeda's star turn is the Plaza de Vázquez de Molina, a stunning Renaissance square surrounded by dazzling buildings. The Palacio de las Cadenas is now the town hall and at the end of the plaza is the Capilla del Salvador, a lovely church with plateresque façade, and an over-the-top *retablo* inside.

➕ 201 D3

Renaissance façades abound in Baeza

Tourist Information Offices

✉ Plaza del Pópulo, Baeza ☎ 953 74 04 44; www.andalucia.org ⏰ Apr–Sep Mon–Fri 9:30–7, Sat–Sun 10–1, 5–7; Oct–Mar Mon–Fri 9:30–2:30, 4–6, Sat 10–2, Sun 10–1

✉ Palacio Marqués de Contadero, Calle Baja del Marqués 4, Úbeda ☎ 953 75 08 97; www.andalucia.org ⏰ Mon–Fri 9–8, Sat–Sun 10–2

Capilla del Salvador

✉ Plaza de Vázquez de Molina, Úbeda ☎ 953 75 08 97 ⏰ Mon–Sat 10–2, 4:30–7, Sun 10:45–2, 4:30–7 🚻 Moderate

➎ Las Alpujarras

The high valleys across the southern slopes of the Sierra Nevada are known as Las Alpujarras. They were first settled by the North African Berbers and later were the final stronghold of the Moors. The area is mountainous, well-watered and fertile, its ancient terraces still used for agriculture. The cube-like houses with flat roofs and secret courtyards are North African in style, and rug-making, introduced by the Berbers, is still an important local industry. The spa town of **Lanjarón**, whose bottled water is drunk all over Spain, is the gateway, and the market settlement **Órgiva** the "capital". Most people head for the High Alpujarras and the picturesque villages of **Pampaneira, Bubión** and **Capileira**. All three cling to the steep slopes above the **Poqueira** gorge, with the snow-capped tops of the southern Sierra rising behind. This is superb walking country, with great views and sparklingly clear air.

➕ 201 D2

Tourist Information Office

✉ Avenida de Madrid s/n, Lanjarón ☎ 958 77 02 82; www.andalucia.org ⏰ Summer Thu–Tue 10–2, 4:30–8:30

6 Costa del Sol

The Costa del Sol (Sunshine Coast) stretches along the Mediterranean coast from Gibraltar to the province of Almería. Its capital is **Málaga**, an attractive city with an historic quarter, sophisticated shops and the excellent Museo Picasso. To the east are the mass-market resorts of **Torremolinos, Benalmádena, Fuengirola** and **Marbella**. This was Spain's first area to be developed for "sun and sand" holidays, and attracts northern Europeans looking for good-value vacations, villas in the sun and retirement homes. Marbella, home to the super-rich, is the pick of the bunch on the western stretch; to the east of Málaga, the coast is steeper and prettier and the development less intense.

➕ 200 C1

Tourist Information Offices
Málaga
➕ 200 C2 ✉ Pasaje de Chinitas 4
☎ 952 21 34 45;
www.malagaturismo.com ⏰ Mon–Fri 9–8, Sat–Sun 10–2

Marbella
➕ 200 C2 ✉ Plaza de los Naranjos
☎ 952 82 35 50;
www.marbella.com ⏰ Mon–Fri 9–9, Sat 10–2

7 Ronda

Ronda's setting is its principal attraction, for the ridge on which it's built is split by a gorge more than 100m (328-feet) deep called El Tajo, and spanned by a superb 18th-century arched bridge, the Puente Nuevo. The old town still retains some Moorish buildings – superb baths, a bridge and a ruined Alcázar. The best way to explore here is simply to wander, but be sure to take in the **Casa de Mondragón**, a beautiful Moorish palace now housing the local museum. Across the gorge lies the Mercadillo quarter, developed after the Christian reconquest. Here you'll find the theatrical **Plaza de Toros**, built in 1785, one of Spain's most important bullrings and the

birthplace of the modern *corrida*. Behind it runs the Paseo de Blas Infante, a lovely walkway which skirts the edge of the gorge. Aim to spend the night here, to enjoy night falling and the peace that descends once the daily coach tours have departed.

➕ 200 B2
www.turismoderonda.es

Tourist Information Office
✉ Plaza de España 1 ☎ 952 87 12 72; www.andalucia.org ⏰ Mon–Fri 9–8, Sat–Sun 10–2

Casa de Mondragón
✉ Plaza de Mondragón ☎ 952 87 84 50 ⏰ Apr–Sep Mon–Fri 10–7, Sat– Sun 10–3; Oct–Mar Mon–Fri 10–6
✋ Inexpensive

Plaza de Toros
✉ Calle Virgen de la Paz ☎ 952 87 41 32 ⏰ Apr–Sep daily 10–8; Oct–Mar 10–6 ✋ Moderate

8 Costa de la Luz

Costa de la Luz (Coast of Light) is an apt name for the beautiful, and blessedly undeveloped, Atlantic coast of Andalucía. From Tarifa, with its fantastic views to Gibraltar and

The Puente Nuevo in Ronda spans the dramatic gorge that divides the town

across the straits to Morocco, past vast sandy beaches, pinewoods and cliffs, this whole coastal stretch is suffused with windy sunshine and radiant light. Wind- and kitesurfers flock to Tarifa, a base for whale and dolphin spotting and visiting the Roman ruins at Baelo Claudia. Further west and a little inland lies Vejer de la Frontera, one of the loveliest of the "white towns", with a fabulous hilltop setting and a maze of narrow streets. From here, more laid-back fishing and holiday villages run along the coast west of Cabo Trafalgar, scene of Nelson's great sea victory in 1805. Neighbouring Conil de la Frontera has great beaches, while west again, beyond Cádiz, the little towns of Chipiona and Sanlúcar de Barrameda are a world away from the Mediterranean resorts.
200 A1/A2

Tourist Information Office, Tarifa
200 B1 Paseo de la Alameda
956 68 09 93: www.aytotarifa.com
Summer Mon–Fri 10–2, 6–8, Sat–Sun 10–3; winter Mon–Fri 10–2, 5–7, Sat–Sun 10–3

9 Jerez de la Frontera

South of Seville you're in sherry country, and sedate and appealing Jerez is its capital. It's a prosperous and elegant city with streets and plazas shaded by orange trees and lined with the *bodegas* (warehouses) of the great wine-producing dynasties. You can take a tour – González Byass and Pedro Domecq are the best known – and listen to an explanation of the *solera* system of wine production before sampling the finished product. Flamenco enthusiasts will learn much at the **Centro Andaluz de Flamenco**; Jerez is an important centre of the art. Near the central Plaza del Arenal lies the lovely Gothic-Renaissance cathedral and an archaeological museum, while further out of town you can experience Jerez's equine love affair at a musical performance at the **Real Escuela Andaluz del Arte Ecuestre** (Royal Andalucían School of Equestrian Art).
200 B2

Tourist Information Office
Calle Larga 39 956 32 47 47; www.turismojerez.com Jun–Sep Mon–Fri 10–3, 5–7, Sat–Sun 10–2:30, Oct–May Mon–Fri 9:30–3, 4:30–6:30, Sat–Sun 9:30–2:30

González Byass
Calle Manuel María González 12
956 35 70 16; www.gonzalezbyass.es
Daily tours every hour from 11:30
Expensive (admission includes tastings and *tapas*). Advance reservations required

Pedro Domecq
Calle San Ildefonso 3
956 15 15 00; www.domecq.es
Mon–Fri 10–12, Sat 12–2. Advance reservations required
Moderate

Centro Andaluz de Flamenco
Plaza San Juan 1 956 32 27 11; http://caf.cica.es/flamenco Mon–Fri 9–2 Free

Real Escuela Andaluz del Arte Ecuestre
Avenida Duque de Abrantes
956 31 80 08; www.realescuela.org
Performances: Mar–Oct Tue and Thu 12; Nov–Feb Tue 12. Stable visits: Mon, Wed and Fri 10–1 (varies seasonally)
Expensive

PUERTA DE JEREZ TO THE CATHEDRAL AND SIERPES

Walk

This varied walk takes you along some of Seville's most spacious boulevards, through the Parque de María Luisa and along the Guadalquivir river then back to the commercial heart of the city. There's plenty to see en route, so allow time for museum visiting, relaxing in the shade and a spot of retail therapy to finish off.

DISTANCE 3km (2 miles) **TIME** Allow around 3 hours to give time for sight-seeing en route
START POINT Puerta de Jerez
END POINT Calle de Sierpes

1–2

Start your walk in Calle de San Fernando with the **Hotel Alfonso XIII**, Seville's ritziest hotel, on your right. Walk up **Calle de San Fernando**, (where a metro stop has been built) and past the grandiose **Fábrica de Tabacos**. This massive building, constructed in the 1750s, was the setting for Bizet's *Carmen*. During the 19th century over 3,000 women *cigarreras* were employed here; today, it houses part of the University. At the junction, turn right down Avenida del Cid to the next busy intersection.

2–3

Cross the road here and bear right along Avenida de Isabel la Católica. You're now in the spacious area of the city that was developed for the 1929 Ibero-American Fair. One block down, on the left, is the **Plaza de España**, popular with both locals and tourists. This wide semicircular complex, complete with fountains, waterways, monumental staircases and dazzling tilework, was the centrepiece of the Americas Fair and where Spanish industry and crafts were exhibited.

3–4

Cross the road and walk

down Avenida de Rodríguez Caso which runs into the **Parque de María Luisa**. The park, shady, green and cool, was laid out in the 19th century, and it's scattered with sumptuous pavilions and mansions that were intended to house more exhibits at the Fair. Take any of the footpaths on the left and head through the park, past the lake, and on to the **Plaza de América**. This is surrounded by opulent 1929 structures, two of which house museums, the **Museo Arqueológico** (Archaeological Museum) and the **Museo de Artes y Costumbres Populares**, devoted to traditional everyday life in Andalucía.

4–5

From the plaza, walk west (straight ahead) towards the Canal de Alfonso XIII then turn right down Paseo de las Delicias. Continue to the second bridge (Puente de San Telmo), where the road becomes Paseo de Cristobal Colón. Across the canal lies the vibrant

CALLE DE SIERPES

7

0 — 500 metres
0 — 500 yards

in Spain. Once built of wood, the present 14,000-seat ring was constructed around the imposing Prince's Balcony, and is actually oval, rather than round.

5–6

To the south of the bullring, cut down Calle de Antonia Díaz then turn right on to Calle de Adriano, and continue straight on until you hit the Avenida de la Constitución with the cathedral across the road in front of you.

6–7

Turn left, cross the road, and walk down to the Plaza San Francisco, where you can turn left to walk down **Calle de Sierpes**, a wide pedestrianised street which lies at the heart of Seville's shopping district.

Triana district, the traditional home of Seville's gypsy flamenco dynasties. Continue down Paseo de Cristoba Colón.

Places to Visit

Museo Arqueológico
🗺 Plaza de América ☎ 954 23 24 01 ⏰ Wed–Sat 9–8, Tue 3–8, Sun 9–2 💶 Inexpensive, free for EU citizens

Museo de Artes y Costumbres Populares
🗺 Plaza de América ☎ 954 23 25 76 ⏰ Wed–Sat 9–8, Tue 3–8, Sun 9–2 💶 Inexpensive, free for EU citizens

Torre del Oro
🗺 Paseo de Cristobal Colón s/n ☎ 954 22 24 19 ⏰ Sep–Jul Tue–Fri 10–2, Sat–Sun 11–2 💶 Inexpensive, free for EU citizens

Plaza de Toros
🗺 Paseo de Cristobal Colón 12 ☎ 954 50 13 82 ⏰ Daily 9:30–7; bullfight days 9:30–3; guided tours every half-hour in Spanish 💶 Moderate

On your left is the **Torre del Oro** (Tower of Gold), once aptly covered in gold, which was built in 1220 by the Almohad dynasty as part of a defence system running from the Alcázar across the river. It now houses Seville's maritime museum. Further down, across the road, lies the **Plaza de Toros**, one of the oldest and most prestigious bullrings

Catedral Santa María de la Sede

Fábrica de Tabacos

Museo de Artes y Costumbres Populares

Museo Arqueológico

PLAZA DE ESPAÑA

AV DE ISABEL LA CATÓLICA

AV DEL CID

Parque de María Luisa

PLAZA DE AMÉRICA

CALLE DE S FERNANDO

Hotel Alfonso XIII

PUERTA DE JEREZ

DE LA CONSTITUCIÓN

PASEO DE CRISTOBAL COLÓN

PUENTE DE SAN TELMO

Torre del Oro

Guadalquivir

PASEO DE LAS DELICIAS

TRIANA

Toros

THE PUEBLOS BLANCOS AND THE SIERRAS

Drive

This beautiful drive takes you from within a stone's throw of the Atlantic through fertile countryside to the high inland sierras behind the coast. En route you can explore some of Andalucía's prettiest settlements – the *pueblos blancos*, the white towns, and enjoy some of the finest mountain scenery in southern Spain.

DISTANCE 201km (125 miles) **TIME** 4.5 hours driving, but allow all day. You could spread this drive over 2 days, with an overnight stop at Grazalema or Ronda
START POINT Vejer de la Frontera ⊞ 200 B1
END POINT Jimena de la Frontera ⊞ 200 B1

1–2

At the bottom of the hill below **Vejer de la Frontera** (▶ 175), turn left inland off the N340 on to the A393 across rolling, fertile, agricultural land to **Medina-Sidonia**. Medina is an Arabic word for city, and this is one of the least-known and loveliest of the white towns. It's best to park outside and explore the narrow streets on foot, making sure you see the spacious tree-lined main square, the Moorish castle ruins and the parish church, built on the site of a mosque.

2–3

Stay on the A393 (signposted Paterna de Rivera, then Arcos de la Frontera) all the way to **Arcos de la Frontera**, turning left on to the A382 as you approach the town. Dramatically situated Arcos sprawls down a ridge, a warren of dazzling white streets, fine churches and splendid mansions. Walk up through the town, following the signs to the *conjunto histórico* (historic quarter), and you'll arrive in the Plaza del Cabildo, where there's a stunning *mirador* (viewpoint) overlooking the surrounding countryside.

3–4

Leave **Arcos** on the A372 and head east towards **El Bosque**. You'll pass tiny **Benamahoma** before climbing steadily into the mountains of the **Parque Natural Sierra de Grazalema** and the pass at **Puerta del Boyar** (1,103m/3,618 feet). This pass is an important funnel for bird migration and you can see griffon vultures wheeling overhead at any time of year. Through the pass, picturesque

Taking a Break

Pause in Grazalema, one of the prettiest *pueblos blancos* on the route, and perhaps have lunch at the **Restaurante Cádiz el Chico** (Plaza de España 8), where you can sample local venison and other typical mountain dishes.

When

Choose a clear day to make the most of the spectacular views once you're in the mountains.

Grazalema lies ahead. Its setting against a rocky backdrop, the ochre tiled roofs, sparkling white houses and its lovely main plaza all combine to make this one of the prettiest of the *pueblos*.

4–5

Leave **Grazalema** on the A372. Continue through the cork forest on the A372, turning right on to the A376 at the junction just after you leave the Parque (signposted Ronda 17). After 2km (1 mile) turn right towards **Montejaque, Benaoján** and **Cueva de la Pileta.** If you want to visit **Ronda** (➤ 174) as part of the drive, continue straight on here and backtrack later.

At **Montejaque,** turn left following signs to **Benaoján** and **Ronda** and **Cueva de la Pileta,** a labyrinthine system of caves where you can see a series of spectacular prehistoric paintings (hourly tours).

5–6

Continue on same road for 5.5km (3.5 miles) then turn left (signposted **Jimena de la Frontera).** After 7km (4.5 miles) turn right on to A369, a spectacular ridge route, to **Gaucín.** With its crag-top setting and superb defensive position, it's easy to see why this village was once renowned as a bandit's stronghold – from its castle you can see Gibraltar on a clear day.

6–7

Re-join the A369 and continue to **Jimena de la Frontera,** topped by a Moorish castle, branching on to the C3331 to reach the town, or continuing on the A369 to the coast.

Where to... Stay

Prices
Expect to pay per person per night
€ up to €50   €€ €50–€90   €€€ €91–€120   €€€€ over €120

Hostería del Laurel €€

This characterful hotel is on a small square lined with orange trees in the heart of the Barrio de Santa Cruz. The Hostería's *bodega* is mentioned in Zorilla's famed *Don Juan Tenorio*; these days the restaurant and *tapas* bar are equally famed among locals in the know. The rooms are a relatively recent addition, spread between two floors. They are simply furnished in bright colours and spotlessly clean; several have views of the plaza.
➕ 200 B2 ⊠ Calle Venerables 5,
☎ 954 22 02 95;
www.hosteriadellaurel.com

Las Casas de la Judería €€€

This is one of the prettiest hotels in Seville, tucked down an alleyway on the edge of the Barrio de Santa Cruz, but close to the shops and commercial centre. The rooms are set around three classic courtyards, which were once incorporated into three palaces. The predominant colours are warm ochre and white and the rooms, which are individually decorated in subdued pastel colours, are appropriately palatial with high ceilings and plush furniture
➕ 200 32 ⊠ Callejón de Dos Hermanas ☎ 954 41 51 50;
www.casasypalacios.com

Los Omeyas €

This hotel is in a superb setting, amid the tangle of back streets in the Judería, the former Jewish quarter. It has been refurbished to reflect the city's Moorish heritage with Mezquita-style arches, white marble and latticework. A central patio provides access to comfortable, tastefully decorated rooms with air conditioning. Try for one of the rooms on the top floor for a panoramic view of the Mezquita (▶ 168–169). Breakfast is a reasonable extra.
➕ 200 C3 ⊠ Calle Encarnación 17,
☎ 957 49 22 67;
www.hotel-losomeyas.com

Mezquita Hotel €€

Formerly the 16th-century palace of renowned Córdoban painter, Julio Romero de Torres, the hotel has retained an evocative historical ambience with magnificent paintings and antiques. There are original columns and stonework, plus a gracious central patio that is used for dining during the summer. The rooms have all modern conveniences and are furnished in a suitably regal fashion with satin drapes and ornately carved furniture. The location – right opposite the main entrance to the Mezquita – is ideal for sightseeing.
➕ 200 C3 ⊠ Plaza Santa Catalina 1
☎ 957 47 55 85;
www.hotelmezquita.com

Casa del Aljarife €€

This hotel is a gem, set in a sensitively refurbished 17th-century house on a tiny square in the heart of the Albaicín (the city's old Moorish quarter), with soul-stirring views of the surrounding rooftops, 9th-century city walls and the Alhambra. Typical of the area, there is a delightful shady central courtyard, as well as a rooftop terrace. The rooms are small but have plenty of character with interesting angles and use of space.

200 C2 ⊠ **Placeta de la Cruz Verde 2, Albaicín** ☎ **958 22 24 25;** www.casadelajarife.com

Hostal Britz €

This small hotel, within walking distance of the Alhambra, gives excellent value for money. Rooms, although basic, are comfortable, and some have terraces and adjoining bathrooms. Its location on the bustling Plaza Nueva means that it may be noisy on a Saturday night but on the plus side that there's a choice of pavement cafés for a short stroll away.

200 C2 ⊠ **Cuesta de Gomérez 1,** ☎ **958 22 36 52; www.lisboaweb.com**

COSTA DEL SOL

La Fonda €

On a pretty pedestrian street in the centre of the relatively unspoiled village of Benalmádena, this hotel doubles as a cookery school which

gives it the added attraction of cut-price, top culinary fare. There are cool patios shaded by palms, pebbled floors and fountains, and the rooms are light and airy with terraces and views. A downstairs seating area is uncannily quiet for a hotel near the coast.

200 C2 ⊠ **Calle Santo Domingo 7, Benalmádena** ☎ **952 56 83 24;** www.fondahotel.com

RONDA

Alavera de Los Baños €

This small hotel, next to Ronda's 13th-century Moorish baths, was used as a backdrop for the film classic *Carmen*. It has super views of the Serranía de Ronda and city walls, plus grown-up facilities like a reading room, library, lounge and dining room where there is an emphasis on fresh, organically grown foods.

200 B2 ⊠ **Hoyo de San Miguel, Ronda** ☎ **952 87 91 43;** www.alaveradelosbanos.com

Where to...
Eat and Drink

Prices

Expect to pay per person for a meal, including wine and service
€ up to €12   €€ €12–€30   €€€ over €30

SEVILLE

Habanita €–€€

This is one of Seville's few vegetarian restaurants, tucked down a side street in the buzzing Alfalfa *barrio*. The menu is vast, with an emphasis on Cuban and Mediterranean dishes. There are some real one-offs like yucca with garlic, as well as black beans, tamales and strict vegan fare. They're not too pious to serve alcohol and sugar-laden desserts though!

200 B2 ⊠ **Calle Golfo 3, Seville** ☎ **606 71 64 56** ⏰ **Mon–Sat 12:30–4:30, 8–1:30**

La Albahaca €€€

Set on one of the city's prettiest squares, this wonderful old building was once a family manor house. It has been subtly converted into one of the best-known restaurants in the city, with an attractive outdoor patio, as well as four intimate dining rooms, decorated with dazzling *azulejos* (tiles), antique oil paintings, chandeliers and plenty of plants. The well-rounded menu includes several truly decadent puddings.

200 B2 ⊠ **Plaza de Santa Cruz 12** ☎ **954 22 07 14** ⏰ **Mon–Sat 12–4, 8–midnight**

Restaurante Vallina €€–€€€

At the back of the Mezquita, the building housing the Vallina dates back an awesome 1,600 years, with Roman columns and an ancient well to prove it. Meat dishes take pride of place here, with steaks cooked on a griddle at the table. Vegetarians have a tasty, if limited, selection, and the choice of puddings is vast.

➕ 200 C3 ⬛ Corregidor Luis de la Cerda 83 ☎ 957 49 87 50 🕑 Daily 8:30pm–1am

Taberna Plateros €

Dating from the 17th century, the large patio restaurant leads to more rooms and a traditional marbled bar where blue-collar workers and businessmen meet. Black-and-white pictures line the walls, and the patio is decorated with patterned tiles and bricks. The food is solid home-style cooking with starters such as deep-fried aubergines

(eggplant) served with a spicy tomato sauce a meal in themselves.

➕ 200 C3 ⬛ San Francisco 6 ☎ 957 47 00 42 🕑 Tue–Sat 8am–4pm, 7:30pm–midnight

Mirador de Morayma €€

Buried in the Albaicín, this restaurant may be hard to find and you have to ring the doorbell to get in. Once inside, you have unbeatable views from the wisteria-covered terrace across the gorge to the Alhambra with the Sierra Nevada backdrop. The menu is mainly traditional with a few surprises, such as *ensalada de remojón granadino* (salad of cod, orange and olives). After your meal wander up to the Mirador San Nicolás for more views.

➕ 200 C2 ⬛ Pianista García Carrillo 2 ☎ 958 22 82 90 🕑 Daily noon–late

Rabo de Nube €

Rabo de Nube is the best-value bar of several on this scenic stretch with

stunning views of the Alhambra. For a quick meal, order a drink for a complimentary *tapa* of *jamón serrano* or crumbly, aged Manchego cheese. Alternatively, you can select from an extensive sandwich menu. The best value of all are the groaning plates of pasta.

➕ 200 C2 ⬛ Paseo de Los Tristes 1 ☎ 958 22 04 21 🕑 Daily noon–late

Bar Logueño €

Shoehorned into a deceptively small space, this is one of Málaga's best-loved *tapas* bars. There is a tantalising array of *tapas* from which to choose, including many Logueño originals, like sautéed oyster mushrooms with garlic, parsley and goats' cheese. There is also an excellent range of Rioja wines. The service is fast and good, despite the lack of elbow-room.

➕ 200 C2 ⬛ Calle Marín García 9, Málaga ☎ 952 22 30 48 🕑 Mon–Sat 1–4, 7–late

El Chinitas €–€€

Traditional Andalucian decor in a century-old building with original paintings of local bullfighters lining the walls. The cuisine is predictably macho with oxtail and calf sirloin. Several *serrano* hams and Manchego cheese. The best *tapas* bar next door is equally popular.

➕ 200 C2 ⬛ Calle Moreno Monroy 4, Málaga ☎ 952 21 09 72 🕑 Daily 1–4, 7–midnight

La Mesa Redonda €€

Owner José Valdespino spent years researching the classic recipes once served in aristocratic Jerez for this, one of the town's most famous restaurants. These days his son greets diners and advises on the menu and choice of wines. There are just eight tables in the dining room.

➕ 200 B2 ⬛ Manuel de la Quintana 3 ☎ 956 34 00 69 🕑 Daily 1:30–4, 9–11:30; closed part Jul–Aug

Where to...
Shop

FASHION

For clothes and shoe shops in **Málaga** head for Calle Marqués de Larios. In **Marbella** try Calle Ramon y Cajal, where you'll find Versace, Armani, Donna Karan and Gucci within a few doors of each other.

Granada city's Calle Reyes Católicos has plenty of high street chains and boutiques. If you can't find what you want here, try El Corte Inglés off Acero del Darro (a continuation of the same street).

Seville's swanky Calle Sierpes has a number of splendid, if pricey boutiques. For fashion in **Córdoba**, head for the area surrounding the pedestrianised Avenida del Gran Capitan, where you'll find chic dress shops to match any in Seville.

SOUVENIRS AND CRAFTS

You can buy souvenirs that range from tacky T-shirts to traditional pottery in just about every city and large town in Andalucia. Most shops that are wholly dedicated to mass-produced souvenirs are concentrated around major attractions and big resorts. If you head inland, however, you can often find more unusual crafts.

In **Málaga** province the Artesania Grazalema (Plaza de España, Grazalema, tel: 956 13 20 08) sells an intriguing range of goods.

Las Alpujarras in **Granada** province is well known for the brightly coloured woven *jarapas* (rugs and bedcovers) that are made there. Worth seeking out is Bodega La Moralea (Calle Verónica, Pampaneira, tel: 958 76 32 25) which carries a vast stock of artefacts, as well as tempting local food products.

In **Seville**, head across the river to Triana if you're seeking the colourful tiles and ceramic ware so distinctive of the city. Azulejos Santa Isabel (Alfarería 12, tel: 954 34 46 08) is just one of several outlets that sells everything from a 6m (20-foot) tiled picture of the *Last Supper* to exquisite hand-painted tiles.

Córdoba is celebrated for its leather crafts. In the centre, Meryan (Calleja de las Flores, tel: 957 47 59 02) sells a good range of leather goods, and other artefacts.

ANTIQUES AND ART

If you are looking for interesting pieces with a genuine Spanish pedigree, search the antiques and fine arts shops scattered throughout the centres of main cities like **Granada** and **Seville.**

FOOD AND DRINK

The hill regions of the Alpujarras in Granada province and the Sierra Morena in Seville province are famous for their *jamón serrano*; villages such as Trevélez in the Alpujurras (▶ 173) have shops devoted to *jamón* and other cured meats.

You can find own-label brands of sherry in the big-name *bodegas* of **Jerez de la Frontera** (▶ 175), while in specialist shops in the main towns and the wine-producing areas, you will find every kind of sherry, wine and liqueur on sale – and you can often sample before deciding what to buy.

MARKETS

The best market for fresh fish is at Sanlúcar de Barrameda (▶ 175), on the Costa de la Luz, although the markets in other coastal towns are also worth visiting.

For mixed fish, meat, fruit and vegetables, try the markets in Cádiz and Málaga (▶ 174), and for clothing and general goods, Fuengirola (▶ 174) and Córdoba (▶ 168–169).

Where to...
Be Entertained

NIGHTLIFE

The club scene in Malaga province is at its most intense on the Costa del Sol. In **Puerto Banús**, the waterfront Sinatra Bar (Muelle Ribera 2, tel: 952 81 09 50) is a top spot for celebrity spotting, while in neighbouring **Marbella**, Olivia Valere (Carretera de Istán, tel: 952 82 88 61) and La Notte (Camino de la Cruz s/n, tel: 952 86 69 96) are similarly glitzy hotspots. Pick up a free copy of the monthly glossy *Essential Marbella* to see what's going on, or the *Guía Marbella – Día y Noche*, a Spanish/English listings guide.

Granada's nightlife largely caters for a student crowd who tend to hang out at the discobars around the Plaza del Príncipe. For more sophistication, try El Camborio

(Camino del Sacromonte), which has several dance floors and views of the Alhambra from the terrace.

Seville's music bars are clustered around the Plaza de la Alfalfa and along El Torneo, parallel to the river. The Bulebar and the Barqueta bars are particularly lively in the summer. Although less cosmopolitan than Seville, Granada and Malaga, **Córdoba** has some lively dance and music bars on Calle Cruz Conde, just north of Plaza de las Tendillas.

FLAMENCO

In **Malaga**, there are regular flamenco shows at Vista Andalucía (Avenida de los Guindos, tel: 952 23 11 57), and frequent top calibre performers appear at Teatro Miguel de Cervantes (Calle Ramos Marín,

tel: 952 22 41 00). **Jerez de la Frontera** has a strong flamenco tradition and there are excellent shows at El Laga (Plaza del Mercado, tel: 956 22 83 34). One of the most popular flamenco venues in **Granada** is Jardines Neptuno (Calle Arabial, tel: 958 52 25 33), while **Seville's** La Carbonería (Calle Levíes 18, tel: 954 21 44 60) is an atmospheric bar with flamenco on Monday and Thursday nights. In **Córdoba**, Tablao Cardenal (Calle Torríjos 10, tel: 957 48 33 20) is one of the best venues for "classical" flamenco.

BULLFIGHTING

The main bullfight season runs from Easter to October, but there are novice fights into November on the Costa del Sol. Bullfights are advertised by garish posters about three weeks before the event, and resort hotels often organise bus pickups. For major rings, tickets are often booked well ahead by locals. Prices

can be as high as €120 and start at about €20. Even Costa del Sol *novilladas* may cost you from €30 to €60 for a ticket, although they should be much less.

OUTDOOR ACTIVITIES

The windier Atlantic coast, especially at Tarifa between Gibraltar and Cádiz, is one of the world's best wind- and kitesurfing venues, while the opportunities for scuba diving, water-skiing and paragliding are increasing.

Andalucía's magnificent mountains offer endless opportunities for adventure holidaying, whether it's basic walking in Las Alpujarras (▶ 173) and the Sierra de Grazalema (▶ 178–179), or horse riding and bicycling on organised trips with expert guides. Ask for information at tourist offices. You can also go for the wilder edges of adventure sport and try rock climbing, abseiling, canoeing, paragliding and hang-gliding.

Practicalities

Websites

- www.tourspain.es
- www.spain.info is the Spanish National Tourist Office website, available in English.

- Go Spain (links to large number of Spanish sites): www.gospain.org
- Icom (Spanish museums and art galleries): www.spanish-living.com/art_galleries.htm

In the UK

Spanish National Tourist Office, PO Box 4009, London W1A 6NB
☎ (020) 7486 8077; brochure line 08459 400 180. Visits by appointment

BEFORE YOU GO

WHAT YOU NEED

	Required — Some countries require a passport to	UK	Germany	USA	Canada	Australia	Ireland	Netherlands	New Zealand
●	Required								
○	Suggested	remain valid for a minimum period							
▲	Not required	(usually at least six months) beyond							
△	Not applicable	the date of entry – check beforehand.							
Passport/National Identity Card		●	●	●	●	●	●	●	●
Visa (regulations can change – check before you travel)		▲	▲	▲	▲	▲	▲	▲	▲
Onward or Return Ticket		▲	▲	●	●	●	▲	▲	●
Health Inoculations (tetanus and polio)		▲	▲	▲	▲	▲	▲	▲	▲
Health Documentation (▶ 190, Health)		○	○	△	△	△	○	○	△
Travel Insurance		○	○	○	○	○	○	○	○
Driving Licence (international/national) for car hire		●	●	●	●	●	●	●	●
Car Insurance Certificate (if using own car)		●	●	△	△	△	●	●	
Car Registration Document (if using own car)		●	●	△	△	△	●	●	△

WHEN TO GO

Madrid

▭ High season   ▭ Low season

JAN	FEB	MAR	APR	MAY	JUN	JUL	AUG	SEP	OCT	NOV	DEC
6°C	10°C	14°C	17°C	20°C	26°C	32°C	30°C	24°C	18°C	12°C	10°C
43°F	50°F	57°F	62°F	68°F	79°F	90°F	86°F	75°F	64°F	54°F	50°F

☀ Sun   🌧 Wet   ⛅ Sun/Showers

Because of its size and geography, Spain has a **very varied climate**. The Mediterranean coast and the south generally have **mild, wet winters and long hot summers**, with most of the rainfall occurring in the autumn. The winter months, after the rain, are ideal here, when spring comes early. It can rain throughout the year in the northern regions, with Cantabria and Galicia having the highest rainfall in the country. This makes high summer in the north less searingly hot than in central Spain or further south, where the heat is punctuated throughout the summer months by **dramatic thunderstorms**. July and August in the south bring a **hot, dry wind** from Africa. Winter in inland Spain can be bitter, with **heavy snow and biting winds** across the central plateau. Central and southern Spain are at their best in spring, while the optimum time to visit the northern coast and the mountainous regions is the summer.

GETTING THERE

By Air Spain's international **airports** include Madrid, Barcelona, Alicante, Bilbao, Oviedo, Santiago, Málaga, Seville, Valencia, Jerez and Murcia.

From the UK these are served by Spain's international carrier, Iberia (tel: 0845 601 2584; www.iberia.com), British Airways (tel: 0845 77 333 77; www.british-airways.com), EasyJet (tel: 0870 600 0000; www.easyjet.com), and numerous no-frills airlines including Ryanair (tel: 807 22 00 222; www.ryanair.com), Air 2000 (tel: 0870 750 0001; www.firstchoice.co.uk) and AVRO plc (tel: 020 8695 4440; www.avro.co.uk). Flying time is 2–3 hours.

From the US Iberia (tel: toll free 800/772-4642) flies non-stop from New York, Miami and Chicago to Madrid, with connecting flights on to other Spanish airports. Other US airlines fly direct from the east coast to Madrid, while Delta Airlines also operates a non-stop service to Barcelona. Flying time from New York is around 7 hours.

Ticket prices are lower from November to March, excluding Christmas and Easter. All airport taxes are normally included in the ticket price.

By Sea Ferries run from the UK direct to Santander and Bilbao. Brittany Ferries (tel: 0870 901 1500; www.brittanyferries.com) operates from Plymouth to Santander with a sailing time of 24 hours, while P & O ferries (tel: 0870 242 4999; www.poferries.com) run from Portsmouth to Bilbao and take 36 hours. An alternative is to cross the Channel by ferry or through the Eurotunnel and either drive or take the train through France to Spain. You should allow roughly two days for a comfortable drive south through France.

By Rail UK travellers can get to Spain by train, either making the Channel crossing by ferry or taking the Eurostar as far as Paris. Journey times are around 28 hours to Barcelona by ferry and train, and 32 hours to Madrid. The Eurostar option takes roughly 20–22 hours. **Prices** vary according to your age and the time of year. If you plan to use trains in Spain, try an InterRail Global FlexiPass, which allows for 5- or 10-days travel within either a 10-day or 22-day period.

TIME

 Spain is one hour ahead of Greenwich Mean Time (GMT).

CURRENCY AND FOREIGN EXCHANGE

Currency The Spanish unit of currency is the euro (€). There are seven euro bank **notes**: €5, €10, €20, €50, €100, €200 and €500. **Coins** come in denominations of 1, 2, 5, 10, 20 and 50 cents and €1 and €2. There are 100 cents in €1.

Traveller's cheques are a convenient way to carry money. **Credit cards** are widely accepted and can also be used for cash advances at banks as well as for withdrawing money from ATMs.

Exchange You can exchange foreign currency and traveller's cheques at *bancos* (banks), *cajas de ahorros* (savings banks) and *casas de cambio* (bureaux de change). Banks generally offer better rates and lower commission charges. In large towns and cities, the department store chain, El Corte Inglés, has excellent exchange facilities. You will need your passport.

GMT
12 noon

Spain
1pm

USA New York
7am

Germany
1pm

France
1pm

Australia
Sydney 10pm

WHEN YOU ARE THERE

CLOTHING SIZES

UK	Spain/Europe	USA	
36	46	36	
38	48	38	
40	50	40	Suits
42	52	42	
44	54	44	
46	56	46	
7	41	8	
7.5	42	8.5	
8.5	43	9.5	Shoes
9.5	44	10.5	
10.5	45	11.5	
11	46	12	
14.5	37	14.5	
15	38	15	
15.5	39/40	15.5	Shirts
16	41	16	
16.5	42	16.5	
17	43	17	
8	34	6	
10	36	8	
12	38	10	Dresses
14	40	12	
16	42	14	
18	44	16	
4.5	38	6	
5	38	6.5	
5.5	39	7	Shoes
6	39	7.5	
6.5	40	8	
7	41	8.5	

NATIONAL HOLIDAYS

1 Jan	New Year's Day
6 Jan	Epiphany
Mar/Apr	Good Friday, Easter Monday
1 May	Labour Day
15 Aug	Assumption of the Virgin
12 October	National Day
1 Nov	All Saints' Day
6 December	Constitution Day
8 Dec	Feast of the Immaculate Conception
25 Dec	Christmas Day

The autonomous regions have their own additional public holidays, and every town in Spain celebrates its patron saint's feast day.

OPENING HOURS

○ Shops
● Offices
● Banks
● Main Post Offices
◐ Museums/Monuments
◑ Pharmacies

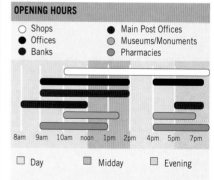

□ Day ▨ Midday ▨ Evening

Shops Large shops and department stores 10–8; smaller shops 10–1:30, 5–8; closed Sat pm. Tourist-oriented shops and hypermarkets may have longer opening hours and be open on Sun, especially in summer.
Offices 10–2, 4–7:30.
Banks 9–2; closed Sat Apr–Oct. *Casas de cambio* are open until late daily and some also on Sun.
Post Offices 8–12, 5–7:30; closed Sun.
Museums 10–1:30, 4–7. Museum opening hours vary considerably; many are closed on Mon.
Pharmacies 9–1, 4–8; closed Sat pm – at least one chemist in town is open on Sat pm, Sun and at night.

POLICE 091

FIRE 085 or 080

AMBULANCE Varies from place to place: contact the operator

PERSONAL SAFETY

Spain is generally safe for travellers, but street crime is on the increase. To be sure, take sensible precautions:

• Don't carry too much cash; women should wear bags slung across their chests rather than hanging from the shoulder.

• Keep an eye on your belongings in public places and crowded tourist areas.

• Be aware of ploys to distract your attention by thieves working in pairs.

• Stick to main thoroughfares at night to avoid getting lost in poorly lit alleys.

• Don't leave belongings on view in a parked car and take the car radio with you.

Police assistance:
 091

TELEPHONES

as internal and international dialling codes displayed inside. The international operator number is 1182 5. Directory enquiries can be reached on 1181 8. If your mobile phone SIM card is removable, it makes sense to buy a Spanish card on arrival to allow you to use the Spanish mobile system at local rates.

Most payphones operate with coins and phone cards (*tarjeta telefónica* or *credifone*), available from *tabacos*, and have English instructions, as well

International Dialling Codes
Dial 00 followed by:

UK	44
USA/Canada	1
Ireland	353
Australia	61
New Zealand	64

POST

Post offices (*correos*) are normally central; post boxes are yellow. *Poste restante* letters can be sent to any Spanish post office; put the surname in capitals and underlined and send them to *Lista de Correos* followed by the name of the town and province. Buy stamps (*sellos*) at any *tabacos*.

ELECTRICITY

The power supply in Spain is 220/230 volts AC. Sockets accept two-pin round plugs so British appliances will need a two-pin adaptor. North Americans will need this plus a transformer; these are hard to find in Spain, so it's best to bring one with you.

TIPS/GRATUITIES

Tipping is expected for all services. As a general guide, the following applies:

Restaurants (if service not included)	5–10%
Bar Service	Change
Tour Guides	Optional
Hairdressers	Change–5%
Taxis	2–3%
Chambermaids	€6
Porters	€6

CONSULATES IN MADRID

UK	**USA**	**Canada**	**Australia**	**Germany**
☎ 91 308 52 01	☎ 91 587 2200	☎ 91 431 43 00	☎ 91 441 93 00	☎ 91 557 90 00

HEALTH

 insurance Citizens of EU countries receive free or reduced-cost medical treatment with relevant documentation (European Health Insurance Card), but private medical insurance is still advised and essential for all other visitors; without this, EU citizens are charged at private rates. Private medical insurance is strongly recommended, particularly for visitors from the US, Australia and New Zealand.

 Dental Services Dental treatment is expensive, so check your medical insurance before you go to see if it covers dental treatment.

 Weather High temperatures and humidity are common throughout the summer months. Protect against sunburn and dehydration by dressing suitably, applying sunscreen and drinking plenty of water – about 1.5–2 litres daily in hot weather.

 Drugs Prescription and non-prescription drugs and homeopathic remedies, as well as medical advice, are available from pharmacies. Many drugs that are on prescription in other countries are also available over the counter in Spain. Chemists operate a rota so there is always one open 24 hours a day; notices in pharmacy windows give details. If you need to renew a prescription, ask your doctor for the chemical name of the drug, as it may be marketed in Spain under another name.

 Safe Water Tap water is generally safe to drink. Mineral water (*agua mineral*) is cheap and widely available.

CONCESSIONS

Students An International Student Identity Card (ISIC) will help obtain free or reduced entry to many museums and sites as well as other discounts.

Senior Citizens Senior citizens can get reductions on some museum entry charges on production of an identity document.

TRAVELLING WITH A DISABILITY

Major cities and resorts have hotels adapted for people with disabilities and all new buildings are now, by law, disabled-friendly. Transport remains a problem, as buses are difficult to access, and only the more modern trains have wheelchair facilities. Accommodation out of the main tourist centres is also a problem. SNTO offices (► 186–187) can provide a variety of useful addresses.

CHILDREN

Children are welcome everywhere in Spain. The under 4s travel free on RENFE trains and at a 40% discount between 4–12 years. Local tourist boards have lists of child-friendly attractions. Nappies and baby food are widely available.

TOILETS

Public toilets (*Los Servicios*) are highly variable and sometimes lack paper. Those in museums and galleries are generally clean and free.

CUSTOMS

Importing wildlife souvenirs from rare or endangered species may be illegal or require a permit. You should check your home country's customs regulations before purchase.

Spanish (*español*), also known as Castilian (*castellano*) to distinguish it from other tongues spoken in Spain, is related to the French and Italian languages. Apart from certain local and regional variations, every letter is pronounced, with the emphasis usually on the last syllable.

GREETINGS AND COMMON WORDS

Do you speak English? **¿Habla inglés?**
I don't understand **No entiendo**
I don't speak Spanish **No hablo español**
Yes/No **Sí/no**
OK **Vale/de acuerdo**
Please **Por favor**
Thank you (very much) **(Muchas) gracias**
You're welcome **De nada**
Hello/Goodbye **Hola/adiós**
Good morning **Buenos días**
Good afternoon/evening **Buenas tardes**
Good night **Buenas noches**
How are you? **¿Qué tal?**
Excuse me **Perdón**
How much is this? **¿Cuánto vale?**
I'd like... **Quisiera/me gustaría**

EMERGENCY!

Help! **¡Socorro!/¡Ayuda!**
Could you help me please? **¿Podría ayudarme por favor?**
Could you call a doctor? **¿Podría llamar a un médico por favor?**

NUMBERS

0	cero	20	veinte
1	uno/una	21	veintiuno
2	dos	30	treinta
3	tres	40	cuarenta
4	cuatro	50	cincuenta
5	cinco	60	sesenta
6	seis	70	setenta
7	siete	80	ochenta
8	ocho	90	noventa
9	nueve	100	cien
10	diez	101	ciento uno
11	once	110	ciento diez
12	doce	120	ciento veinte
13	trece		
14	catorce	200	doscientos/cienta
15	quince		
16	dieciséis	500	quinientos/quinientas
17	diecisiete		
18	dieciocho	1000	mil
19	diecinueve	5000	cinco mil

DIRECTIONS AND TRAVELLING

Aeroplane **Avión**
Airport **Aeropuerto**
Car **Coche**
Boat **Barco**
Bus **Autobús**
Bus stop **Parada de autobús**
Station **Estación**
Ticket (single/return) **Billete (de ida/de ida y vuelta**
I'm lost **Me he perdido**
Where is...? **¿Dónde está...?**
How do I get to...? **¿Cómo llego a...?**
  the beach **la playa**
  the telephone **el teléfono**
  the toilets **los servicios**
Left/right **Izquierda/derecha**
Straight on **Todo recto**

ACCOMMODATION

Do you have a single/double room available? **¿Tiene una habitación individual/doble?**
with/without bath/toilet/shower **con/sin baño/lavabo/ducha**
Does that include breakfast? **¿Incluye el desayuno?**
Could I see the room? **¿Puedo ver la habitación?**
I'll take this room **Cojo esta habitación**
One night **Una noche**
Key **Llave**
Lift **Ascensor**
Sea views **Vistas al mar**

DAYS

Today	**Hoy**
Tomorrow	**Mañana**
Yesterday	**Ayer**
Later	**Más tarde**
This week	**Esta semana**
Monday	**Lunes**
Tuesday	**Martes**
Wednesday	**Miércoles**
Thursday	**Jueves**
Friday	**Viernes**
Saturday	**Sábado**
Sunday	**Domingo**

Useful words and phrases 191

RESTAURANT

I'd like to book a table **Quisiera reservar una mesa**
A table for two please **Una mesa para dos, por favor**
Could we see the menu, please? **¿Nos trae la carta, por favor?**
What's this? **¿Qué es esto?**
A bottle/glass of... **Una botella/copa de...**

Could I have the bill please? **¿La cuenta, por favor?**
Service charge included **Servicio incluido**
Waiter/waitress **Camarero/a**
Breakfast **Desayuno**
Lunch **Almuerzo**
Dinner **Cena**
Menu **La carta**

MENU READER

a la plancha grilled
aceite oil
aceituna olive
agua water
ajo garlic
almendra almond
anchoas anchovies
arroz rice
atún tuna

bacalao cod
berenjena aubergines
bistec steak
bocadillo sandwich

café coffee
calamares squid
cangrejo crab
carne meat
cebolla onion
cerdo pork
cerezas cherries
cerveza beer
champiñones mushrooms
chocolate chocolate
chorizo spicy sausage
chuleta chop
conejo rabbit
cordero lamb
crema cream
crudo raw
cubierto(s) cover (cutlery)
cuchara spoon
cuchillo knife

embutidos sausages
ensalada salad
entrante starter
espárragos asparagus

filete fillet
flan crème caramel
frambuesa raspberry
fresa strawberry
frito fried
fruta fruit

galleta biscuit
gambas prawns
gazpacho andaluz gazpacho (cold soup)
guisantes peas

habas broad beans
helado ice cream
hígado liver
huevos fritos/ revueltos fried/ scrambled eggs

jamón serrano ham (cured)
jamón York ham (cooked)
judías beans
judías verdes French beans
jugo fruit juice

langosta lobster
leche milk
lechuga lettuce
legumbres pulses

lengua tongue
lenguado sole
limón lemon
lomo de cerdo pork tenderloin

mantequilla butter
manzana apple
mariscos seafood
mejillones mussels
melocotón peach
melón melon
merluza hake
mero sea bass
miel honey

naranja orange

ostra oyster

pan bread
patata potato
patatas fritas chips
pato duck
pepinillo gherkin
pepino cucumber
pera pear
perejil parsley
pescado fish
pez espada swordfish
picante hot/spicy
pimientos red/ green peppers
piña pineapple
plátano banana
pollo chicken
postre dessert
primer plato first course
pulpo octopus

queso cheese

rape monkfish
relleno filled/ stuffed
riñones kidneys

salchicha sausage
salchichón salami
salmón salmon
salmonete red mullet
salsa sauce
seco dry
segundo plato main course
solomillo de ternera fillet of beef
sopa soup

té tea
tenedor fork
ternera beef
tocino bacon
tortilla española Spanish omelette
tortilla francesa plain omelette

uva grape

verduras green vegetables
vino blanco/ rosado/tinto white/rosé/red wine

zanahorias carrots

Atlas

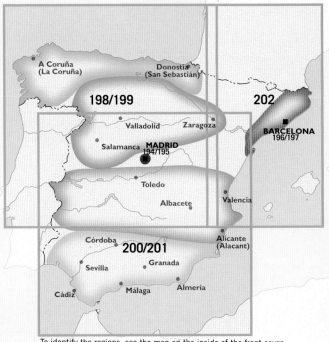

A Coruña
(La Coruña)

Donostia
(San Sebastián)

198/199

Valladolid   Zaragoza

Salamanca   **MADRID**
              194/195

202

BARCELONA
196/197

Toledo

Albacete

Valencia

Córdoba   **200/201**

Alicante
(Alacant)

Sevilla   Granada

Cádiz   Málaga   Almería

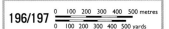

To identify the regions, see the map on the inside of the front cover

Regional Maps

—··— International boundary	✈ Airport
······ Regional boundary	🔳 Featured place of interest
▬▬▬ Major route	■ Place of interest
▦▦▦ Motorway	○ Town
─── Main road	∘ Village
─── Other road	🗺 Built up area
········ Pilgrimage route to Santiago de Compostela	🗺 National Park
─┼─ Canal	
☐ City	

198/202	0 20 40 60 80 100 km
	0 20 40 60 miles

Streetplans

─── Main roads	▦ Important building
········ Other roads	🔳 Featured place of interest
─── Rail line	● Metro station
─◆─◆─ Cable car	◎ FGC station
▦ Park	ⓘ Information

194/195	0 100 200 300 metres
	0 100 200 300 yards

196/197	0 100 200 300 400 500 metres
	0 100 200 300 400 500 yards

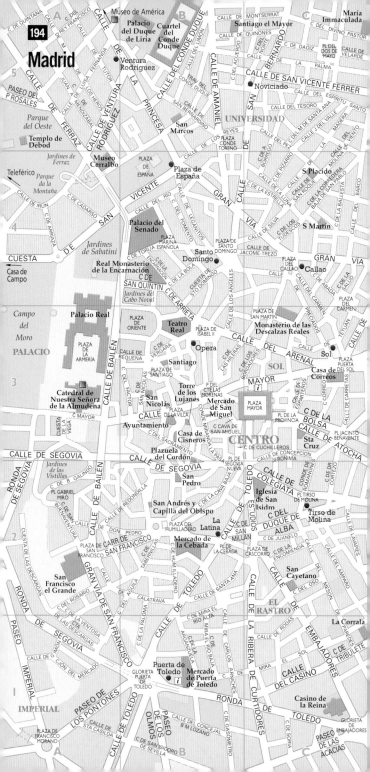

5

A   B   C

Cabo Ortegal
Punta da Estaca de Bares

Costa Verde

Costa da Morte
(Costa de la Muerte)

Cabo Prior
Cedeira
Ortigueira

Viveiro

A Coruña (La Coruña)
Ferrol
Mondoñedo
Foz
Ribadeo
Luarca (Luarca)
Navia (Luarca)
Cudillero (Cuideiru)
Cabo de Peñas
Salinas
Lastres (Llastres)

Foxas (Fene)
Betanzos
Villalba
Taramundi
Castropol
Vegadeo (A Veiga)
Tineo (Tinéu)
Pravia
Salas
Gijón (Xixón)
La Is

Carballo
Ordes (Ordenes)
N634
Rábade
Meira
A Fonsagrada
ASTURIAS
Cangas del Narcea
Oviedo (Uviéu)
Mieres
N634

Cabo Vilán
Santa Comba
Guitiriz
GALICIA
N640
Cordillera

Camariñas
Negreira
A52
Santiago de Compostela
Lugo
Becerreá
Villablino
Puerto de Pajares
La Robla

Fisterra (Finisterre)
Cee
Muros
Noia
Monterroso
Embalse de Belesar
NVI
Porto de Pedrafita
O Cebreiro
N630
A66
Pomar

Ría de Muros e Noia
Padrón
A Estrada
Chantada
Monforte de Lemos
Bembibre
León
Astorga

Santa Eugenia (Ribeira)
Vagarcia
Lalin
Carballiño
A Rúa
Ponferrada
León

Rías Baixas (Rías Bajas)
Ría de Arousa
Grove
Arousa
Cerdedo
Ourense (Orense)
Las Médulas
O Barco

Pontevedra
Ribadavia
Embalse de San Esteban
La Bañeza
NG

Ría de Vigo
Redondela
A Caniza
Allariz
1707m
Viana do Bolo
Eria
Esla
N610

Vigo
Porriño
A Caniza
Xinzo de Limia (Ginzo de Limia)
A Gudiña
Puebla de Sanabria
CASTILLA-

Baiona
Tui
Miño
Embalse das Conchas
N525
Verín
Benavente
NVI

A Guarda (La Guardia)
N13
Chaves
Bragança
Sierra de la Culebra
LEÓN

Viana do Castelo
A3/IP1
N2
200
N122
Embalse de Ricobayo
Zamora

Braga
ICI
IP4/E82
Duero
Tor

Póvoa de Varzim
Guimarães
Fermoselle
Embalse de Almendra
N630

A4/IP4
Vila Real
Vitigudino
Fuentesaúco
Ledesma
Salamanca

PORTO
A1/E01
Huebra
Lumbrales
N620/E80
Peñaranda de Bracamonte

P
Viseu
La Fuente de San Esteban
Alba de Tormes

Aveiro
IP5/E80
Fuentes de Oñoro
Ciudad Rodrigo
La Alberca
Embalse de Santa Teresa

N17
Guarda
El Barco de Ávila

Figueira da Foz
Coimbra
Covilhã
Sierra de Gata
Béjar
N630/E803
Sierra de Gredos
2592m

IP2/E802
Moraleja
Montehermoso
Jerte
Monasterio de Yuste
Jarandilla de la Vera

Leiria
Castelo Branco
Zarza la Mayor
Coria
Alagón
Plasencia
Navalmoral de la Mata
Oropes

Caldas da Rainha
Tajo
Alcántara
PARQUE NATURAL DE MONFRAGÜE
Embalse de Valdecañas

A1/E01
Santarém
Brozas
Cáceres
Embalse de Alcántara
Trujillo
Sierra de Guadalupe

Sierra de San Pedro
Arroyo de la Luz
N521
Guadalupe

Portalegre
Alburquerque
NV/E90
Alcuéscar
Embalse de García de Sola

IP2/E802
EXTREMADURA
La Roca de la Sierra
Miajadas
N430
Embalse de Orellan

A6/E90
Montijo
Mérida
Villanueva de la Serena
Embals del Zújc

LISBOA
N4
Badajoz
Don Benito
Campanario

A6/IP7
Guadiana
Olivenza
N432
Almendralejo
Castuera

Setúbal
Évora
Barcarrota
Villafranca de los Barros
Cabeza del Buey

Jerez de los
Zafra

A   B   C

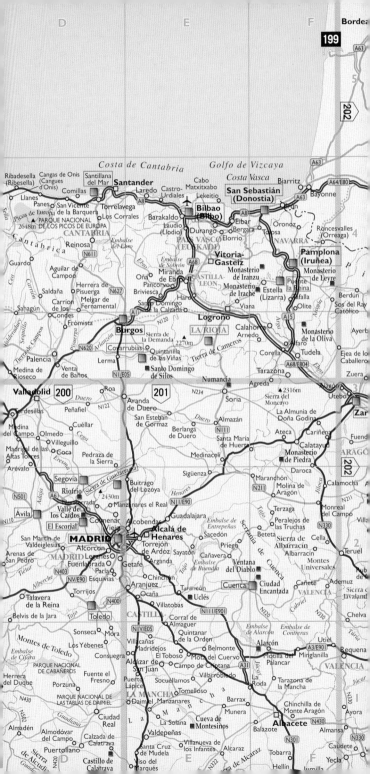

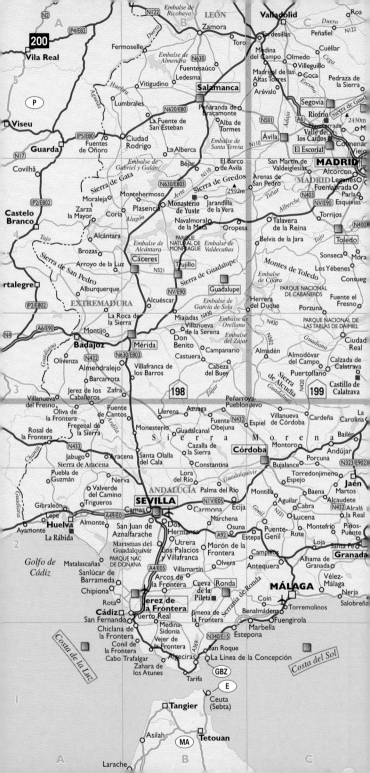

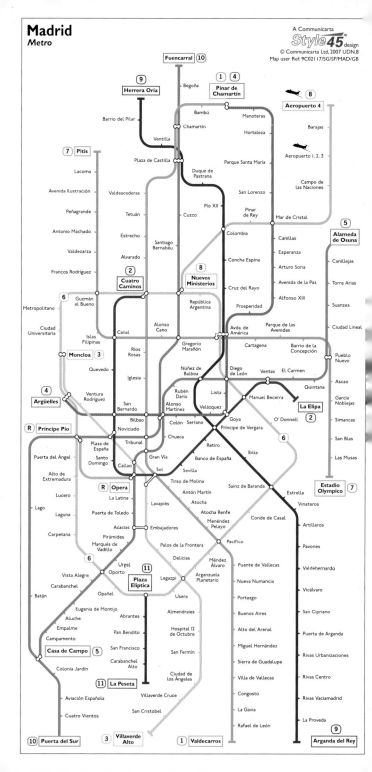

SPIRAL GUIDES

Questionnaire

Dear Traveler
Your comments, opinions and recommendations are very important to us.
So please help us to improve our travel guides by taking a few minutes to complete this simple questionnaire.

Send to: **Spiral Guides,
MailStop 66, 1000 AAA Drive,
Heathrow, FL 32746–5063**

About this guide...

Which title did you buy? _____

Where did you buy it? _____

When? m m / y y

Why did you choose a AAA Spiral Guide?
_____
_____

Did this guide meet your expectations?
Please give your reasons.

Exceeded ☐   Met all ☐   Met most ☐

Fell below ☐
_____
_____
_____

Were there any aspects of this guide that you
particularly liked or thought could have been done better.
_____
_____
_____
_____

About you...

Name (Mr/Mrs/Ms) _____

Address _____
_____

Zip _____

Daytime tel nos. _____

Which age group are you in?

Under 25 ☐ 25–34 ☐ 35–44 ☐ 45–54 ☐

55–64 ☐ 65+ ☐

How many trips do you make a year?

Less than one ☐ One ☐ Two ☐ Three or more ☐

Are you a AAA member? Yes ☐   No ☐

Name of AAA club _____

About your trip...

When did you book? m m / y y

When did you travel? m m / y y

How long did you stay? _____

Was it for business or leisure? _____

Did you buy any other travel guides for your trip?

☐ Yes   ☐ No

If yes, which ones? _____
_____

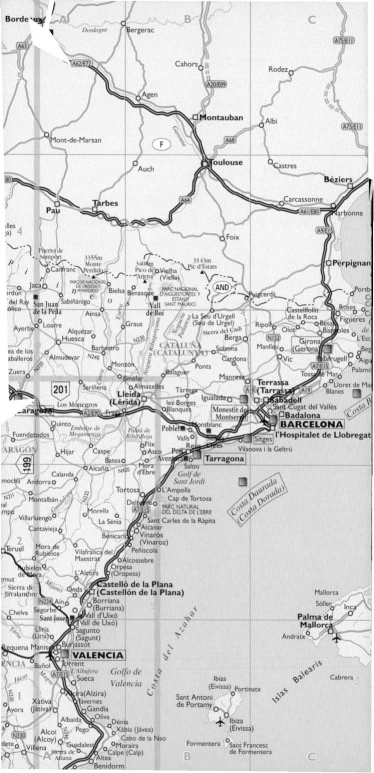

Picture credits

The Automobile Association wishes to thank the following photographers and libraries for their assistance in the preparation of this book:

ART ARCHIVE 8; BRIDGEMAN ART LIBRARY 119t Menu from 'Els Quatre Gats', 1899 by Pablo Picasso (1881–1973), Museo Picasso, Barcelona, Spain/Index, 123 Madonna and Child, fresco from the Apse of Santa Maria de Taull, Vall de Boi, 12th century by Master of St Maria (12th century), Museu de Arte de Catalunya, Barcelona, Spain/Index; CORBIS UK 99 (Gianni Dagli); DACS, LONDON 53, 119t, 120 © Succession Picasso/DACS 2003; MARY EVANS PICTURE LIBRARY 9t; GETTY IMAGES 18/19, 20/21; HULTON ARCHIVES 9br; IMAGESTATE 11t, 11c; ILLUSTRATED LONDON NEWS 120; INDEX FOTOTECA 119b; NATURE PICTURE LIBRARY 20b; NICK INMAN 11b, 149; PICTURES COLOUR LIBRARY 10, 28tl, 28c, 71, 76, 77, 78, 79, 94/5, 142b, 148, 150b; TRAVEL LIBRARY 14t (Stuart Black), 150r, 155; WORLD PICTURES 105, 143t, 147, 153, 170/1.

All remaining pictures are held in the Association's own library (AA PHOTO LIBRARY) and were taken by MAX JOURDAN with the exception of the following:
PETE BENNETT 3(v), 185; MICHELLE CHAPLOW F/Cct, F/Ccb, 2(ii), 3(iv), 19t, 27c, 29, 47, 53, 56, 111, 130, 143b, 154, 159, 164, 166, 187tl, 187tr, 187b; JANIE COWHAM 21c; STEVE DAY 3(ii), 17l, 113, 114, 117, 118, 122, 128; JERRY EDMANSON 3(iii), 139, 141, 142t, 144/5, 146, 163t, 168, 173; PHILIP ENTICKNAP 6t, 7tl, 7tr, 59, 68, 69, 75, 81, 92, 94, 132; ERIC MEACHER 28bl, 28br; ANDREW MOLYNEUX 6b, 162, 165t; DOUGLAS ROBERTSON 14b, 170; RICK STRANGE 16tl, 17r, 44; JAMES TIMS 27t, 160; HARRY WILLIAMS 20t; PETER WILSON 16tr, 115b, 161, 163b, 174.